QUILTS FOR Rosie

Paper Piecing Patterns from the '40s

By Carolyn Cullinan McCormick

Introduction

When selecting the patterns for this book, I found that *The Kansas City Star* only printed 261 patterns during the 1940s. Paper was rationed, and one of the chemicals used to make paper was also used to make bombs. The newspaper even had to turn down profitable advertisements because of the paper shortage.

The names of some of the blocks show support for the troops: A Salute to the Colors and Army Star. The Army Star block was submitted to *The Kansas City Star* by two young men who were in the Army. The tagline under the pattern read, "In appreciation of the many thoughtful deeds of American women for soldiers, two young men in an army training camp have sent The Weekly Star this pattern of their own origination. They are Eugene Aubuchan and Earl J. Faxton. Their addresses may not be revealed. Red, white, and blue are the colors they chose for the design. They suggest placing a white strip across the top of the quilt and stitching in the letters 'USA.'"

Paper piecing was pretty much unheard of back in the 1940s unless one was making a "string" quilt or a crazy quilt. I have redrafted 20 patterns from *The Kansas City Star* collection and changed them into paper piecing patterns in two different sizes, 10-inch and 4-inch for those of you who enjoy miniatures. I hope you enjoy making these traditional quilts in this non-traditional manner.

—*Carolyn Cullinan McCormick*

About the Author

Carolyn McCormick currently lives outside of Denver, Colorado, with her husband, Larry. They have a son, Ryan, and a daughter, Jennifer. Ryan and his wife, Megan, will soon become parents, making Carolyn and Larry first-time grandparents.

Carolyn started to quilt in 1985 when she and her husband moved to Bozeman, Montana. There she worked and taught a variety of quilting and craft classes at The Patchworks from 1987 to 1995. In 1995, she invented the Add-A-Quarter ruler to make rotary cutting templates easier. The Add-A-Quarter has now become a standard tool when paper piecing.

Now Carolyn has invented another tool called the Add-Enough. The Add-Enough makes it easy to determine the size of the piece of fabric one needs for their own paper piecing patterns.

Acknowledgments

Thanks to the love of my life, Larry. You are always there for me and I cannot tell you how much I love you.

I am so very blessed to have a wonderful family. A very special thanks to Carol Netwal, Castle Rock, Colorado, for testing all the 4" blocks. Thanks also go to my daughter-in-law, Megan McCormick, Parker, Colorado, and my sister Marie Huber, Glendive, Montana.

I am lucky to have very special friends that made projects for this book. Diane Donnelly, Bozeman, Montana; Kathy Braun, Rosholt, South Dakota; Kelly Collins, Littleton, Colorado; Jennie Maze, Parker, Colorado; and Sandra Reinke, Lakewood, Colorado.

Thank you so very much to the following friends who took time out of their busy lives to test the 10" blocks. Mona's Choice and Sunlight and Shadow made by Ginny Rafferty, Sedalia, Colorado. New Four Pointer made by Carol Bonetti, Castle Rock, Colorado. A Salute to the Colors made by Jeanette Davis, Castle Rock, Colorado. A Flash of Diamonds made by Polly Somers, Sedalia, Colorado. Colorado Quilt and The Spider Web made by Brenda Phillips, Sedalia, Colorado. Anna's Choice made by Kathy Rutkosky, Larkspur, Colorado. The Army Star and Return of the Swallows made by Jeannine Glendenning, Castle Rock, Colorado. A Basket quilt in Triangles and The North Star made by Evie Scott, Kiowa, Colorado. Crazy Anne made by Nancy Orth, Kiowa, Colorado. Christmas Star and Kansas Star made by Marilyn Vap, Castle Rock, Colorado. Mother's Favorite Star and A Quilt Mosaic made by Meriellen Joga, Castle Rock, Colorado. Shepherd's Crossing made by Carol Herriek, Kiowa, Colorado. The 1941 Nine Patch made by Claudia Harrison, Kiowa, Colorado. The Bright Jewel made by Julie Lilly, Monument, Colorado.

Dedication

To my dad, John, who served in the U.S. Army. Because of you, I am not afraid to dream.

I love you, Carolyn

I would also like to thank Tracy Peterson Yadon, Manhattan, Montana, Carol Willey and Jan Korytkowski, Castle Rock, Colorado, for their wonderful long arm quilting.

I would also like to thank the following people and companies for their generous donations of fabric for this book, Margo Krager from Reproductionfabrics.com, Leah Nelson from In The Beginning Fabrics and Emily Cohen from Timeless Treasures.

Thanks to the staff at *The Kansas City Star*. Doug Weaver for giving me the opportunity to work with *The Kansas City Star* patterns. Edie McGinnis, my editor, who does such a tremendous job. I appreciate her friendship as well as her advice and expertise.

Thanks to Amy Robertson for her fabulous design work on this book. Thanks to Aaron Leimkuehler, our photographer, for the great photos and Eric Craven for his excellent technical illustrations.

—*Carolyn Cullinan McCormick*

Quilts for Rosie

Paper Piecing Patterns from the '40s

Author: Carolyn Cullinan McCormick
Editor: Edie McGinnis
Technical Editor: Jane Miller
Designer: Amy Robertson
Photography: Aaron T. Leimkuehler
Illustration: Lon Eric Craven
Production Assistance: Jo Ann Groves

Published by:

Kansas City Star Books
1729 Grand Blvd.
Kansas City, Missouri, USA 64108

First edition, first printing
978-1-933466-52-1
Printed in the United States of America
by Walsworth Publishing Co., Marceline, MO

To order copies, call StarInfo at (816) 234-4636 and say "Books."

KANSAS CITY STAR QUILTS
Continuing the Tradition

www.PickleDish.com

Contents

1940–1949

It seemed as though the world had gone crazy. With the bombing of Pearl Harbor, America was propelled into World War II. London was already a shambles with Germany dropping enough bombs to kill 300 to 600 people per day and injuring 1,000 to 3,000. In a time when great changes hovered on the horizon, quilters stepped up and volunteered and kept their fingers flying. Quilting was, and always has been, a comfort, not just for the recipient of the result, but for the peace of mind that comes with being engaged in the process of making a quilt.

During the early 1940s, women quilted not only to warm their own beds but to help the war effort as well. They made quilts to raise money for the Red Cross and quilts to send to family and friends in Europe. Ladies Circles affiliated with various churches pitched in with their scraps and time and talents. Sometimes it became more of an issue to find the money for the postage to send a quilt overseas than it was to get a quilt made.

Dorothy Cozart, author of "A Century of Fundraising Quilts: 1860 – 1960," tells the saga of one fundraising quilt in Uncoverings, Volume 5, 1984. Cozart wrote, "The quilt was probably made in 1944, during World War II. The Women's Missionary Union of a Baptist Church in Clark County, Missouri, made a quilt, putting the names of each woman and man then in the Armed Forces in the center of an album block. The only one killed in World War II whose name was on the quilt was Raymond S. Grinstead. In 1946 it was decided to raffle the quilt." People in the county must have thought highly of the Grinstead family, because friends bought tickets in the family's name. When the ticket was drawn, Raymond's fathers name was on it.

Dorothy Tiegs carrying shocks of wheat to the threshing machine circa 1941. Two of her brothers served in World War II.

BLUE STAR BANNERS

No one knows how many quilters made Blue Star Banners during the 1940s. We do know the first Blue Star Banner was designed in 1917 by Capt. Robert Queissner, who had two sons serving on the front line. The service flag was adopted quickly as the unofficial symbol of having a child serving in active duty. The banner became official when an Ohio congressman read a proclamation into the congressional record claiming, "The world should know of those who give so much for liberty. The dearest thing in all the world to a father and mother – their children."

One could always tell how many members in a family were actively serving their country by looking at the Blue Star Banners hanging in the windows of the homes lining the streets of any city. Each blue star on the banner signified a loved ones absence. When a smaller gold star was appliquéd on top of a blue star, it indicated that a serviceman had made the ultimate sacrifice and a family filled with grief now occupied the home.

During World War I and World War II, the banners were hand made by mothers and wives across America. Probably the most famous Blue Star Banner hung in the window of the Sullivan home in Waterloo, Iowa. The Sullivan family was made up of parents Thomas and Alleta, daughter Genevive, and five sons, George, Francis, Joseph, Madison and Albert. Outraged at the death of close friend Bill Ball at Pearl Harbor, all five brothers enlisted in the Navy, the branch the two oldest brothers had already served in. The boys pleaded to stay together. The Navy honored their request and all were assigned to the USS Juneau.

Friday the Thirteenth has always been considered a day of ill fortune. That February day of 1942 enforced the superstition for the Sullivan family when a torpedo hit the Juneau. Having survived an earlier hit, a second torpedo struck in almost the same place and split the hull in half. Four of the brothers were killed instantly. George was killed by sharks when he got out of the life raft to bathe in the oily water surrounding the survivors. Due to security reasons, the Sullivans were listed as missing in action. It wasn't until later that the family discovered they had lost all five of their sons in one fell swoop. The Sullivans had the heart-rending task of adding five gold stars to their window banner.

The deaths of the five brothers resulted in a new military policy being put into effect. No longer would members of the same family be allowed to serve in the same area or ship during wartime.

Mulvaney knew that boredom and lack of morale could be every bit as big an enemy as lack of food or nutrition to prisoners. A talented and skilled embroiderer, Mrs. Mulvany came up with the idea of having the women make quilt squares. Each woman would sign her name and use the project to pass on hidden messages to family members so they would know the women were alive.

WOMEN IN THE SERVICE

For the first time in the history of the United States, women were encouraged to enlist in branches of the armed services. Not only did they serve as nurses in the Army Nurse Corps but they joined the WAACS, the WAVES, the WASP and the WAF. Even though they were anxious to do their part, wages and rights fell far short of the compensation men received. Women who served in the WAACS worked with the Army but were not considered a part of the Army. The Army provided up to 150,000 "auxiliaries" with food, shelter, clothing and pay. Even though WAACS were allowed to serve overseas, the Army failed to provide them with overseas pay, life insurance, veteran's medical coverage or death benefits such as their male counterparts received. If WAACS became prisoners of war, they had no protection under international agreements. Still the women enlisted. Still they served their country. Still they died in battle.

WOMEN AS PRISONERS OF WAR

Europe was not the only front seeing women in uniform for the first time. In 1942 when Singapore fell, thousands of Allied troops surrendered to the Japanese. The Japanese, who had been trained to fight to the death, were totally unprepared to feed and house prisoners. Not only were there soldiers to be taken care of but civilians as well. Four hundred women and children had failed to evacuate and were taken prisoner.

Along with civilian men, the women and children were housed in Changi Prison. Originally designed to hold about 600 people, there were over 2,000 inmates. The best that could be said for the prison was that it had running water and flushable toilets. The women of Changi came from all over – the majority from the United Kingdom, but others were from the Netherlands, Australia, New Zealand, Canada and the United States.

The Japanese left the inmates to the task of administrating their sections. Canadian internee, Mrs. Ethel Mulvaney was chosen to be the Red Cross representative for the women. Mulvaney knew that boredom and lack of morale could be every bit as big an enemy as lack of food or nutrition to prisoners. A talented and skilled embroiderer, Mrs. Mulvany came up with the idea of having the women make quilt squares. Each woman would sign her name and use the project to pass on hidden messages to family members so they would know the women were alive.

She petitioned for and received permission from the Japanese commandant to have the ladies make the blocks, then after the blocks were made and sewn into quilts, they were destined to go to the wounded in Changi hospitals. Each quilt was embroidered on the back and indicated for whom it was made and where it was to go after the war. The back of one of the quilts in the War Memorial in Australia reads, "Presented by the women of Changi internment camp 1942 to the wounded Australian soldiers with our sympathy for their suffering. It is our wish that on the cessation of hostilities that this quilt be presented to the Australian Red Cross Society. It is advisable to dryclean this quilt." The ladies supposedly made four quilts, including one quilt specifically for the Japanese wounded. It was a shrewd move on Mulvaney's part to provide a quilt for the Japanese since it most likely secured the necessary permission required for the project.

Each woman who wanted to participate was given a square of white fabric. Some squares came from sheets and others from cot-

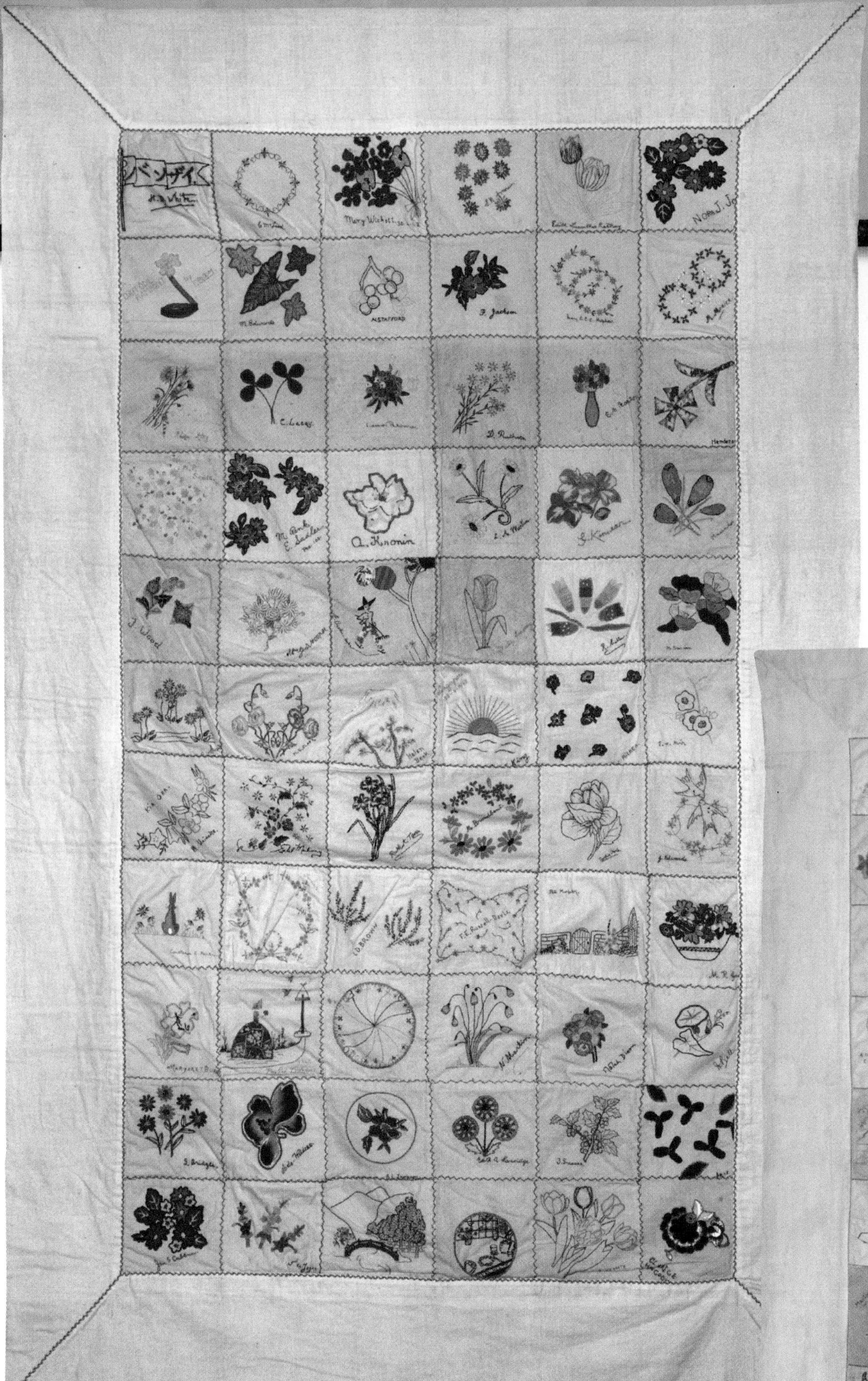

We are deeply grateful to the Australian War Memorial for allowing us to print the photographs of these quilts. The photo of the Australian Changi quilt can be viewed block by block on the following Web site: http://www.awm.gov.au/encyclopedia/quilt/detail.htm

PHOTOS COURTESY OF AUSTRALIAN WAR MEMORIAL, CANBERRA, ACT, AUSTRALIA

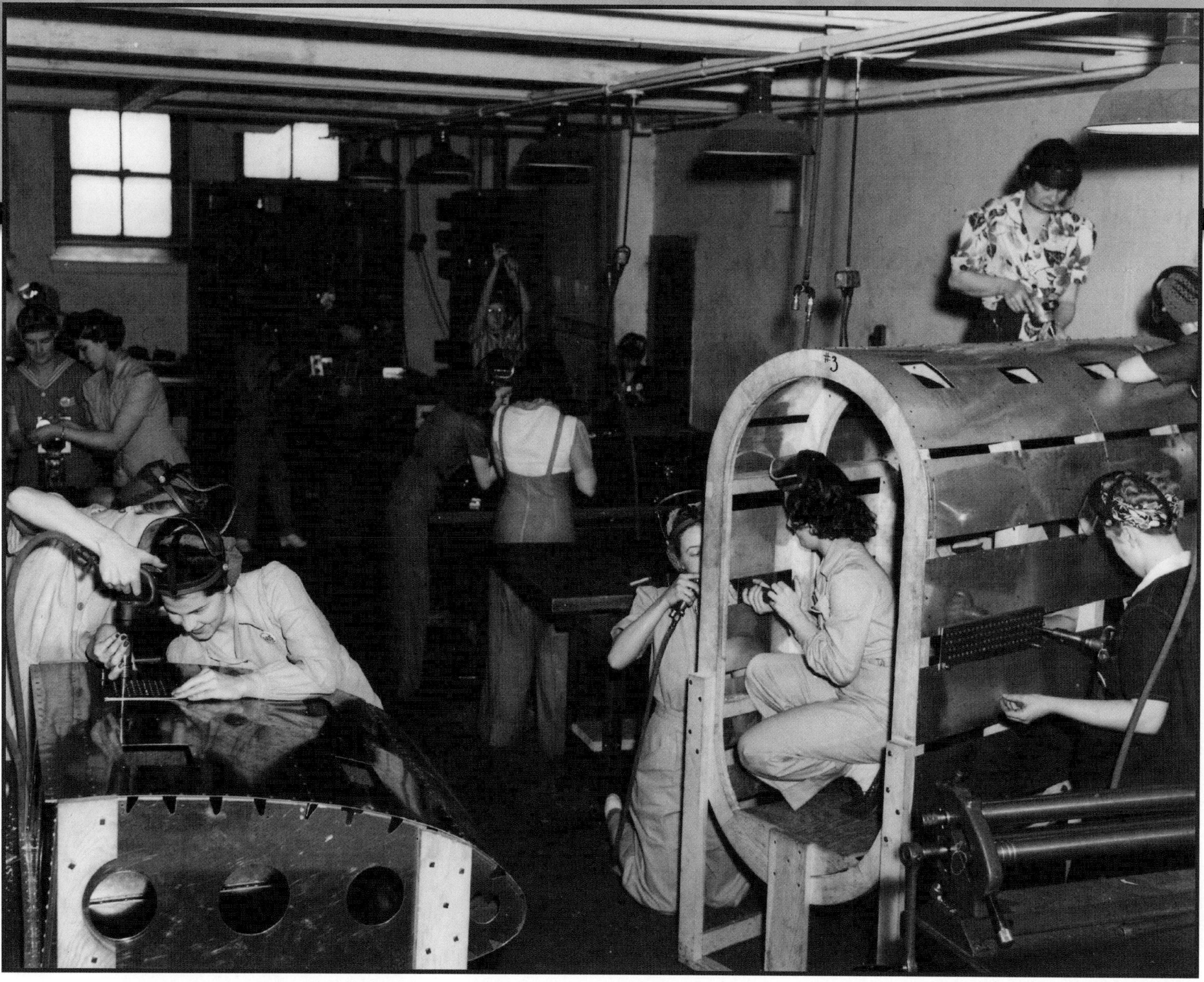

PHOTO COURTESY OF THE KANSAS CITY STAR

Women work on aircraft in a plant near Kansas City, Missouri.

ton flour sacks. Each woman was asked to put "something of herself" in her block as well as signing it. In the quilt, there are embroidered thistles, Disney cartoon characters, lazy daisy embroidered flowers, children's toys and animals.

The quilt made for the Japanese had no messages. Instead the designs contained the rising sun, flowers and Mount Fuji, all designs that would appeal to the Japanese. The reverse side of the quilt made for the Japanese read, "Presented by the women of Changi internment camp 2602 [the Japanese year that corresponded with 1942] to the wounded Nipponese soldiers with our sympathy for their suffering. It is our wish that on the cessation of hostilities that this quilt be presented to the Japanese Red Cross Society. It is advisable to dryclean this quilt."

After the war, the quilts eventually came to Colonel Collins, a British medical officer. He passed the quilts on to Lieutenant Webster, an Australian, who eventually gave the quilt intended for the Australian wounded to the Australian Red Cross. Webster gave the Japanese quilt to his wife who donated it to the Australian War Memorial in 1968. The quilt made for the British wounded was taken to England after the war and is now at the headquarters of the British Red Cross in Surrey. Only the three quilts are accounted for. No one knows what happened to the fourth.

WOMEN IN THE WORKFORCE

For the first time ever, women played an enormous role in the workforce taking over jobs that had been previously held only by men. Rosie the Riveter became the icon representing the working woman during the war years. Not only were single women encouraged to work in the factories, so were married women. Publicity campaigns were directed at women who had never held a job. The

Office of War Information said, "These jobs will have to be glorified as a patriotic war service if American women are to be persuaded to take them and stick to them. Their importance to a nation engaged in total war must be convincingly presented." Posters depicting working women portrayed them as confident and attractive as well as being resolved to do their duty to help the war effort.

Factories were not the only places where laborers were needed. The agricultural community also cried out for help. The Women's Land Army was formed and women stepped forward and sowed and harvested crops to provide food for a hungry nation as well as a massive fighting force. Promoted as a "healthy, happy job," the women were expected to work a minimum of 48 hours per week hoeing in the fields or using horse-drawn, outdated equipment when there wasn't enough machinery available.

Mardell Smith of Anatone, Washington, wrote to a friend who was then in the service, "I'm quite the farmer, Jack. You should see me – I ride the horse after the cows, drive hay trucks and yesterday I even learned to drive the tractor." Dawn Dyer of Sprague, Washington, wrote to her future husband and threatened to break down in tears if she ran into any more problems while trying to harvest the crops. Not only did she have problems with an old Dodge truck but the header on the combine broke.

Even the family backyard was put to use for the war effort as women planted and harvested produce they raised in Victory Gardens. All the vegetables that were harvested and canned saved that much for the war effort.

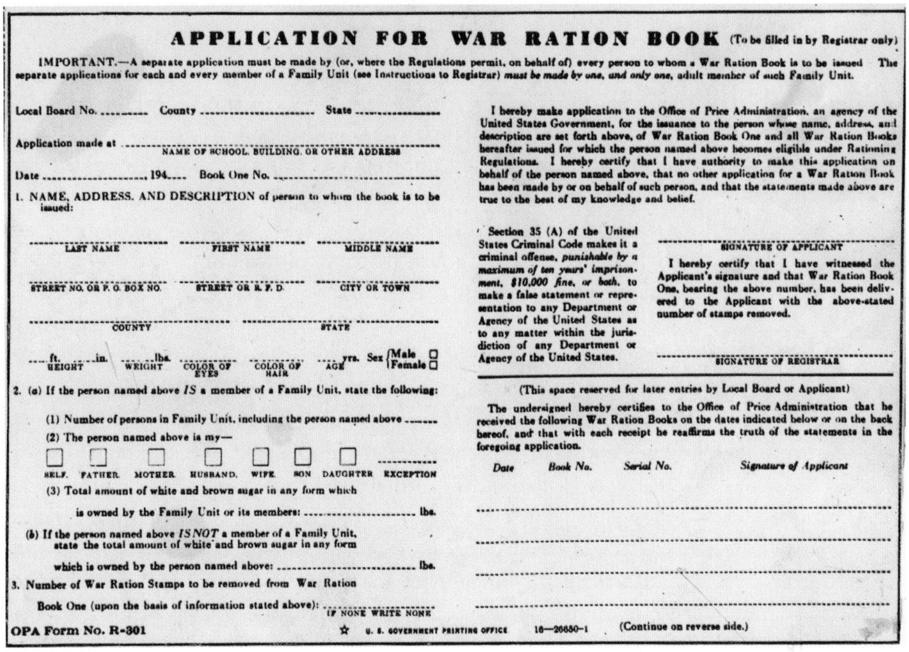

APPLICATION FOR WAR RATION BOOK (To be filled in by Registrar only)

IMPORTANT.—A separate application must be made by (or, where the Regulations permit, on behalf of) every person to whom a War Ration Book is to be issued. The separate applications for each and every member of a Family Unit (see Instructions to Registrar) *must be made by one, and only one*, adult member of such Family Unit.

Local Board No. .... County .... State ....

Application made at ....
NAME OF SCHOOL, BUILDING, OR OTHER ADDRESS

Date ...., 194.... Book One No. ....

1. NAME, ADDRESS, AND DESCRIPTION of person to whom the book is to be issued:

LAST NAME | FIRST NAME | MIDDLE NAME

STREET NO. OR P. O. BOX NO. | STREET OR R. F. D. | CITY OR TOWN

COUNTY | STATE

....ft. ....in. HEIGHT | ....lbs. WEIGHT | COLOR OF EYES | COLOR OF HAIR | ....yrs. AGE | Sex {Male ☐ Female ☐

2. (a) If the person named above *IS* a member of a Family Unit, state the following:

(1) Number of persons in Family Unit, including the person named above ....

(2) The person named above is my—

☐ SELF. ☐ FATHER. ☐ MOTHER. ☐ HUSBAND. ☐ WIFE. ☐ SON ☐ DAUGHTER .... EXCEPTION

(3) Total amount of white and brown sugar in any form which is owned by the Family Unit or its members: .... lbs.

(b) If the person named above *IS NOT* a member of a Family Unit, state the total amount of white and brown sugar in any form which is owned by the person named above: .... lbs.

3. Number of War Ration Stamps to be removed from War Ration Book One (upon the basis of information stated above): .... IF NONE WRITE NONE

I hereby make application to the Office of Price Administration, an agency of the United States Government, for the issuance to the person whose name, address, and description are set forth above, of War Ration Book One and all War Ration Books hereafter issued for which the person named above becomes eligible under Rationing Regulations. I hereby certify that I have authority to make this application on behalf of the person named above, that no other application for a War Ration Book has been made by or on behalf of such person, and that the statements made above are true to the best of my knowledge and belief.

Section 35 (A) of the United States Criminal Code makes it a criminal offense, *punishable by a maximum of ten years' imprisonment, $10,000 fine, or both*, to make a false statement or representation to any Department or Agency of the United States as to any matter within the jurisdiction of any Department or Agency of the United States.

....
SIGNATURE OF APPLICANT

I hereby certify that I have witnessed the Applicant's signature and that War Ration Book One, bearing the above number, has been delivered to the Applicant with the above-stated number of stamps removed.

....
SIGNATURE OF REGISTRAR

(This space reserved for later entries by Local Board or Applicant)

The undersigned hereby certifies to the Office of Price Administration that he received the following War Ration Books on the dates indicated below or on the back hereof, and that with each receipt he reaffirms the truth of the statements in the foregoing application.

Date | *Book No.* | *Serial No.* | *Signature of Applicant*

OPA Form No. R-301 ☆ U. S. GOVERNMENT PRINTING OFFICE 16—26650-1 (Continue on reverse side.)

PHOTO COURTESY OF THE KANSAS CITY STAR

Application for rationing card.

RATIONING

Rationing affected everyone in the country. Clothing, shoes, rubber, gas, meat, sugar and butter had to be bought using coupons. No longer were silk stockings or nylons available to the women, instead that material was used for making parachutes. The ever ingenious women began to draw a line up the back of their legs to make it appear as though they were wearing stockings.

"Eking out and making do" became one of the mottos of the home front. The National Cotton Council issued booklets on sewing with cotton bags to encourage homemakers to use feedsacks, flour sacks and sugar sacks for fabric for their sewing projects. The feedsacks and flour sacks were a bonanza for the seamstress and quilter alike.

The Cotton Council had all manner of suggestions for ways to use cotton bags. Since the bags came in all kinds of prints, you could find ones that were suitable for just about any kind of garment. There were plaids and stripes to turn into wonderful men's shirts. Lovely floral fabrics were perfect for ladies dresses, blouses and skirts. Cowboy prints for the boys, ballerinas for the girls and nursery rhymes for the babies meant a world of fabric choices for clothing, curtains and quilts. It was more a sign of loyalty to our country to wear garments made of cotton bags than it was a sign of poverty.

After culling all one could for garments from the bags, the scraps went into quilts. Charm quilts and scrap quilts using small pieces were very much in vogue during the 40s. String quilts that used the smallest strips decorated the bedrooms of the frugal.

RECONSTRUCTION

After the armistice was signed, rebuilding war-torn Europe became a priority. The call came out asking for quilts as well as other supplies. Quilters were advised to make quilts using wool rather than cotton to send to Europe. Unlike cotton, wool remained warm even when wet. With a lack of heat and blown out windows, warmth became a priority while Europe struggled to rebuild.

Two days after the peace treaty was signed with Japan, President George Albert Smith of the Church of Jesus Christ of Latter-Day Saints met with 6,000 people of various faiths to show their gratitude of being a nation at peace. One of the speakers reminded the people of the responsibilities victors owed those they had vanquished.

The Relief Society of the L.D.S. Church took those responsibilities to heart. Women made Crazy Quilts out of warm wool suiting material, sometimes taking clothing apart so they would have enough pieces. Wool batting went on the inside and soft flannel on the back. Generally these wool quilts were tied rather than quilted because of the denseness of the layers. Also time was of the essence and the process of tying took much less time than actually quilting them.

Joyce Peaden, in her article, "Donated Quilts," Uncoverings, Vol. 9, 1988, estimated that 38,000 to 40,000 quilts were made and donated by the L.D.S. Relief Society after World War II had ended.

THE DECLINE

After the end of the war, the popularity of quilting appeared to be on the decline. People seemed to connect quilting with the hard times of the depression and the war. Household goods were no longer rationed. Pretty blankets could be readily purchased and those lovely chenille bedspreads were a "must have" in stylish homes.

Women had gotten used to working and earning their own money. Even though many women were laid off of the factory jobs to make way for returning soldiers, it had become acceptable for them to be in the workforce. The face of the world had changed and so had the roles of women.

It would be over twenty years before women would again find comfort in going back to their roots and picking up a needle to stitch on some patchwork. New inventions such as the rotary cutter, mat and rulers took much of the tedious labor out of making a quilt. Women have again found the pleasure in creating and the comfort of working with beautiful fabrics. Quilting has soared to new heights and has been established as a "new" tradition to be passed from one quilter to another. — *Edie McGinnis*

How to Paper Piece

WHY PAPER PIECE?

Paper piecing is great for beginners as well as experienced quilters. One can make a wonderful quilt on their very first try since complicated patterns are broken down into easily managed steps. Sewing the fabric to paper makes matching points relatively easy and the paper stabilizes the fabric, enabling one to use even the smallest of scraps.

HOW TO PAPER PIECE: GET READY...

Use a copy machine to copy your pattern. Make all of your copies from the same original and use the same copy machine. All copy machines distort to some extent so check your pattern by holding the original and the copy together with a light source behind the two sheets of paper. Make as many copies as necessary. It's nice to have a few extras in case you make an error. Use the lightest weight paper you can find. The heavier the paper, the more difficult it is to remove.

Set up your sewing machine. Use a 90/14 size needle and set the stitch length to 18–20 stitches per inch. The larger needle perforates the paper making it easier to tear off. The smaller stitches keep the seams from ripping out when you remove the paper.

Place a piece of muslin or scrap fabric on your ironing board. When you press the pieces, the ink from the copies can transfer onto your ironing board cover.

Make sure you have a light source nearby. The light on your sewing machine is usually adequate.

Remember when paper piecing, your pattern will be reversed.

GET SET...

Here is a familiar pattern... see Fig. A. Instead of templates with seam allowances as many of us are used to seeing, we have lines and numbers. The lines indicate where to sew and the numbers indicate the sequence in which to sew. The only seam allowances that are shown are the ones that go around a block or a unit.

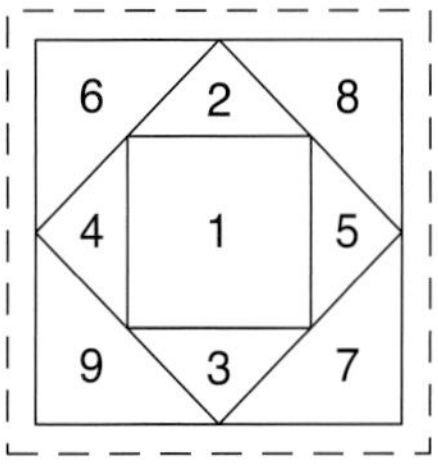

Figure A

The front of the pattern is where the lines and numbers are printed. This is the side you sew on.

The back of the pattern is the side that is blank. This is where your fabric will be placed.

Cut your fabric pieces by following the cutting chart for each block. Always make sure the piece of fabric you are using is at least one-quarter of an inch larger all the way around than shown on the foundation pattern.

SEW!

Put fabric number 1 right side up on the blank side of the pattern. You may either pin the piece in place or use double–sided tape

PAPER PIECING SUPPLIES:

- Add–A–Quarter Ruler – 10" Blocks
- Add–An–Eighth Ruler – 4" Blocks
- Rotary Cutter and Mat
- Rulers for Rotary Cutting
- Sewing Machine
- 90/14 Sewing Machine Needles
- Thread
- Iron and Ironing Board
- Straight Pins (Regular, Silk and/or Flower Head)
- Double–Sided tape (Optional)
- Index Card or Piece of Template Plastic Measuring 3" x 10"
- Tweezers (For removing small pieces of paper)
- Paper for Foundation Piecing (This should be relatively thin)
- Piece of Muslin or Scrap Fabric (For Ironing Board)

to hold the fabric in place. The tape makes the fabric lie flat on the paper. The pin can make a small rise in the paper. See Fig. B.

Turn the foundation pattern over, look through the paper towards your light source and make sure the fabric extends over the lines on each side by at least one–quarter of an inch. See Fig. C.

Place an index card or template plastic on the sewing line between piece number 1 and piece number 2. Fold back the foundation pattern over the edge of the card. You can now see the excess fabric from piece number 1. See Fig. D.

Place the Add–A–Quarter ruler up against the fold of the foundation paper with lip side down. Use the rotary cutter to trim the extra fabric from piece number 1. You will now have a straight line to help you place fabric piece number 2. See Fig. E.

Now place the fabric that goes in position number 2 of the pattern on the trimmed edge of piece number 1 with the right sides facing each other. See Fig. F.

Turn the foundation paper over and stitch on the line between piece number 1 and piece number 2. Sew a few stitches before the line begins and a few stitches after the line ends. Make sure piece number 2 does not slip. See Fig. G.

Flip the paper back over and open piece number 2. Press the piece open using a dry iron. See Fig. H.

Fold the foundation paper back along the line between piece number 1 and piece number 3 using the index card or the template plastic. Butt the Add–A–Quarter ruler up against the paper and trim the excess fabric. See Fig. I.

Turn the foundation back over and position fabric piece number 3, being careful not to displace your fabric. Sew on the line between number 1 and number 3. See Fig. J & K.

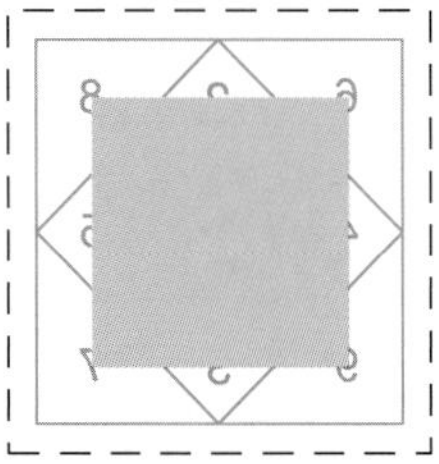

Figure B

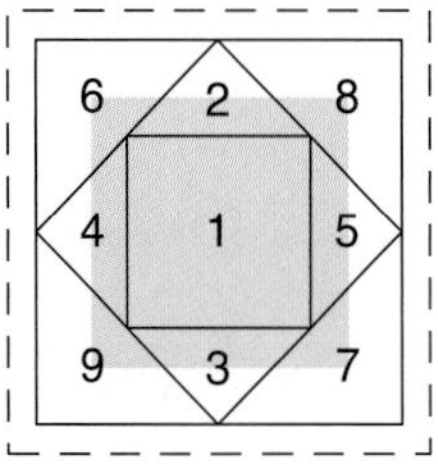

Figure C

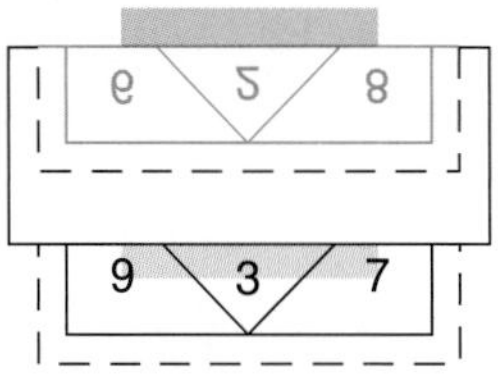

Figure D

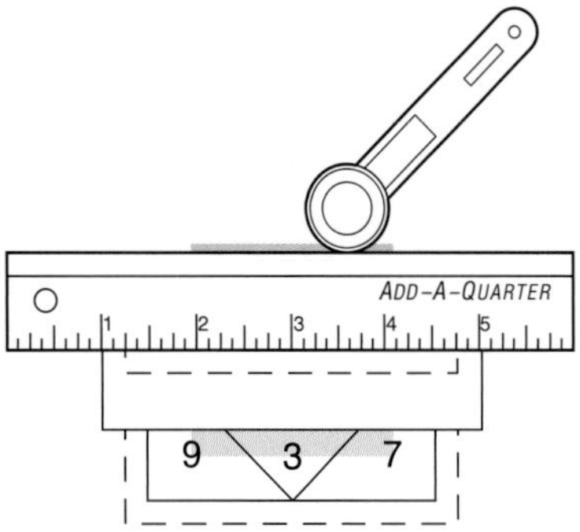

Figure E

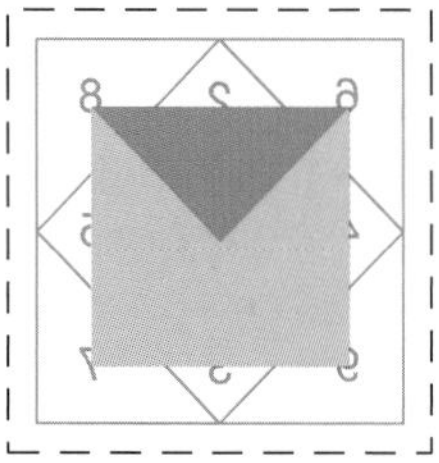

Figure F

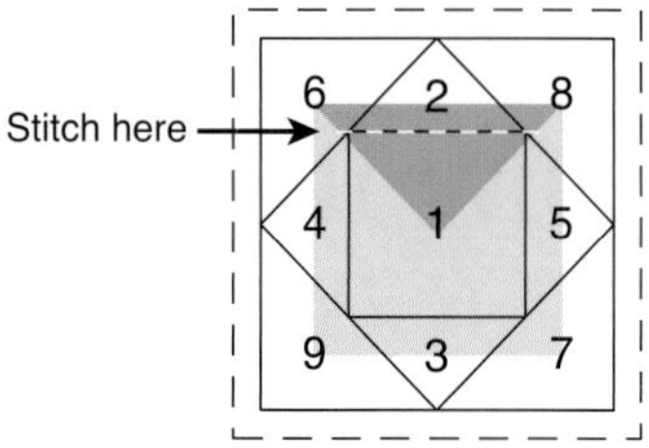

Figure G

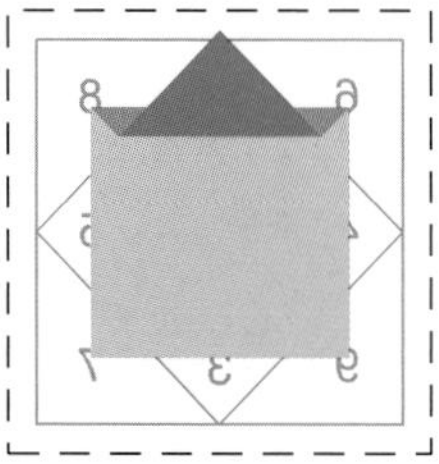

Figure H

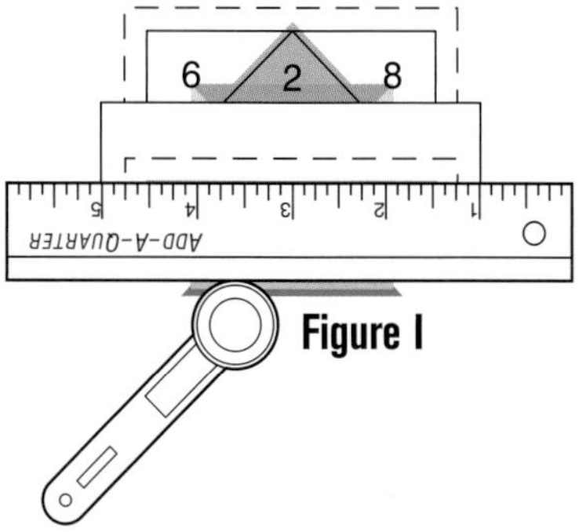

Figure I

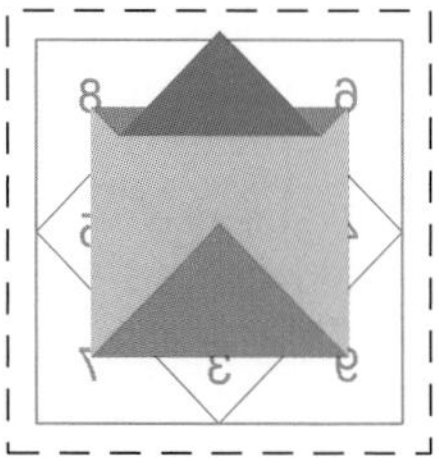

Figure J

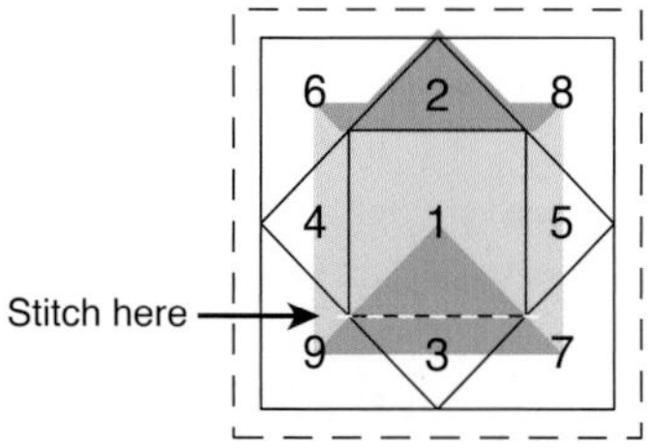

Figure K

Continue sewing each piece in place in the numeric order given until all the pieces are sewn in place and each unit is complete. See Fig. L.

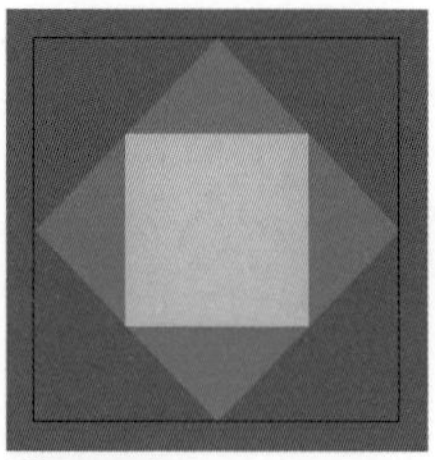

Figure L

After all the pieces are sewn onto the foundation, you will be ready to trim the edges. You will need a 1⁄4" seam allowance around the entire block, no matter the size of the block, when you sew your blocks together. Never trim on the solid line! Line up the ruler with the solid line on the foundation. Trim off the excess fabric using your rotary cutter.

If you are paper piecing a block that is made up of multiple units, the time has come to sew them together. Pin the units together. Make sure the lines you are sewing match on the top and the bottom of the units. This can be accomplished by putting a pin straight through both lines at each intersection. Always check to make sure the seam is directly on the top line and the underneath line as well, otherwise your block will be off.

When the block is finished, do not remove the paper! It is best to join the blocks before you remove the paper. This gives you a line to follow when you sew the blocks together. Remove the paper after the blocks are sewn together. You might want to remove the really small pieces with a pair of tweezers.

A FEW VARIATIONS...

Since these patterns from *The Kansas City Star* have been adapted to a paper pieced pattern from traditional blocks, you will have a few things crop up that you might not run into with blocks that were originally designed with paper piecing in mind.

You may have triangles that are either sewn to inside or outside corners of the block. These are shown as separate pieces. You may either pin or use double-sided tape to hold your fabric to the triangles. Sew them in the order indicated on the pattern leaving the paper in place.

Use half-square triangles where you see this symbol: 

JUST A FEW SUGGESTIONS...

If you have to unsew and the paper foundation separates on the sewing line, use a piece of clear tape to repair the pattern. Sometimes you will notice the stitches from the previously sewn fabric when you fold back the foundation. If this happens, just pull the foundation away from the fabric and trim using the ruler.

After you have sewn two units together and after pressing, remove the paper from the back side of the seam allowance, this will reduce some of the bulk.

To help speed up your paper piecing, place all of your position 1 pieces on multiple units at the same time. Trim and sew multiple units at the same time.

By placing your pattern face down on a white piece of paper you will be able to see the outline of the design for placement of your first fabric.

Ten-inch sampler quilt made by Carolyn Cullinan McCormick, Franktown, Colorado, quilted by Carol Willey, Castle Rock, Colorado.

1940s Sampler Quilt

SEWING INSTRUCTIONS ★ 72" x 92"

Supply List

FABRIC REQUIREMENTS:

Background:
Blocks: 2 5/8 yd
Solid Blocks: 1 5/8 yd
Total: 4 1/4 yd

Dark:
Blocks 1 3/4 yd
Setting and Corner Triangles: 1 5/8 yd
Total: 4 3/8 yd

Medium:	3/4 yd
Light:	3/4 yd
Various Prints:	1/2 yd each of 5 prints

SASHING:	2 yd
BINDING:	3/4 yd
BATTING:	1 5/8 yd 90" wide
BACKING:	5 1/2 yd

The quilt is set on point and the fabric requirements are based on 40-inches of usable fabric width. Follow the cutting instructions and the position chart for each block. Make all twenty blocks.

SASHING:

From the blue fabric, cut:

★ 34 – 2" strips across the width of the fabric. Cut the strips into 40 – 2" x 10 1/2" rectangles and 40 – 2" x 13 1/2" rectangles.

★ Sew the 2" x 10 1/2" rectangles on two sides of the block. Press toward the sashing. Sew the 2" x 13 1/2" rectangles on the top and bottom of each block. Press toward the sashing.

SOLID BLOCKS:

From the background fabric, cut:

★ 4 – 13 1/2" strips across the width of the fabric. Cut the strips into 13 1/2" squares. You need a total of 12 squares.

SETTING TRIANGLES:

From the red fabric, cut:

★ 2 – 19 5/8" strips across the width of the fabric. Cut the strips into 19 5/8" squares. You need a total of 4 squares. Cut the squares on the diagonal from corner to corner twice, each square will make 4 quarter-square triangles. You need 14 setting triangles.

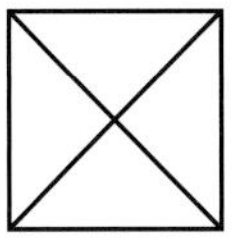

SETTING CORNER TRIANGLES:

From the red fabric, cut

★ 1 – 10 1/8" strip across the width of the fabric. Cut the strip into 10 1/8" squares. You will need two squares. Cut each square on the diagonal from corner to corner for a total of 4 triangles.

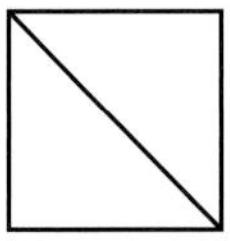

Refer to the diagram and sew the quilt blocks together as shown.

Quilt as desired, trim excess fabric from edges and sew on binding.

For the binding, cut:

★ 9 – 2 1/2" strips across the width of the fabric.

Mother's Favorite Star

May 1940 ★ 10" Block

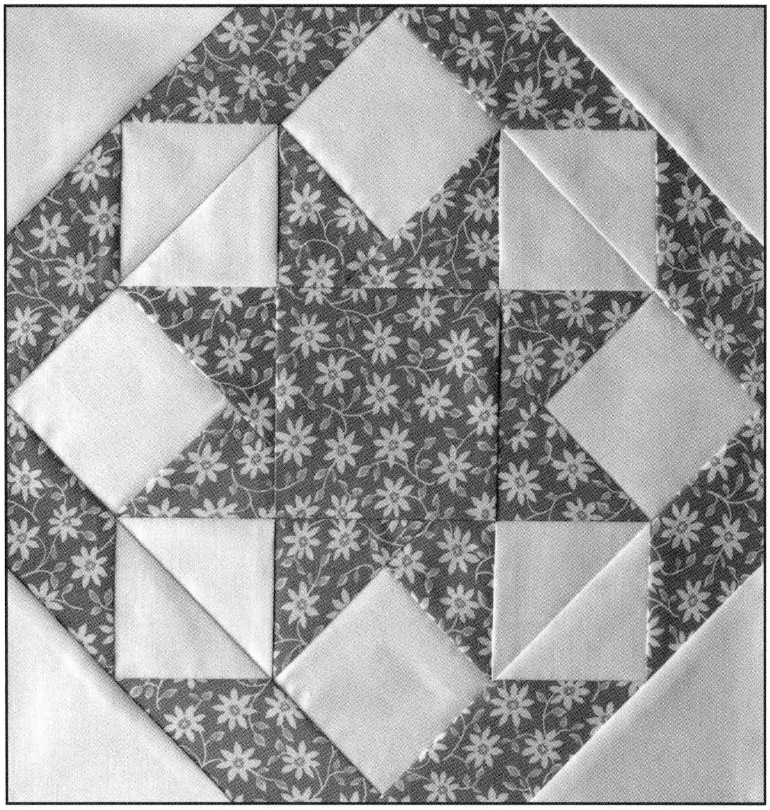

CUTTING INSTRUCTIONS

FROM THE BACKGROUND FABRIC, CUT:

★ 1 – 4 1/2" x 9" strip.
Cut the strip into 2 – 4 1/2" squares.
Cut the squares into half-square triangles.

★ 1 – 3 1/2" x 14" strip.
Cut the strip into 4 – 3 1/2" squares.
Cut the squares into half-square triangles.

★ 1 – 3" x 12" strip.
Cut the strip into 4 – 3" squares.

FROM THE PRINT FABRIC, CUT:

★ 1 – 4" square.

★ 1 – 3 1/2" x 14" strip.
Cut the strip into 4 – 3 1/2" squares.
Cut the squares into half-square triangles.

★ 1 – 2 1/2" x 36" strip.
Cut the strip into 8 – 2 1/2" x 4 1/2" rectangles.

PATTERNS ON PAGES 78–79.

ASSEMBLING THE BLOCK

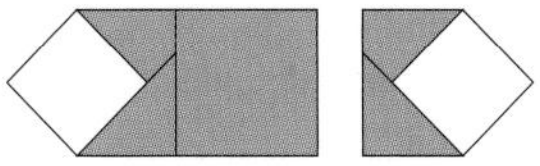

Sew Unit A to Unit B.

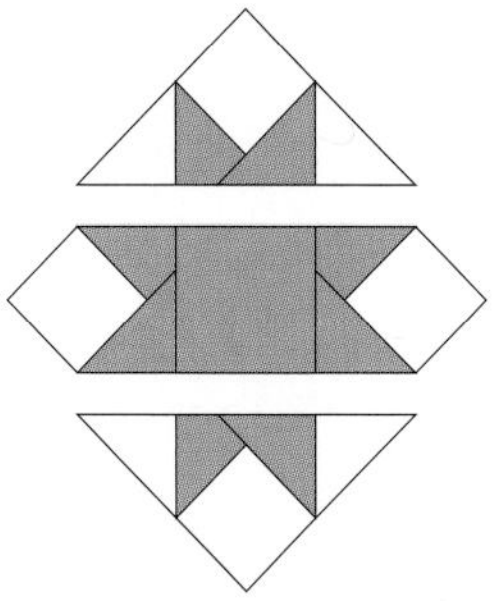

Sew Units C to Unit AB.

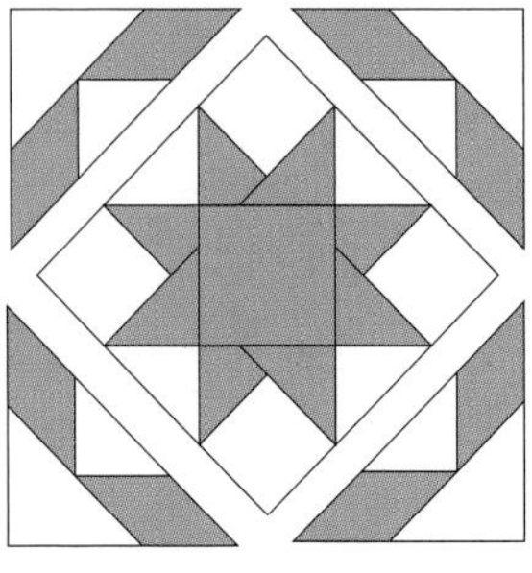

Sew Units D to Unit ABC.

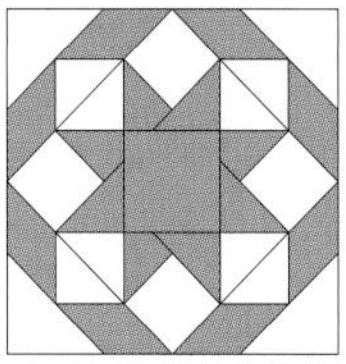

POSITION CHART

FABRIC	POSITION	SIZE
UNIT A - MAKE 1		
Background	1	3" x 3"
Print	2, 3	3½" x 3½"
Print	4	4" x 4"
UNIT B - MAKE 1		
Background	1	3" x 3"
Print	2, 3	3½" x 3½"
UNIT C - MAKE 2		
Background	1	3" x 3"
Print	2, 3	3½" x 3½"
Background	4, 5	3½" x 3½"
UNIT D - MAKE 4		
Background	1	3½" x 3½"
Print	2, 3	2½" x 4½"
Background	4	4½" x 4½"

Mona's Choice

June 1940 ★ 10" Block

CUTTING INSTRUCTIONS

FROM THE LIGHT FABRIC, CUT:

★ 1 – 4 1/4" square.

★ 1 – 3 1/4" x 34" strip.
Cut the strip into 8 – 3 1/4" x 4 1/4" rectangles.

★ 1 – 2 1/4" x 36" and 1 – 2 1/4" x 12" strip.
Cut the strip into 16 – 2 1/4" x 3" rectangles.

FROM THE DARK FABRIC, CUT:

★ 2 – 2" x 35" strips and 1 – 2" x 14" strip.
Cut the strips into 24 – 2" x 3 1/2" rectangles.

PATTERNS ON PAGES 80–81.

POSITION CHART

FABRIC	POSITION	SIZE
UNITS A & B - MAKE 4 EACH		
Dark	1,3	2" x 3½"
Light	2,4	2¼" x 3"
UNITS C & D - MAKE 4 EACH		
Dark	1	2" x 3½"
Light	2	3¼" x 4¼"
UNIT E - MAKE 1		
Light	1	4¼" x 4¼"

ASSEMBLING THE BLOCK

Sew Units A to Units B.

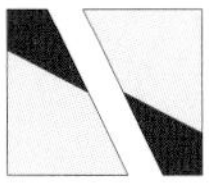

Sew Units C to Units D.

Sew Unit AB to each side of Unit E.

Sew Unit CD to each side of Unit AB. Make two.

Sew together as shown to complete the block.

The Colorado Quilt

JANUARY 1941 ★ 10" BLOCK

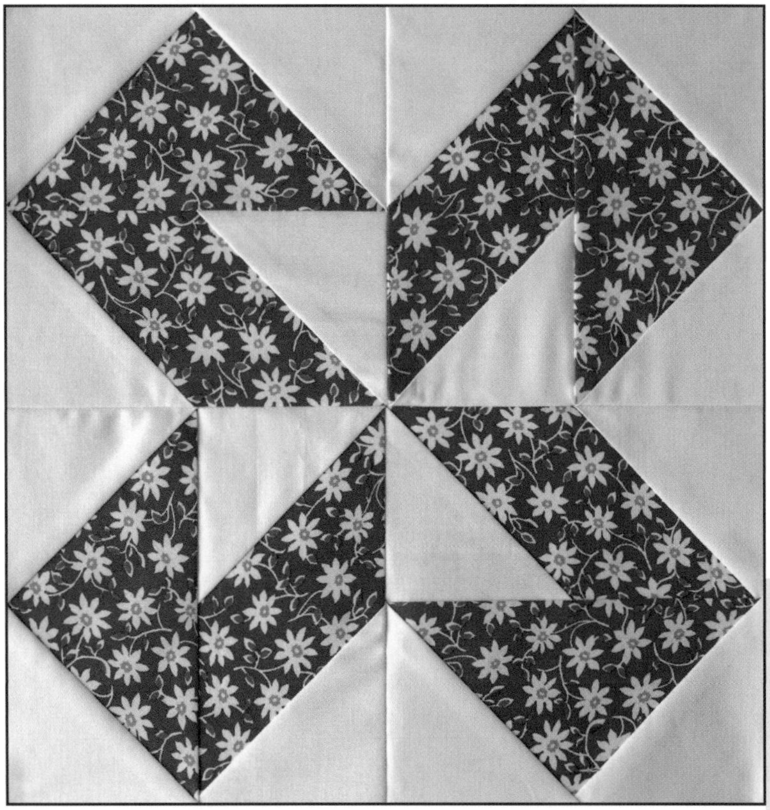

CUTTING INSTRUCTIONS

FROM THE BACKGROUND FABRIC, CUT:

★ 1 – 4" x 32" strip.
Cut the strip into 8 – 4" squares.
Cut the squares into half-square triangles.

FROM THE PRINT FABRIC, CUT:

★ 1 – 5 1/4" x 10 1/2" strip.
Cut the strip into 2 – 5 1/4" squares.
Cut the squares into half-square triangles.

★ 1 – 3 1/2" x 24" strips.
Cut the strip into 4 – 3 1/2" x 6" rectangles.

PATTERNS ON PAGE 84.

POSITION CHART

FABRIC	POSITION	SIZE
UNIT A - MAKE 4		
Print	1	3½" x 6"
Background	2,3,5,6	4" x 4"
Print	4	5¼" x 5¼"

ASSEMBLING THE BLOCK

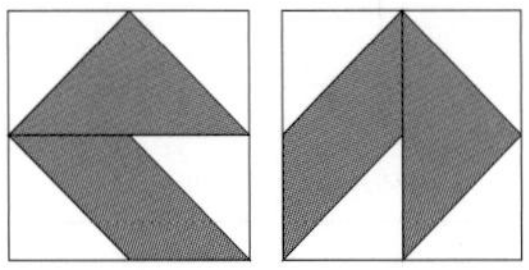

Sew two Units A together. Make two.

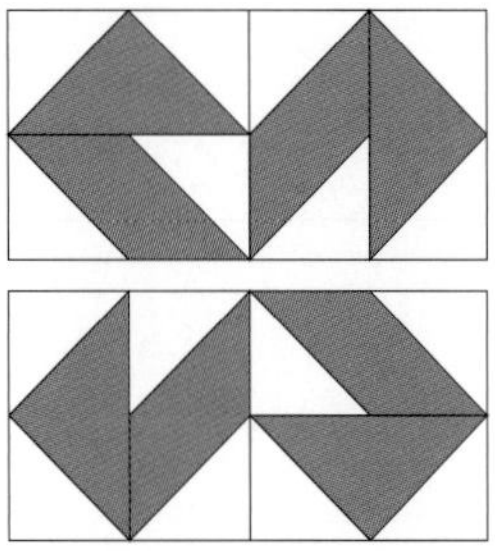

Sew the two halves together to complete the block.

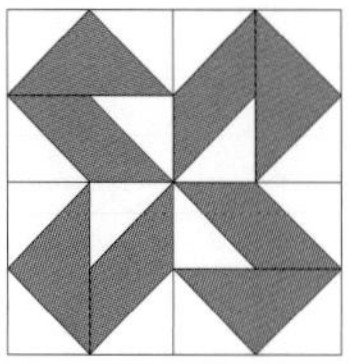

Anna's Choice

FEBRUARY 1941 ★ 10" BLOCK

CUTTING INSTRUCTIONS

FROM THE DARK FABRIC, CUT:

★ 1 – 4" x 32" strip.
Cut the strip into 8 – 4" squares.
Cut the squares into half-square triangles.

FROM THE LIGHT FABRIC, CUT:

★ 1 – 4" x 32" strip.
Cut the strip into 8 – 4" squares.
Cut the squares into half-square triangles.

PATTERNS ON PAGES 82–83.

POSITION CHART

FABRIC	POSITION	SIZE
UNIT A - MAKE 2		
Dark	1,3,5,7	4" x 4"
Light	2,4,6,8	4" x 4"
UNIT B - MAKE 2		
Dark	1,4,6,7	4" x 4"
Light	2,3,5,8	4" x 4"

ASSEMBLING THE BLOCK

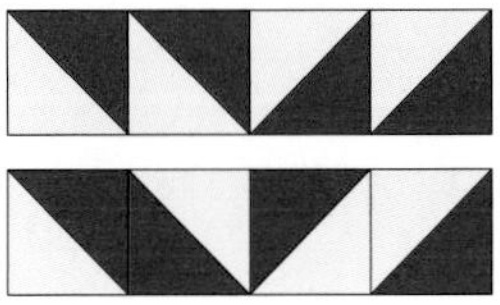

Sew each Unit A to each Unit B.

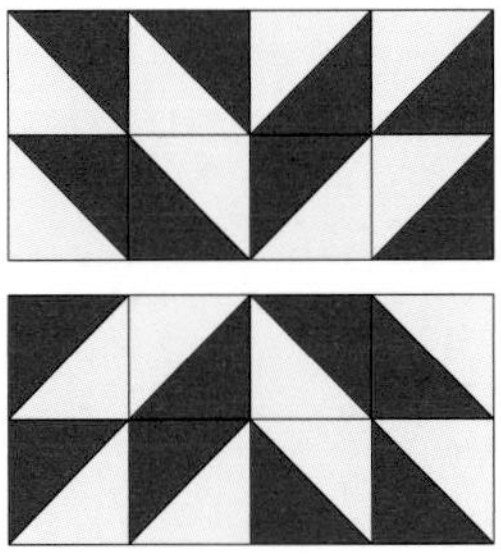

Sew the AB Units together as shown.

The 1941 Nine Patch

SEPTEMBER 1941 ★ 10" BLOCK

CUTTING INSTRUCTIONS

FROM THE DARK FABRIC, CUT:

★ 1 – 4 1/4" x 17" strip.
Cut the strip into 4 – 4 1/4" squares.

★ 1 – 2" x 17" strip.
Cut the strip into 4 – 2" x 4 1/4" rectangles.

FROM THE PRINT FABRIC, CUT:

★ 1 – 4 1/4" square.

★ 1 – 3 1/2" x 22" strip.
Cut the strip into 4 - 3 1/2" x 5 1/2" rectangles.

★ 1 – 3" x 13" strip.
Cut the strip into 4 – 3" x 3 1/4" rectangles.

PATTERNS ON PAGES 85-86.

POSITION CHART

FABRIC	POSITION	SIZE
UNIT A – MAKE 1		
Dark	1	2" x 4¼"
Print	2	3" x 3¼"
Print	3	3½" x 5½"
Print	4	4¼" x 4¼"
UNIT B –MAKE 1		
Dark	1	2" x 4¼"
Print	2	3" x 3¼"
Print	3	3½" x 5½"
UNIT C – MAKE 2		
Dark	1	2" x 4¼"
Print	2	3" x 3¼"
Print	3	3½" x 5½"
Dark	4,5	4¼" x 4¼"

ASSEMBLING THE BLOCK

Sew Unit A to Unit B.

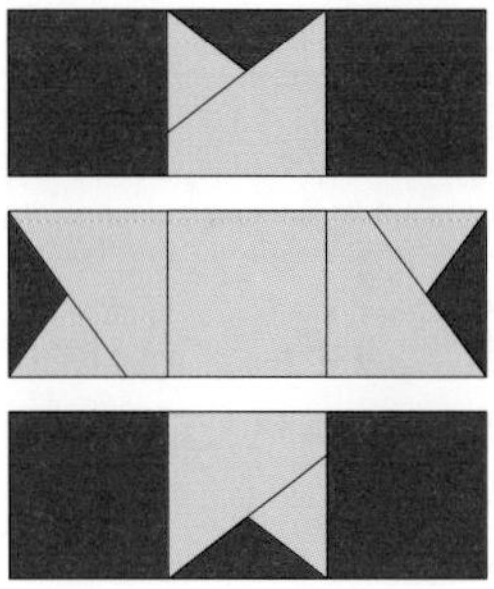

Sew Units C to Unit AB.

Sunlight and Shadows

January 1942 ★ 10" Block

CUTTING INSTRUCTIONS

FROM THE DARK FABRIC, CUT:

★ 1 – 3 3/4" x 7 1/2" strip.
Cut the strip into 2 – 3 3/4" squares.

★ 1 – 3" x 19 1/2" strip.
Cut the strip into 2 – 3" x 3 3/4" rectangles and 2 – 3" x 6" rectangles.

FROM THE MEDIUM FABRIC, CUT:

★ 1 – 3 1/2" x 14" strip.
Cut the strip into 4 – 3 1/2" squares.
Cut the squares into half-square triangles.

FROM THE LIGHT FABRIC, CUT:

★ 1 – 3 3/4" x 7 1/2" strip.
Cut the strip into 2 – 3 3/4" squares.

★ 1 – 3" x 19 1/2" strip.
Cut the strip into 2 – 3" x 3 3/4" rectangles and 2 – 3" x 6" rectangles.

PATTERNS ON PAGES 87–88.

OSITION CHART

FABRIC	POSITION	SIZE
NIT A - MAKE 2		
Dark	1	3¾" x 3¾"
Light	2	3" x 3¾"
Light	3	3" x 6"
Medium	4,5	3½" x 3½"
NIT B - MAKE 2		
Light	1	3¾" x 3¾"
Dark	2	3" x 3¾"
Dark	3	3" x 6"
Medium	4,5	3½" x 3½"

ASSEMBLING THE BLOCK

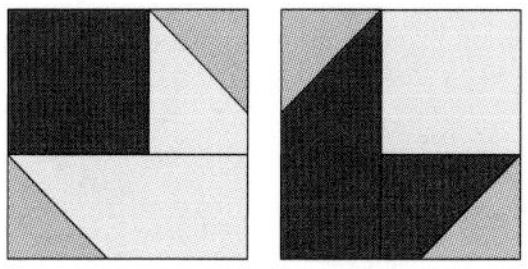

Sew Units A to Units B.

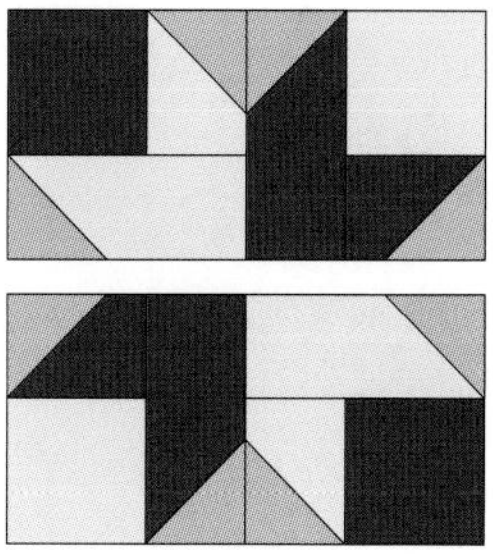

Sew the two halves together to complete the block.

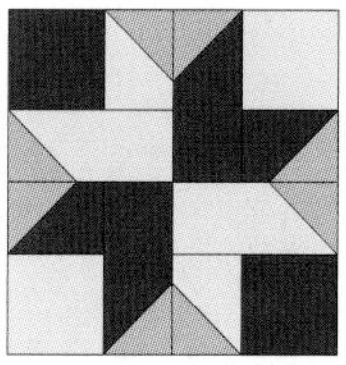

A Salute to the Colors

May 1942 ★ 10" Block

CUTTING INSTRUCTIONS

FROM THE LIGHT FABRIC, CUT:

★ 1 – 4" x 32" strip. Cut the strip into 8 – 4" squares.
Cut the squares into half-square triangles.

FROM THE DARK FABRIC, CUT:

★ 1 – 3 1/2" x 14" strip.
Cut the strip into 4 – 3 1/2" squares.
Cut the squares into half-square triangles.

★ 1 – 2 3/4" x 5 1/2" strip.
Cut the strip into 2 – 2 3/4" squares.

★ 1 – 2 1/2" x 5" strip.*

FROM THE PRINT FABRIC, CUT:

★ 1 – 3 1/2" x 14" strip.
Cut the strip into 4 – 3 1/2" squares.
Cut the squares into half-square triangles.

★ 1 – 2 3/4" x 5 1/2" strip.
Cut the strip into 2 – 2 3/4" squares.

★ 1 – 2 1/2" x 5" strip.*

* Sew the print 2 1/2" x 5" strip to the dark 2 1/2" x 5" strip using a 1/4" seam allowance. Press towards the dark fabric.
Cut the strip into 2 – 2 1/2" pieces.

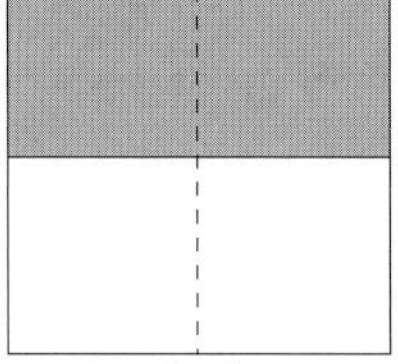

PATTERNS ON PAGES 89–90.

ASSEMBLING THE BLOCK

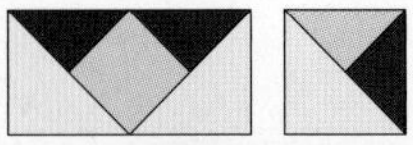

Sew Units A to Units B.

Sew Units AB to Units C.

Sew one Unit E to each side of Unit D.

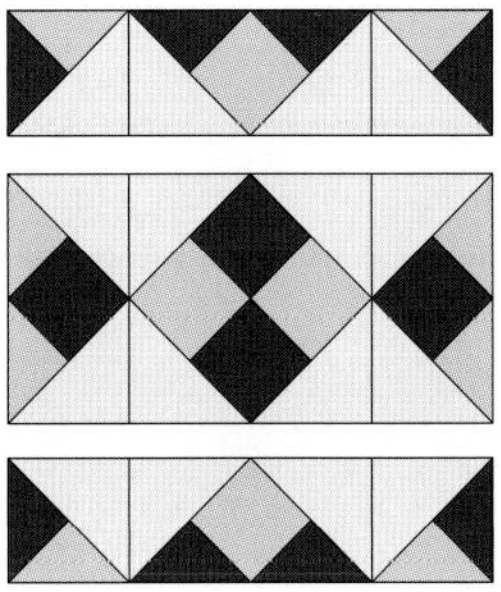

Sew together as shown.

POSITION CHART

FABRIC	POSITION	SIZE
UNIT A - MAKE 2		
Print	1	2¾" x 2¾"
Dark	2,3	3½" x 3½"
Light	4,5	4" x 4"
UNIT B - MAKE 2		
Dark	1	3½" x 3½"
Print	2	3½" x 3½"
Light	3	4" x 4"
UNIT C - MAKE 2		
Dark	1	3½" x 3½"
Print	2	3½" x 3½"
Light	3	4" x 4"
UNIT D - MAKE 1		
Print/Dark	1,2	*
Light	3,4,5,6	4" x 4"
UNIT E - MAKE 2		
Dark	1	2¾" x 2¾"
Print	2,3	3½" x 3½"
Light	4,5	4" x 4"

* *See cutting instructions.*

Shepherd's Crossing

JUNE 1942 ★ 10" BLOCK

CUTTING INSTRUCTIONS

FROM THE PRINT FABRICS, CUT:

★ 4 – 3 1/2" squares.

FROM THE DARK FABRIC, CUT:

★ 1 – 3 1/2" x 20 1/2" strip.
Cut the strip into 1 – 3 1/2" x 11" rectangle and 2 – 3 1/2" x 4 3/4" rectangles.

FROM THE MEDIUM FABRIC, CUT:

★ 1 – 2 3/4" x 11" strip.
Cut the strip into 4 – 2 3/4" squares.
Cut the squares into half-square triangles.

★ 1 – 2 1/4" x 33" strip.
Cut the strip into 4 – 2 1/4" x 3 1/2" rectangles and 4 – 2 1/4" x 4 3/4" rectangles.

PATTERNS ON PAGES 91–92.

POSITION CHART

FABRIC	POSITION	SIZE
UNIT A - MAKE 1		
Dark	1	3½" x 11"
Medium	2,3,4,5	2¾" x 2¾"
UNIT B - MAKE 4		
Prints	1	3½" x 3½"
Medium	2	2¼" x 3½"
Medium	3	2¼" x 4¾"
UNIT C - MAKE 2		
Dark	1	3½" x 4¾"
Medium	2,3	2¾" x 2¾"

ASSEMBLING THE BLOCK

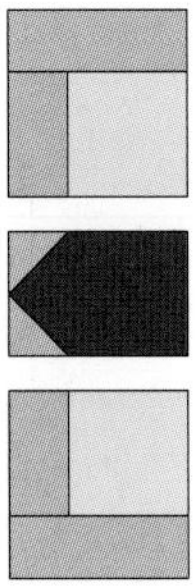

Sew Units B to Units C.

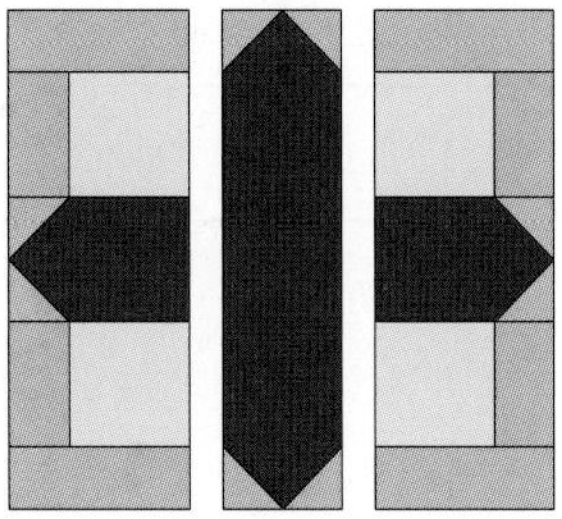

Sew Unit A to Units BCB.

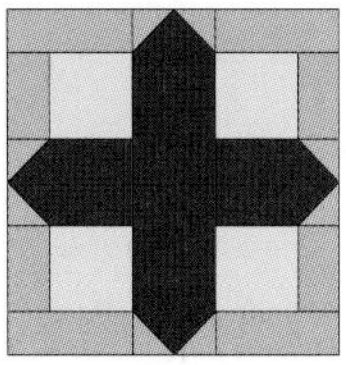

The Army Star

May 1943 ★ 10" Block

CUTTING INSTRUCTIONS

FROM THE BACKGROUND FABRIC, CUT:

★ 1 – 4" x 8" strip.
Cut the strip into 2 – 4" squares.
Cut the squares into half-square triangles.

★ 1 – 3 1/2" x 19" strip.
Cut the strip into 4 – 3 1/2" x 4 3/4" rectangles.

★ 1 – 2 1/4" x 9" strip.
Cut the strip into 4 – 2 1/4" squares.

FROM THE DARK FABRIC, CUT:

★ 1 – 3 1/2" square.

★ 1 – 3" x 12" strip.
Cut the strip into 4 – 3" squares.
Cut the squares into half-square triangles.

★ 1 – 2 3/4" x 11 strip.
Cut the strip into 4 – 2 3/4" squares.
Cut the squares into half-square triangles.

FROM THE PRINT FABRIC, CUT:

★ 1 – 2 1/4" x 28" strip.
Cut the strip into 8 – 2 1/4" x 3 1/2" rectangles.

★ 1 – 1 1/2" x 12" strip.
Cut the strip into 4 – 1 1/2" x 3" rectangles.

PATTERNS ON PAGES 96–97.

POSITION CHART

FABRIC	POSITION	SIZE
UNIT A - MAKE 1		
Background	1	3 1/2" x 4 3/4"
Dark	2,3	2 3/4" x 2 3/4"
Dark	4	3 1/2" x 3 1/2"
UNIT B - MAKE 3		
Background	1	3 1/2" x 4 3/4"
Dark	2,3	2 3/4" x 2 3/4"
UNIT C - MAKE 4		
Print	1	1 1/2" x 3"
Dark	2,3	3" x 3"
Background	4	4" x 4"
Print	5	2 1/4" x 3 1/2"
UNIT D - MAKE 4		
Print	1	2 1/4" x 3 1/2"
Background	2	2 1/4" x 2 1/4"

ASSEMBLING THE BLOCK

Sew Unit A to Unit B.

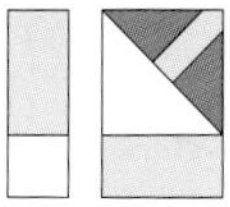

Sew Units C to Units D.

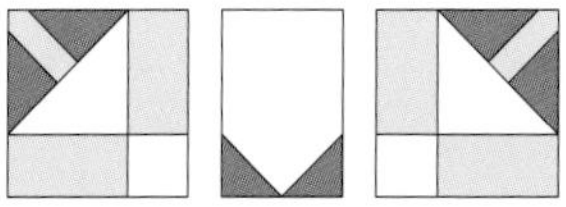

Sew a Unit CD to each side of a Unit B.

Sew together as shown.

A Basket Quilt in Triangles

DECEMBER 1942 ★ 10" BLOCK

CUTTING INSTRUCTIONS

FROM THE BACKGROUND FABRIC, CUT:

★ 1 – 8 1/4" square.
Cut the square into half-square triangles. You will have one half-square triangle left over.

★ 1 – 5" square.
Cut the square into half-square triangles. You will have one half-square triangle left over.

★ 1 - 3 1/4" x 22 3/4" strip.
Cut the strip into 7 – 3 1/4" squares.
Cut the squares into half-square triangles.

★ 1 – 2 1/2" x 17 1/2" strip.
Cut the strip into 1 – 2 1/2" square and 2 – 2 1/2" x 7 1/2" rectangles.

FROM THE MEDIUM FABRIC, CUT:

★ 1 – 3 1/4" x 32 1/2" strip.
Cut the strip into 10 – 3 1/4" squares.
Cut the squares into half-square triangles.

PATTERNS ON PAGES 93–95.

ASSEMBLING THE BLOCK

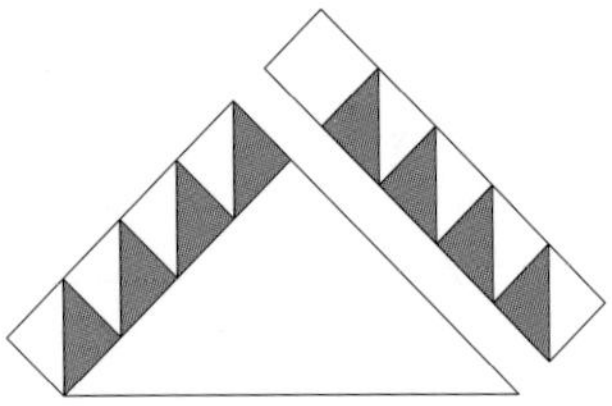

Sew Unit A to Unit B.

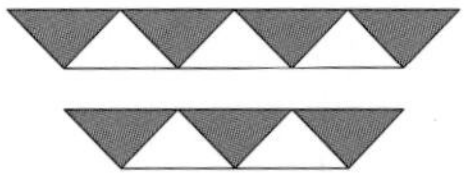

Sew Unit C to Unit D.

Sew Unit E to Unit CD.

Sew Unit AB to Unit CDE.

ASSEMBLING THE BLOCK, CONTINUED

Sew Units F and G to Unit ABCDE.

Add Unit H as shown to complete the block.

POSITION CHART

FABRIC	POSITION	SIZE
UNIT A - MAKE 1		
Background	1	2½" x 2½"
Medium	2,4,6,8	3¼" x 3¼"
Background	3,5,7,9	3¼" x 3¼"
UNIT B - MAKE 1		
Background	1,3,5,7	3¼" x 3¼"
Medium	2,4,6,8	3¼" x 3¼"
Background	9	8¼" x 8¼"
UNIT C - MAKE 1		
Medium	1,3,5,7	3¼" x 3¼"
Background	2,4,6	3¼" x 3¼"
UNIT D - MAKE 1		
Medium	1,3,5	3¼" x 3¼"
Background	2,4	3¼" x 3¼"
UNIT E - MAKE 1		
Medium	1,3,4	3¼" x 3¼"
Background	2	3¼" x 3¼"
UNIT F & G - MAKE 1 EACH		
Background	1	2½" x 7½"
Medium	2	3¼" x 3¼"
UNIT H - MAKE 1		
Background	1	5" x 5"

The New Four Pointer

May 1944 ★ 10" Block

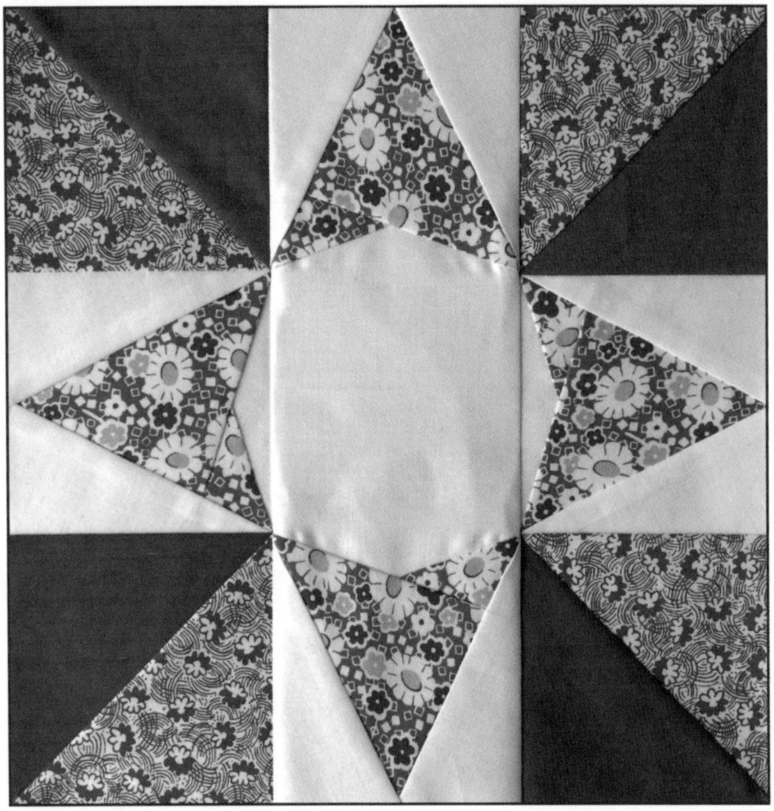

CUTTING INSTRUCTIONS

FROM THE BACKGROUND FABRIC, CUT:

★ 1 – 4 1/4" x 5 1/4" rectangle.

★ 1 – 2 1/2" x 38" strip.
Cut the strip into 8 – 4 3/4" rectangles.

★ 1 – 1 1/2" x 8 1/2" strip.
Cut the strip into 2 – 1 1/2" x 4 1/4" rectangles.

FROM THE DARK FABRIC, CUT:

★ 1 – 5" x 10" strip.
Cut the strip into 2 – 5" squares.
Cut the squares into half-square triangles.

FROM THE MEDIUM FABRIC, CUT:

★ 1 – 5" x 10" strip.
Cut the strip into 2 – 5" squares.
Cut the squares into half-square triangles.

FROM THE PRINT FABRIC, CUT:

★ 1 – 3 1/2" x 16" strip.
Cut the strip into 4 – 3 1/2" x 4" rectangles.

★ 1 – 1 1/2" x 11" strip.
Cut the strip into 4 – 1 1/2" x 2 3/4" rectangles.

PATTERNS ON PAGES 103–104.

ASSEMBLING THE BLOCK

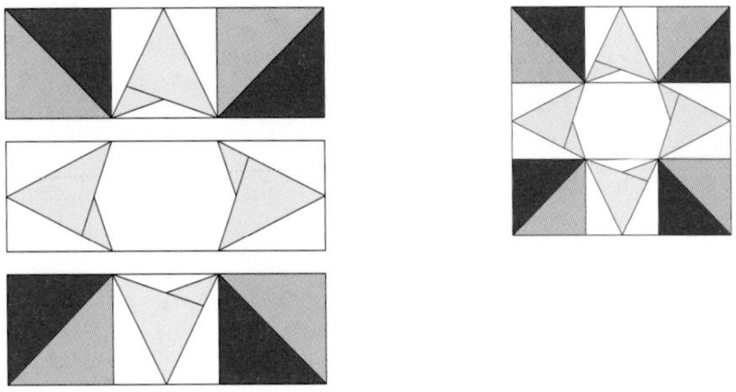

Sew Unit A to Units B.

POSITION CHART

FABRIC	POSITION	SIZE
UNIT A - MAKE 1		
Background	1	4¼" x 5¼"
Print	2,3	1½" x 2¾"
Print	4,5	3½" x 4"
Background	6,7,8,9	2½" x 4¾"
UNIT B - MAKE 2		
Background	1	1½" x 4¼"
Print	2	1½" x 2¾"
Print	3	3½" x 4"
Background	4,5	2½" x 4¾"
Dark	6,9	5" x 5"
Medium	7,8	5" x 5"

A Quilt Mosaic

SEPTEMBER 1945 ★ 10" BLOCK

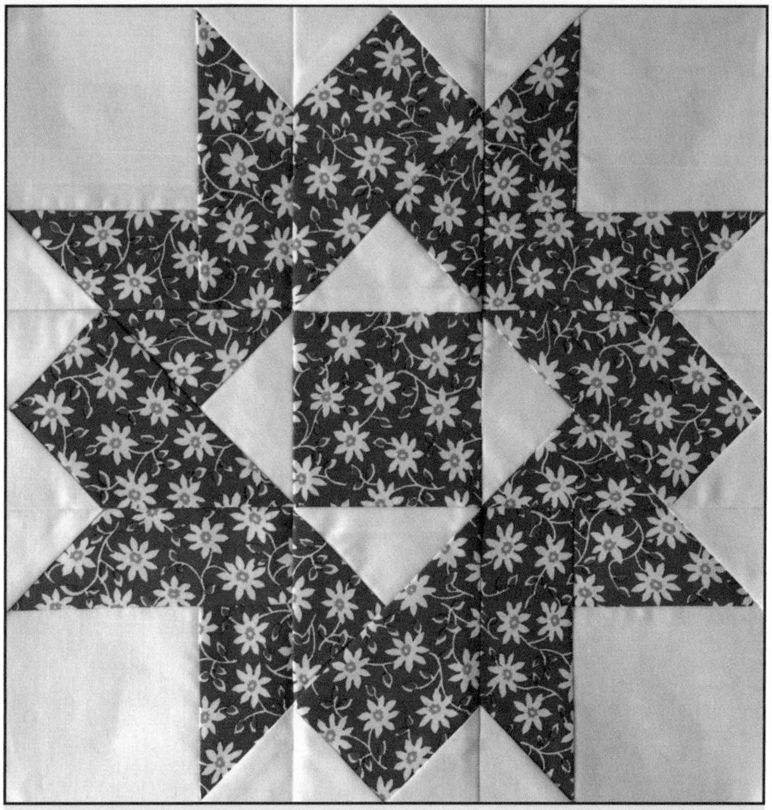

CUTTING INSTRUCTIONS

FROM THE BACKGROUND FABRIC, CUT:

★ 1 - 3 1/2" x 14" strip.
Cut the strip into 4 – 3 1/2" squares.

★ 1 – 3" x 6" strip.
Cut the strip into 2- 3" squares.
Cut the squares into half-square triangles.

★ 1 – 2 3/4" x 22" strip.
Cut the strip into 8 – 2 3/4" squares.
Cut the squares into half-square triangles.

FROM THE PRINT FABRIC, CUT:

★ 1 – 3 1/2" square.

★ 1 – 3" x 6" strip.
Cut the strip into 2 – 3" squares.
Cut the squares into half-square triangles.

★ 1 – 2 1/2" x 18" strip.
Cut the strip into 4 – 2 1/2" x 4 1/2" rectangles.

★ 1 – 2 1/4" x 33" strip.
Cut the strip into 4 – 2 1/4" x 3 1/2" rectangles and 4 – 2 1/4" x 4 3/4" rectangles.

PATTERNS ON PAGES 98-99.

ASSEMBLING THE BLOCK

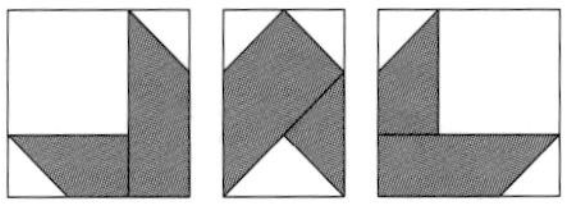

Sew Units C to Units B.

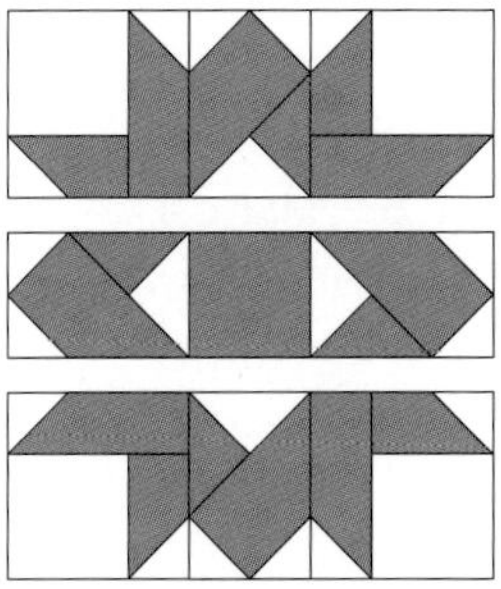

Sew Unit A to Units BC.

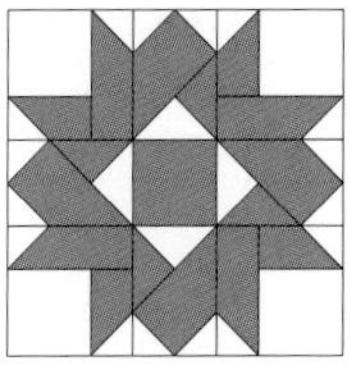

POSITION CHART

FABRIC	POSITION	SIZE
UNIT A - MAKE 1		
Print	1	3½" x 3½"
Background	2,3	3" x 3"
Print	4,5	3" x 3"
Print	6,7	2½" x 4½"
Background	8,9,10,11	2¾" x 2¾"
UNIT B - MAKE 2		
Background	1	3" x 3"
Print	2	3" x 3"
Print	3	2½" x 4½"
Background	4,5	2¾" x 2¾"
UNIT C - MAKE 4		
Background	1	3½" x 3½"
Print	2	2¼" x 3½"
Print	3	2¼" x 4¾"
Background	4,5	2¾" x 2¾"

Return of the Swallows

October 1946 ★ 10" Block

CUTTING INSTRUCTIONS

FROM THE BACKGROUND FABRIC, CUT:

★ 1 – 3 3/4" x 30" strip.
Cut the strip into 8 – 3 3/4" squares.
Cut the squares into half-square triangles.

FROM THE PRINT FABRICS, CUT:

★ 4 – 5" squares.
Cut the squares into half-square triangles.

PATTERNS ON PAGES 100–102.

ASSEMBLING THE BLOCK

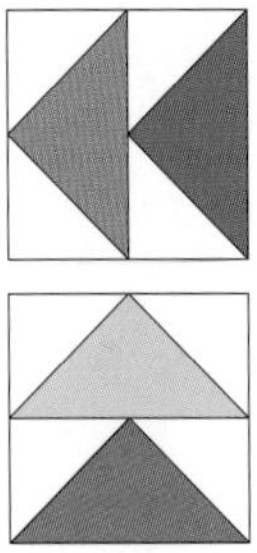

Sew Unit B to Unit C.

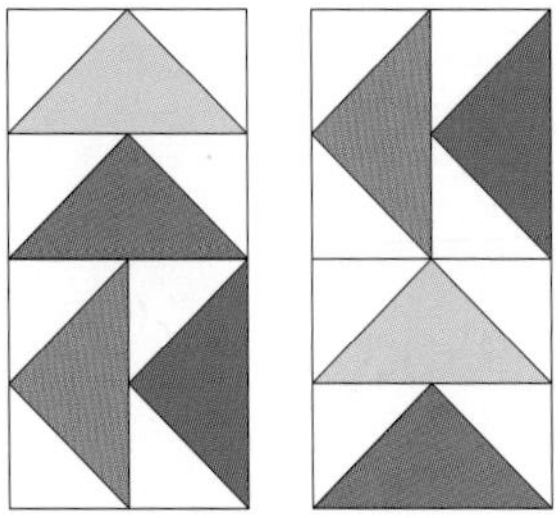

Sew Unit A to Unit BC.

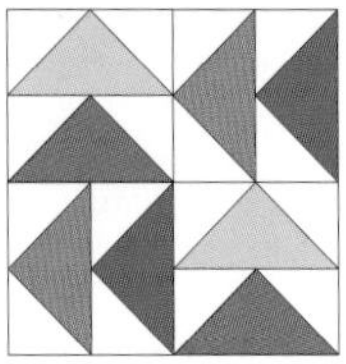

POSITION CHART

FABRIC	POSITION	SIZE
UNIT A - MAKE 1		
Various Prints	1,4,7,10	5" x 5"
Background	2,3,5,6,8,9,	3¾" x 3¾"
	11,12	3¾" x 3¾"
UNIT B - MAKE 1		
Various Prints	1,4	5" x 5"
Background	2,3,5,6	3¾" x 3¾"
UNIT C - MAKE 1		
Various Prints	1,4	5" x 5"
Background	2,3,5,6	3¾" x 3¾"

The North Star

MARCH 1949 ★ 10" BLOCK

CUTTING INSTRUCTIONS

FROM THE BACKGROUND FABRIC, CUT:

★ 1 – 2" x 38" strip.
Cut the strip into 8 – 2" x 4 3/4" rectangles.

FROM THE PRINT FABRIC, CUT:

★ 1 – 3 3/4" x 19" strip.
Cut the strip into 4 – 3 3/4" x 4 3/4" rectangles.

FROM THE DARK FABRIC, CUT:

★ 1 – 3 1/4" x 6 1/2" strip.
Cut the strip into 2 – 3 1/4" squares.
Cut the squares into half-square triangles.

★ 1 – 2" x 24" strip.
Cut the strip into 8 – 2" x 3" rectangles.

★ 2 – 1 3/4" x 24" strips.
Cut the strips into 8 – 1 3/4" x 6" rectangles.

PATTERN ON PAGES 105.

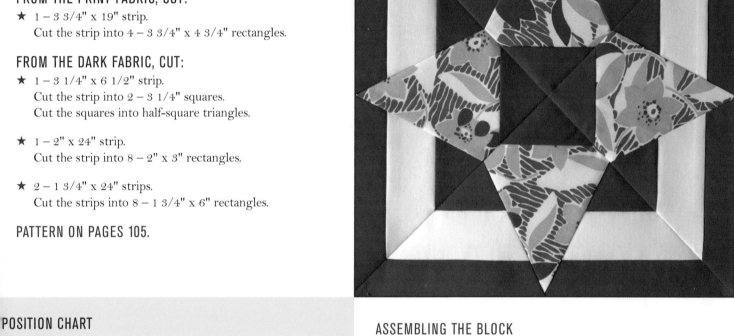

POSITION CHART

FABRIC	POSITION	SIZE
UNIT A - MAKE 4		
Dark	1	1¾" x 6"
Background	2	2" x 4¾"
Dark	3	2" x 3"
Print	4	3¾" x 4¾"
Dark	5	3¼" x 3¼" ◪
UNIT B - MAKE 4		
Dark	1	1¾" x 6"
Background	2	2" x 4¾"
Dark	3	2" x 3"

ASSEMBLING THE BLOCK

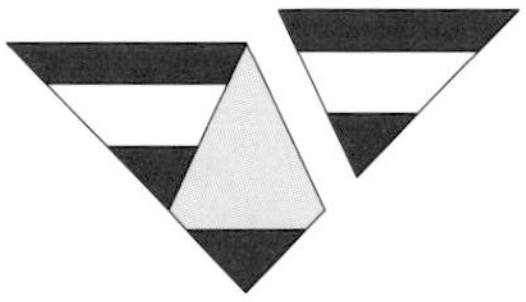

Sew Units A to Units B.

Sew Units AB together.

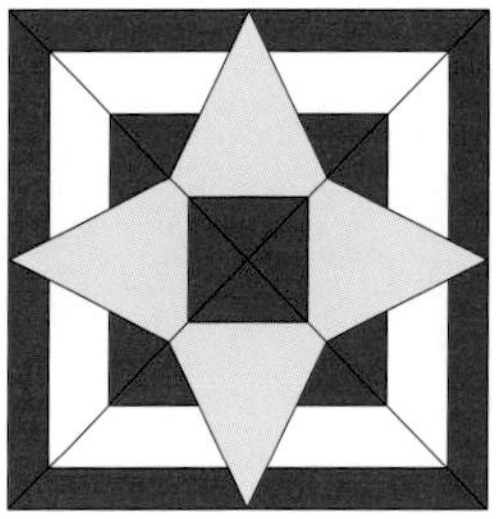

Sew the two halves together to complete the block.

The Christmas Star

DECEMBER 1947 ★ 10" BLOCK

CUTTING INSTRUCTIONS

FROM THE BACKGROUND FABRIC, CUT:

★ 1 – 5" x 20" strip.
Cut the strip into 4 – 5" squares.
Cut the squares into half-square triangles.

★ 1 – 4 1/4" x 8 1/2" strip.
Cut the strip into 2 – 4 1/4" squares.
Cut the squares into half-square triangles.

★ 1 – 2 1/4" x 18" strip.
Cut the strip into 8 – 2 1/4" squares.
Cut the squares into half-square triangles.

FROM THE PRINT FABRIC, CUT:

★ 1 – 1 3/4" x 38 1/2" strip and 1 – 1 3/4" x 5 1/2" strip.
Cut the strips into 16 – 1 3/4" x 2 3/4" rectangles.

FROM THE DARK FABRIC, CUT:

★ 1 – 1 3/4" x 38 1/2" strip and 1 – 1 3/4" x 5 1/2" strip.
Cut the strips into 16 – 1 3/4" x 2 3/4" rectangles.

FROM THE MEDIUM FABRIC, CUT:

★ 1 – 1 3/4" x 38 1/2" strip
and 1 – 1 3/4" x 25 1/2" strip.
Cut the strips into 20 – 1 3/4" x 2 3/4" rectangles
and 4 – 1 3/4" x 2 1/4" rectangles.

PATTERN ON PAGE 77.

ASSEMBLING THE BLOCK

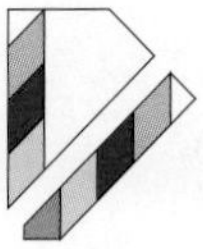

Sew Units A to Units B.

Sew Units C to Units AB.

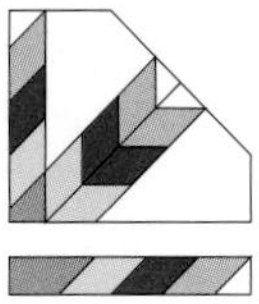

Sew Units D to Units ABC.

Add Units E to Units ABCD.

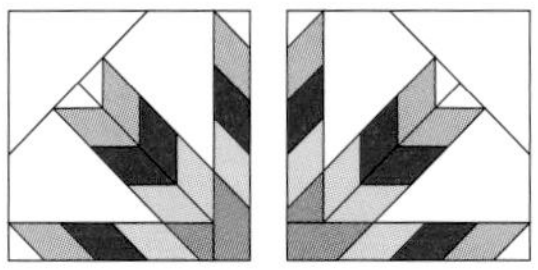

Sew 2 Units ABCDE together.

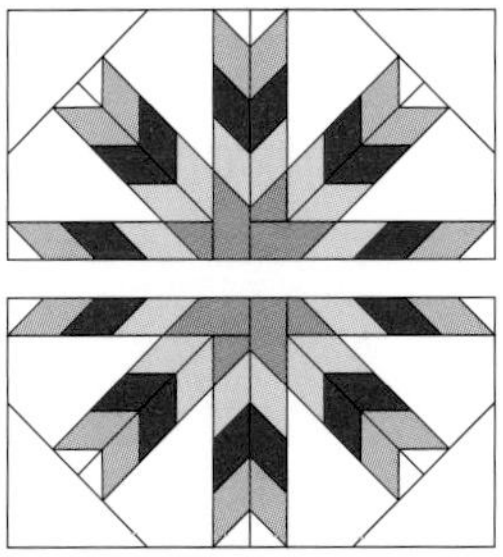

Sew the two halves together to complete the block.

POSITION CHART

FABRIC	POSITION	SIZE	
UNITS A & C - MAKE 4 EACH			
Print	1	1¾" x 2¾"	
Dark	2	1¾" x 2¾"	
Medium	3	1¾" x 2¾"	
Background	4	2¼" x 2¼"	◣
Background	5	5" x 5"	◣
UNIT B - MAKE 4			
Medium	1	1¾" x 2¼"	
Print	2	1¾" x 2¾"	
Dark	3	1¾" x 2¾"	
Medium	4	1¾" x 2¾"	
Background	5	2¼" x 2¼"	◣
UNIT D - MAKE 4			
Medium	1	1¾" x 2¾"	
Print	2	1¾" x 2¾"	
Dark	3	1¾" x 2¾"	
Medium	4	1¾" x 2¾"	
Background	5	2¼" x 2¼"	◣
UNIT E - MAKE 4			
Background	1	4¼" x 4¼"	◣

The Spider Web

June 1943 ★ 10" Block

CUTTING INSTRUCTIONS

FROM THE BACKGROUND FABRIC, CUT:

★ 1 – 4 1/4" x 17" strip.
Cut the strip into 4 – 4 1/4" squares.
Cut the squares into half-square triangles.

★ 1 – 2 3/4" x 5 1/2" strip.
Cut the strip into 2 – 2 3/4" squares.
Cut the squares into half-square triangles.

★ 1 – 2 1/2" x 10" strip.
Cut the strip into 4 – 2 1/2" squares.

★ 1 – 2 1/4" x 38 1/2" strip
and 1 – 2 1/4" x 16 1/2" strip.
Cut the strips into 20 – 2 1/4" x 2 3/4" rectangles.

FROM THE MEDIUM FABRIC, CUT:

★ 1 – 3" square.

★ 1 – 2 3/4" x 11" strip.
Cut the strip into 4 – 2 3/4" squares.
Cut the squares into half-square triangles.

★ 1 – 1 1/2" x 40" strips.
Cut the strips into 16 – 1 1/2" x 2 1/2" rectangles.

FROM THE DARK FABRIC, CUT:

★ 2 – 1 1/2" x 30" strip.
Cut the strip into 24 – 1 1/2" x 2 1/2" rectangles.

PATTERN ON PAGE 106.

ASSEMBLING THE BLOCK

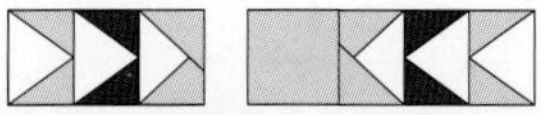

Sew Unit A to Unit B.

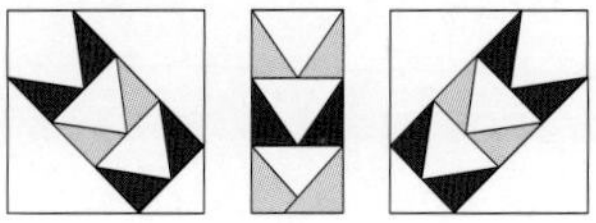

Sew Units B to Units C.

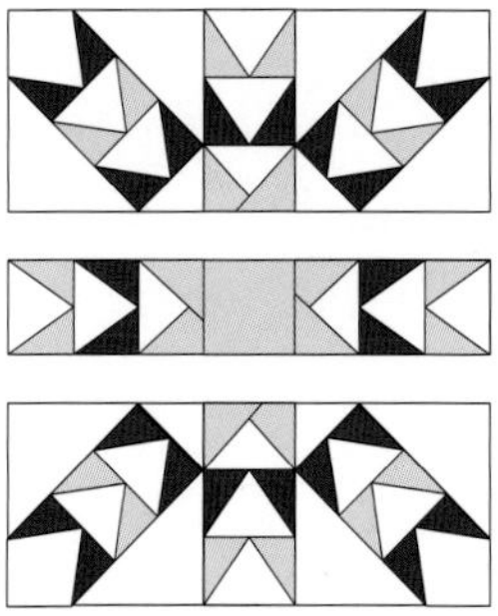

Sew together as shown.

POSITION CHART

FABRIC	POSITION	SIZE
UNIT A- MAKE 1		
Background	1,4,7	2¼" x 2¾"
Medium	2,3	1½" x 2½"
Dark	5,6	1½" x 2½"
Medium	8,9	2¾" x 2¾"
Medium	10	3" x 3"
UNIT B - MAKE 3		
Background	1,4,7	2¼" x 2¾"
Medium	2,3	1½" x 2½"
Dark	5,6	1½" x 2½"
Medium	8,9	2¾" x 2¾"
UNIT C - MAKE 4		
Background	1	2½" x 2½"
Dark	2,3	1½" x 2½"
Background	4,7	2¼" x 2¾"
Medium	5,6	1½" x 2½"
Dark	8,9	1½" x 2½"
Background	10	2¾" x 2¾"
Background	11,12	4¼" x 4¼"

A Flash of Diamonds

APRIL 1949 ★ 10" BLOCK

CUTTING INSTRUCTIONS

FROM THE BACKGROUND FABRIC, CUT:

★ 1 – 3" x 18" strip.
Cut the strip into 6 – 3" squares.
Cut the squares into half-square triangles.

★ 1 - 2 1/2" x 20" strip.
Cut the strip into 8 – 2 1/2" squares.
Cut the squares into half-square triangles.

★ 1 – 2 1/4" x 18" strip.
Cut the strip into 8 – 2 1/4" squares.

FROM THE DARK FABRIC, CUT:

★ 1 – 3" x 15" strip.
Cut the strip into 5 – 3" squares.
Cut 4 of the squares into half-square triangles.

★ 1 – 1 3/4" x 28" strip.
Cut the strip into 8 – 1 3/4" x 3 1/2" rectangles.

FROM THE MEDIUM FABRIC, CUT:

★ 1 – 2 3/4" x 5 1/2" strip.
Cut the strip into 2 – 2 3/4" squares.
Cut the squares into half-square triangles.

★ 1 – 2" x 14" strip.
Cut the strip into 4 – 2" x 3 1/2" rectangles.

FROM THE LIGHT FABRIC, CUT:

★ 1 – 5 1/4" x 10 1/2" strip.
Cut the strip into 2 – 5 1/4" squares.
Cut the squares into half-square triangles.

PATTERNS ON PAGES 108-109.

ASSEMBLING THE BLOCK

Sew Unit A to Unit B.

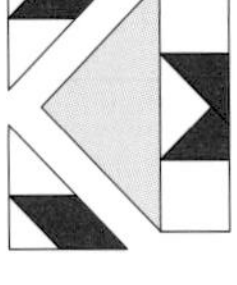

Sew Units D and E to Units C.

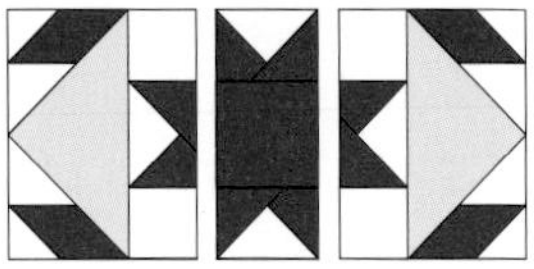

Sew Units CDE to Unit AB.

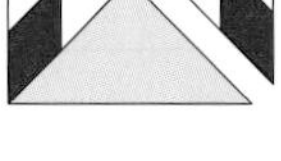

Sew Units D to Units G.

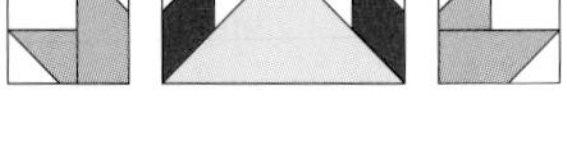

Sew Units F to Units DG.

ASSEMBLING THE BLOCK, CONTINUED

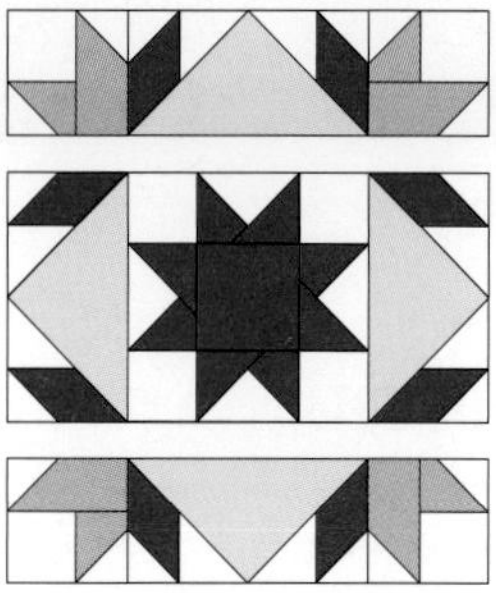

Sew together as shown to complete the block.

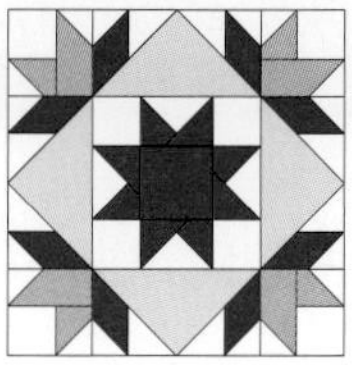

POSITION CHART

FABRIC	POSITION	SIZE	
UNIT A – MAKE 1			
Background	1	3" x 3"	◩
Dark	2,3	3" x 3"	◩
Dark	4	3" x 3"	
UNIT B – MAKE 1			
Background	1	3" x 3"	◩
Dark	2,3	3" x 3"	◩
UNIT C – MAKE 2			
Background	1	3" x 3"	◩
Dark	2,3	3" x 3"	◩
Background	4,5	2¼" x 2¼"	
Light	6	5¼" x 5¼"	◩
UNITS D – MAKE 4			
Dark	1	1¾" x 3½"	
Background	2	2½" x 2½"	◩
Background	3	3" x 3"	◩
UNIT E – MAKE 2			
Dark	1	1¾" x 3½"	
Background	2	2½" x 2½"	◩
Background	3	3" x 3"	◩
UNIT F – MAKE 4			
Background	1	2¼" x 2¼"	
Medium	2	2¾" x 2¾"	◩
Medium	3	2" x 3½"	
Background	4,5	2½" x 2½"	◩
UNIT G – MAKE 2			
Dark	1	1¾" x 3½"	
Background	2	2½" x 2½"	◩
Background	3	3" x 3"	◩
Light	4	5¼" x 5¼"	◩

The Kansas Star

May 1949 ★ 10" Block

CUTTING INSTRUCTIONS

FROM THE BACKGROUND FABRIC, CUT:

★ 1 – 3 1/4" x 19 1/2" strip.
Cut the strip into 6 – 3 1/4" squares.
Cut the squares into half-square triangles.

FROM THE DARK FABRIC, CUT:

★ 1 – 3 1/4" x 13" strip.
Cut the strip into 4 – 3 1/4" squares.
Cut the squares into half-square triangles.

FROM THE PRINT FABRIC, CUT:

★ 1 – 3 1/4" x 16 1/4" strip.
Cut the strip into 5 – 3 1/4" squares.

FROM THE LIGHT FABRIC, CUT:

★ 1 – 3 1/4" x 26" strip.
Cut the strip into 8 – 3 1/4" squares.
Cut 4 squares into half-square triangles.

FROM THE MEDIUM FABRIC, CUT:

★ 1 – 3 1/4" x 13" strip.
Cut the strip into 4 – 3 1/4" squares.
Cut the squares into half-square triangles.

PATTERN ON PAGE 110.

ASSEMBLING THE BLOCK

Sew one Unit A to either side of Unit B. Make two.

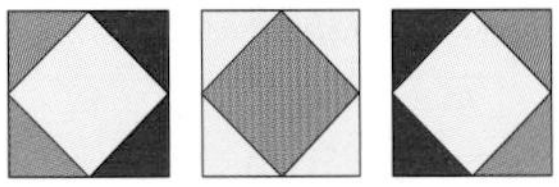

Sew one Unit B to either side of Unit C.

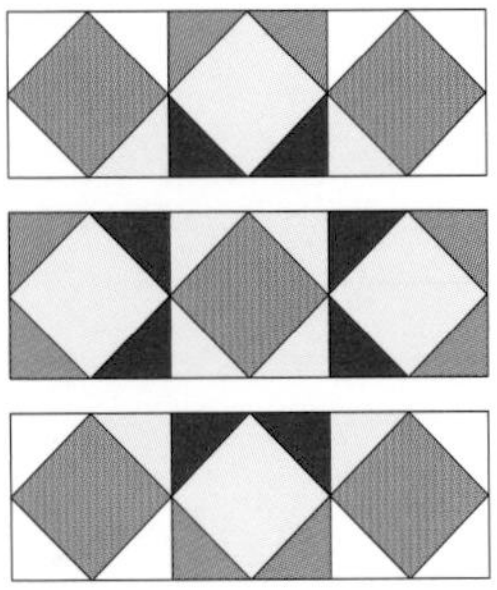

Sew together as shown.

POSITION CHART

FABRIC	POSITION	SIZE
UNIT A - MAKE 4		
Print	1	3¼" x 3¼"
Light	2	3¼" x 3¼" ◩
Background	3,4,5	3¼" x 3¼" ◩
UNIT B - MAKE 4		
Light	1	3¼" x 3¼"
Dark	2,4	3¼" x 3¼" ◩
Medium	3,5	3¼" x 3¼" ◩
UNIT C - MAKE 1		
Print	1	3¼" x 3¼"
Light	2,3,4,5	3¼" x 3¼" ◩

Crazy Anne

JUNE 1949 ★ 10" BLOCK

CUTTING INSTRUCTIONS

FROM THE BACKGROUND FABRIC, CUT:

★ 1 – 3 1/2" x 19" strip.
Cut the strip into 4 – 3 1/2" x 4 3/4".

★ 1 – 3" x 19" strip.
Cut the strip into 4 – 3" x 4 3/4" rectangles.

★ 1 – 2" x 22" strip.
Cut the strip into 8 – 2" x 2 3/4" rectangles.

FROM THE PRINT FABRICS, CUT:

★ 4 – 4 1/2" squares.
Cut the squares into half-square triangles.

★ 8 – 1 1/2" x 3 1/2" rectangles.

PATTERN ON PAGE 107.

POSITION CHART

FABRIC	POSITION	SIZE	
UNIT A - MAKE 4			
Background	1	3" x 4¾"	
Various Prints	2	4½" x 4½"	◩
Various Prints	3	1½" x 3½"	
Background	4	2" x 2¾"	
UNIT B - MAKE 4			
Background	1	3½" x 4¾"	
Various Prints	2	4½" x 4½"	◩
Various Prints	3	1½" x 3½"	
Background	4	2" x 2¾"	

ASSEMBLING THE BLOCK

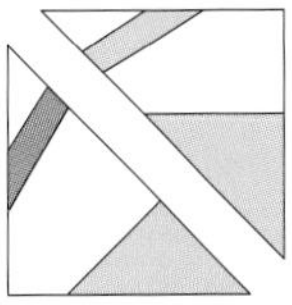

Sew Units A to Unit Bs.

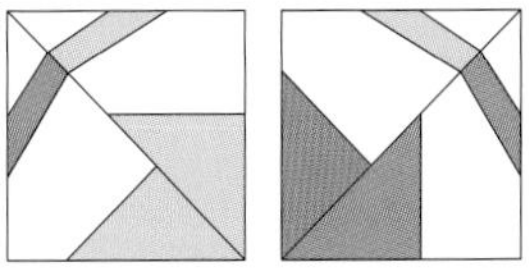

Sew two AB Units together. Make two.

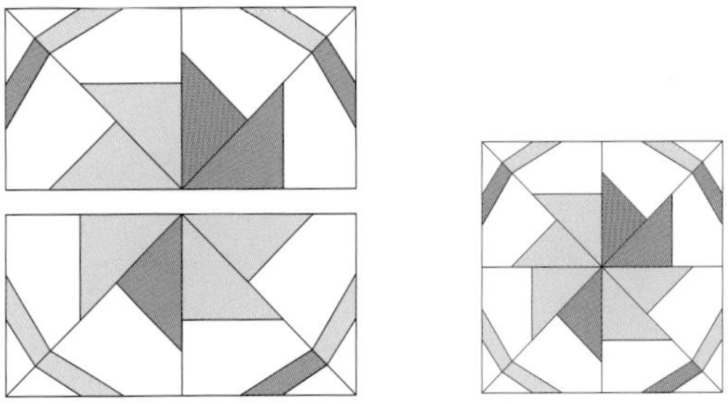

Sew the two halves together.

The Bright Jewel

SEPTEMBER 1949 ★ 10" BLOCK

CUTTING INSTRUCTIONS

FROM THE BACKGROUND FABRIC, CUT:

★ 1 – 3 1/2" x 28" strip.
Cut the strip into 8 – 3 1/2" squares.
Cut the squares into half-square triangles.

★ 1 – 3" square.

FROM THE PRINT FABRIC, CUT:

★ 1 – 3 1/2" x 28" strip.
Cut the strip into 8 – 3 1/2" squares.
Cut the squares into half-square triangles.

★ 1 – 3" x 20" strip.
Cut the strip into 4 – 3" x 5" rectangles.

PATTERNS ON PAGES 111-112.

POSITION CHART

FABRIC	POSITION	SIZE
UNIT A - MAKE 2		
Print	1,3	3½" x 3½"
Background	2,4	3½" x 3½"
Print	5	3" x 5"
UNITS B AND C- MAKE 2 EACH		
Print	1,3	3½" x 3½"
Background	2,4	3½" x 3½"
UNIT D - MAKE 2		
Background	1,3	3½" x 3½"
Print	2,4	3½" x 3½"
UNIT E - MAKE 1		
Background	1	3" x 3"
Print	2,3	3" x 5"

ASSEMBLING THE BLOCK

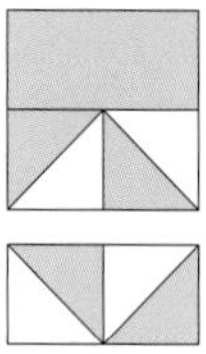

Sew Units A to Units B.

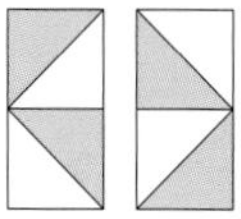

Sew Units C to Units D.

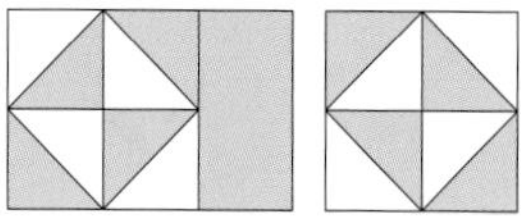

Sew Units AB to Units CD. Make two.

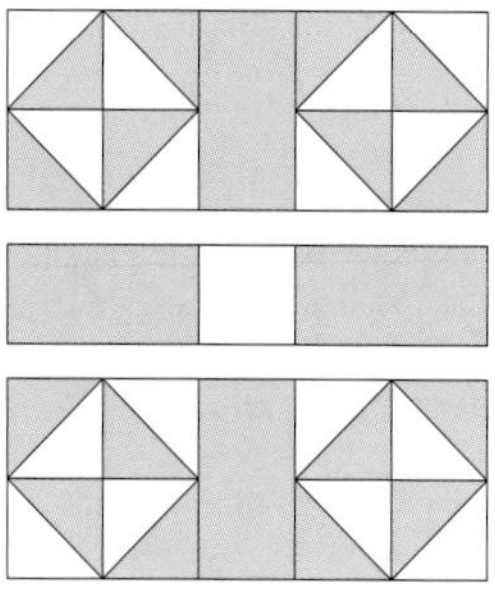

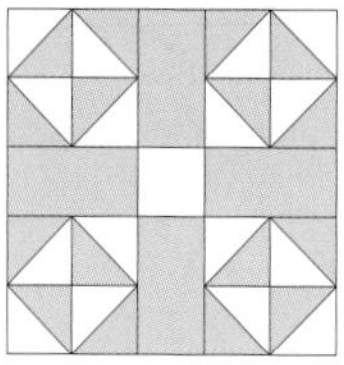

Sew Units ABCD to Unit E.

Projects

Inspired by Patterns from the '40s

Sachet

SEWING DIRECTIONS:

★ Layer the block with the 5" square of batting and muslin. Quilt the layers together. Trim around the block.

★ Using the two 3 1/2" x 4 1/2" pieces of accent fabric for the back of sachet, fold under 1/4" and 1/4" again across the long side of each piece, then press and stitch. This will give a finished edge on both pieces.

★ Place the backing and the block atop each other with right sides together. The finished edges will overlap. Pin into place and stitch around the entire block using a 1/4" seam allowance. Clip the corners and turn right side out.

★ Sew the two 3 1/2" muslin pieces together on three sides. Clip the corners and turn right side out. Fill half full with lavender or potpourri. Turn the raw edges in and stitch closed.

★ Insert into the back of the quilt block.

Supply List

4" Quilt Block
Muslin
1 – 5" Square
2 – 3 1/2" Squares
5" Square Batting
2- 3 1/2" x 4 1/2" Pieces of Accent Fabric for Back of Sachet
Thread
Lavender or Potpourri*
Basic sewing supplies

* *Purchase pre-made potpourri or go on the web for recipes to make your own.*

* *Fabric requirements do not include the blocks.*

Trinket Box

ASSEMBLE THE BOX:

★ Use the fine sandpaper to sand the box, remove any dust from the box with a cloth. Paint the box on the inside and outside with the acrylic paint. You do not have to paint the entire inside of the box since these areas will be covered. Let dry. If the box feels rough when dry, sand lightly.

★ Layer a 4" block with the muslin and batting. Quilt the layers together. Trim around the block. Cut a strip of bias for binding 2 1/4" wide. Fold in half and press. Sew the binding onto the block.

★ Measure the inside top of the lid and the inside bottom of the box. Cut fabric, fusible web and batting to size.

★ Press the fusible web onto the reverse side of the fabric; remove the paper and press onto the batting. Make sure it fits properly. Glue into place on the lid and the bottom of the box.

★ Place a thin line of glue around the outside edge of the block (on the binding). Glue into place. Use trim to decorate as desired.

Supply List

4" Quilt Block
Wood Box
(make sure top of box is at least 4 1/2")
Acrylic Paint
Fine Sandpaper
Small Paint Brush
Small Pieces of Batting
5" Muslin Square
1/4 yd Accent Fabric
(inside of box and binding)
Fusible Web
Tacky Glue
Trim

1940s Apron

SEWING DIRECTIONS:

★ **Skirt:** Sew the three 10" blocks together. Sew the skirt and border to the top and bottom of the blocks using a 1/4" seam allowance. (Fig. A) Press. Remove the paper from the blocks. Place the backing and apron skirt right sides together. Pin in place. Stitch on both sides and the bottom using a 1/4" seam allowance. The 1/4" seam allowance is required so the stitch line does not cut off the points on the blocks.

Clip bottom corners, turn right side out and press. Quilt around the blocks. Stitch 1/4" on both sides and bottom of the skirt

Gather the top of the skirt. The easiest way to gather is to use a piece of crochet thread and the wide zigzag on the sewing machine. Place the crochet thread in the middle of the zigzag (Fig. B). Stitch in place being very careful not to sew on the crochet thread. To adjust the gathers to 18", push the fabric along both ends of the crochet thread, making sure the gathers are even.

★ **Ties:** Fold the right sides together, stitch on one end and the bottom making a tube. Clip the corners (Fig. C) and turn right sides out. Press. Stitch 1/4" on three sides. Leave one end open .

★ **Waistband:** Turn and press a 3/8" seam allowance under both sides and the bottom (Fig. D). Make sure that the skirt is gathered to 18". Pin the waistband to the front of apron right sides together. Baste and remove the pins.

Pin the ties on each end of the waistband (Fig. E). Fold the waistband to the back of the apron, pin in place. Stitch 1/4" around all sides of the waistband.

Supply List

Three 10" Quilt Blocks*
Fabric

Light	3/4 yd.
Medium	3/4 yd.

Thread
Basic Sewing Supplies
* *Fabric requirements do not include the blocks.*

CUTTING INSTRUCTIONS

FROM THE MEDIUM FABRIC, CUT:

★ **Skirt:** 1 — 10 1/2" x 30 1/2" rectangle.

★ **Border:** 1 — 2 1/2" x 30 1/2" strip.

★ **Ties:** 1 — 5" strip across the width of the fabric. Cut the strip into 2 – 5" x 18" pieces.

★ **Waistband:** 1 — 6" x 18 3/4" strip.

FROM THE LIGHT FABRIC, CUT:

★ Backing: 1 –22 1/2" x 30 1/2" rectangle.

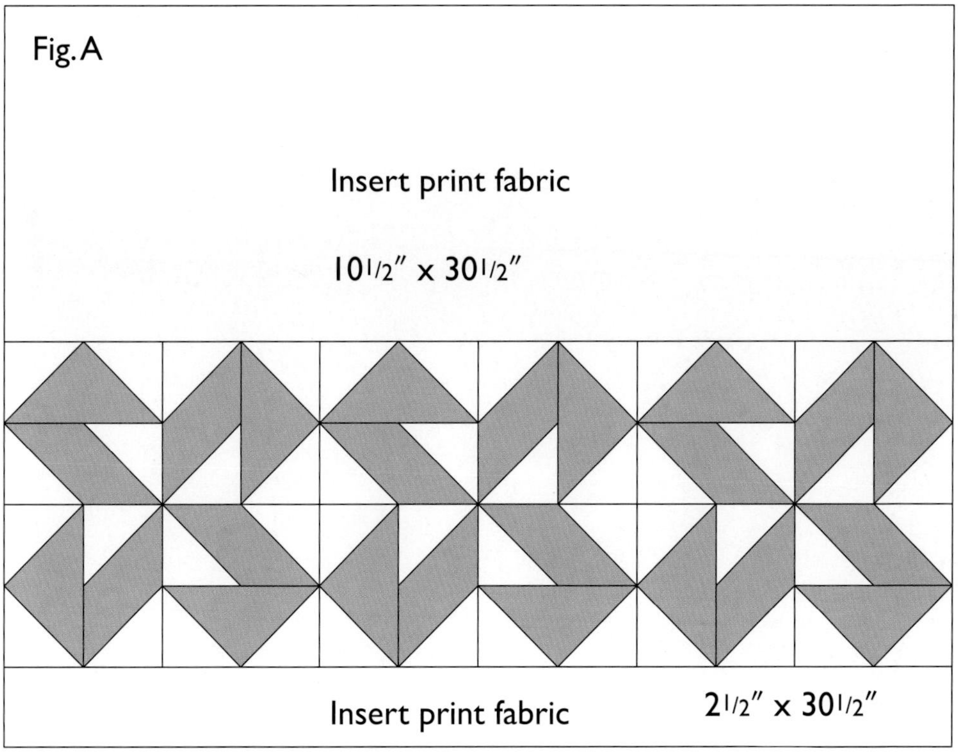

Fig. A

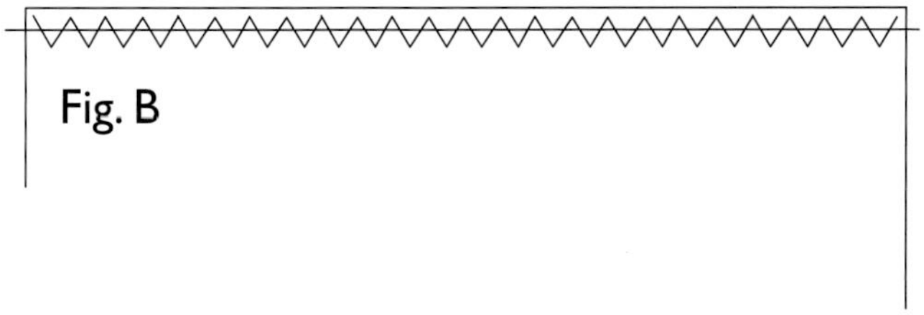
Fig. B

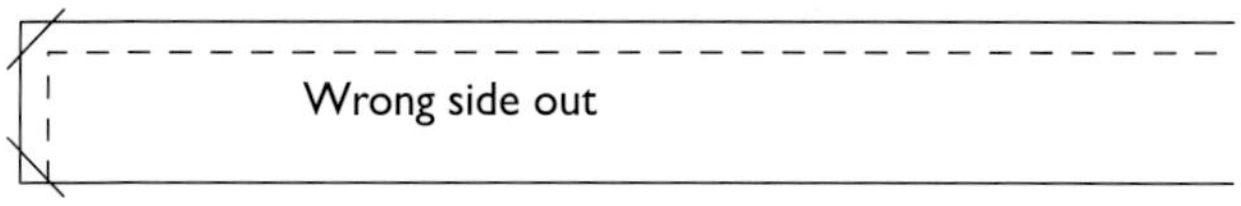

Fig. C

Fig. E

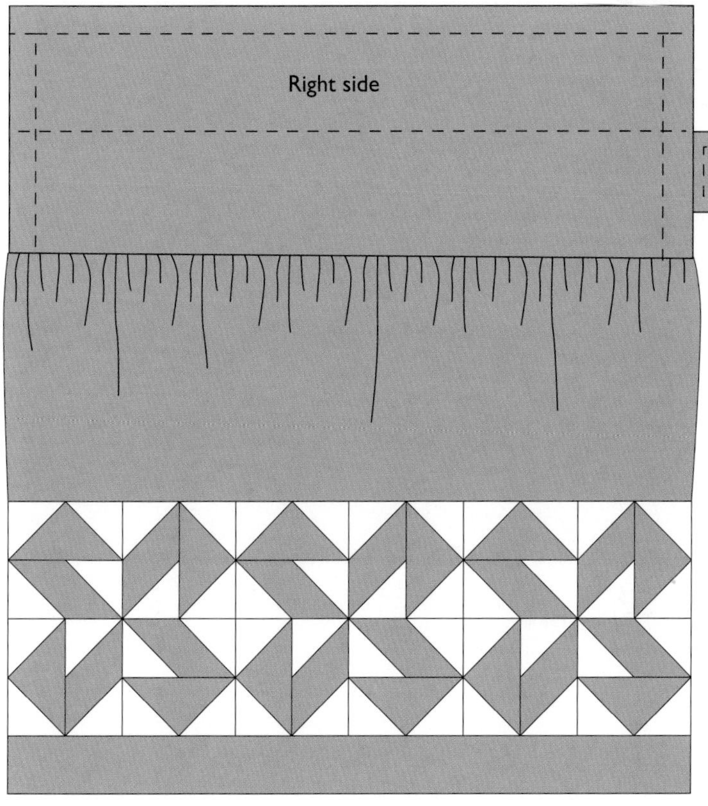

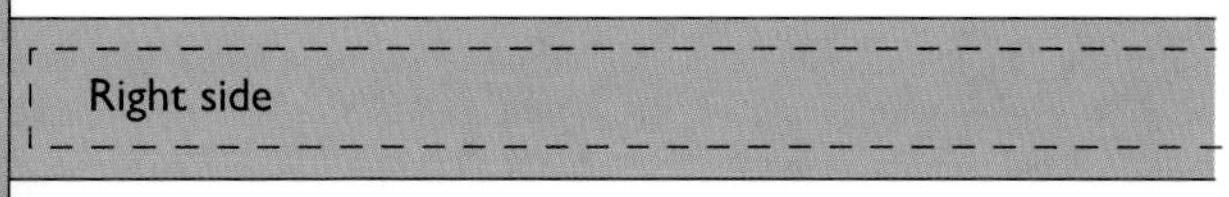

Fig. D

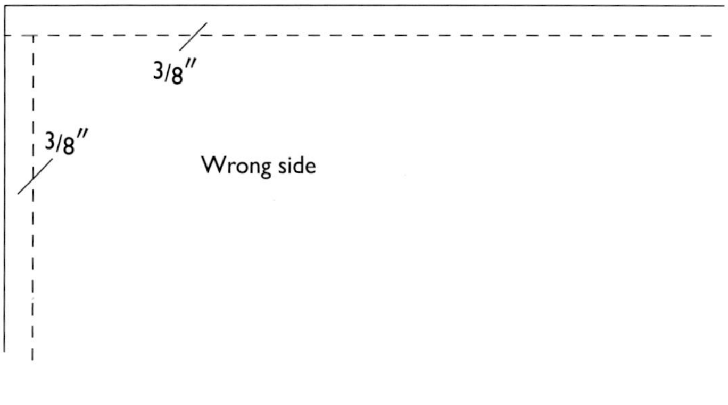

Four-inch sampler quilt made and quilted by Carolyn Cullinan McCormick, Franktown, Colorado.

Miniature 1940s Sampler Quilt

SEWING INSTRUCTIONS ★ 32 1/2" x 34 1/2" QUILTED

Supply List

FABRIC REQUIREMENTS:

Background: 1 1/4 yds.

Dark: (Blocks and Border) 1 1/4 yds.

Medium: 1/2 yd.

Light: 1/4 yd.

Print: 3/4 yd.

Corner Square Triangles:

Dark Green 1/2 yd.

Vertical Sashing and 2nd Border:

Striped Fabric: 1 yd.

Binding: 3/8 yd.

BATTING: Approximately 1 yd. square

BACKING: Approximately 1 yd. square

Follow the cutting instructions and position charts. Make 20 miniature blocks.

CORNER TRIANGLES:

Dark Green Fabric:

★ 4 – 3 3/4" strips. Cut the strips into 40 – 3 3/4" squares. Cut the squares into 80 half-square triangles.

★ Sew the half-square triangles on all four sides of each of the blocks. Press toward the triangles. Remove the paper.
NOTE: By using this method, you will be able to remove the paper before you sew the strips together.

★ Sew the blocks together into 4 vertical rows with 5 blocks in each strip.

★ Measure the length of the rows of block and cut 3 strips from the striped fabric. (I used a fabric that had stripes of various sizes running vertically on the fabric. The width of your strip will be determined by the width of the stripe. Be sure you allow 1/4" on each side of the stripe for seam allowances.) Sew the striped fabric between the vertical block rows. If you prefer to use a fabric other than a stripe, cut 3 – 1 1/2" strips for the vertical sashing.

1ST BORDER:

Dark Fabric:

★ 4 – 1 1/2" strips. Measure the top and bottom of the quilt to determine the length to cut the border. Sew the border to the top and bottom of the quilt. Press the seam allowances toward the borders. Measure the sides to determine the length to cut the borders for the sides. Sew the side borders onto the quilt. Press the seam allowances toward the border.

2ND BORDER:

Striped Fabric:

★ Cut 4 strips from the striped fabric. Measure the quilt to determine the length to cut the strips. (Be sure you allow 1/4" on each side of the strip for seam allowances.)

Fabric without Stripes:

★ Cut 4 – 3 1/2" strips. Measure the quilt to determine the length to cut the strips.

CORNERSTONES:

Background Fabric:

★ 4 squares cut the same width as the striped 2nd border.

★ Sew the striped border onto the top and bottom of quilt. Press towards the 2nd border. Sew the cornerstones onto both ends of the side border. Sew onto both sides of the quilt. Press toward the 2nd border.

★ Layer the top, batting and backing. Quilt as desired.

★ For straight binding, cut 4 – 2 1/2" strips.

Mother's Favorite Star

May 1940 ★ 4" Block

CUTTING INSTRUCTIONS

FROM THE BACKGROUND FABRIC, CUT:

★ 1 – 2 1/4" x 4 1/2" strip.
Cut the strip into 2 – 2 1/4" squares.
Cut the squares into half-square triangles.

★ 1 – 2" x 8" strip.
Cut the strip into 4 – 2" squares.
Cut the squares into half-square triangles.

★ 1 – 1 1/2" x 6" strip.
Cut the strip into 4 – 1 1/2" squares.

FROM THE DARK FABRIC, CUT:

★ 1 – 2" square.

★ 1 – 2" x 7" strip.
Cut the strip into 4 – 2" squares.
Cut the squares into half-square triangles.

★ 1 – 1 1/4" x 18" strip.
Cut the strip into 8 – 1 1/4" x 2 1/4" rectangles.

PATTERN ON PAGE 113.

ASSEMBLING THE BLOCK

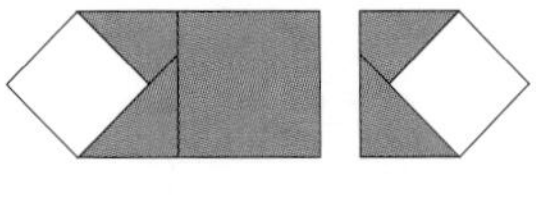

Sew Unit A to Unit B.

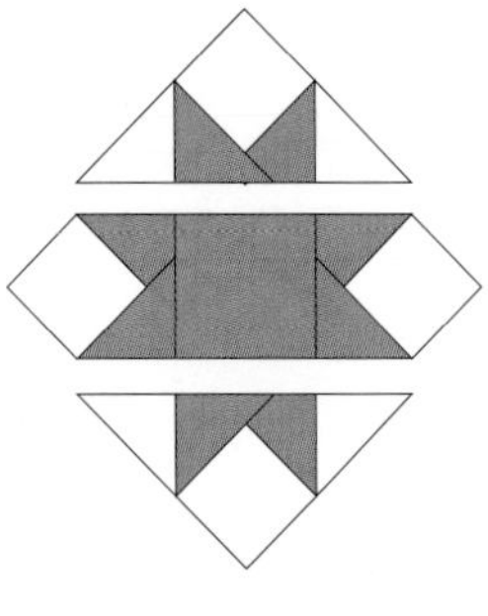

Sew Units C to Unit AB.

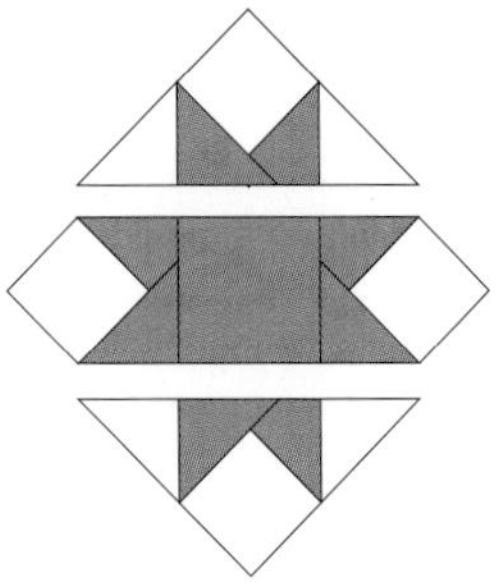

Sew Units D to Unit ABC.

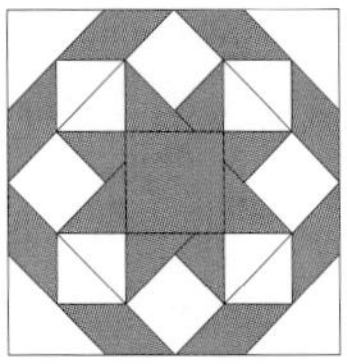

POSITION CHART

FABRIC	POSITION	SIZE
UNIT A – MAKE 1		
Background	1	1½" x 1½"
Dark	2,3	2" x 2"
Dark	4	2" x 2"
UNIT B – MAKE 1		
Background	1	1½" x 1½"
Dark	2,3	2" x 2"
UNIT C – MAKE 2		
Background	1	1½" x 1½"
Dark	2,3	2" x 2"
Background	4,5	2" x 2"
UNIT D – MAKE 4		
Background	1	2" x 2"
Dark	2,3	1¼" x 2¼"
Background	4	2¼" x 2¼"

Mona's Choice

June 1940 ★ 4" Block

CUTTING INSTRUCTIONS

FROM THE BACKGROUND FABRIC, CUT:

★ 1 – 2 1/4" square.

★ 1 – 1 1/2" x 18" strip.
Cut the strip into 8 – 1 1/2" x 2 1/4" rectangles.

★ 1 – 1 1/4" x 24" strip.
Cut the strip into 16 – 1 1/4" x 1 1/2" rectangles.

FROM THE DARK FABRIC, CUT:

★ 1 – 1 1/4" x 40 strip and 1 1/4" x 8" strip.
Cut the strips into 24 – 1 1/4" x 2" rectangles.

PATTERN ON PAGE 115.

POSITION CHART

FABRIC	POSITION	SIZE
UNITS A & B - MAKE 4 EACH		
Dark	1,3	1¼" x 2"
Background	2,4	1¼" x 1½"
UNITS C & D - MAKE 4 EACH		
Dark	1	1¼" x 2"
Background	2	1½" x 2¼"
UNIT E - MAKE 1		
Background	1	2¼" x 2¼"

ASSEMBLING THE BLOCK

Sew Units A to Units B.

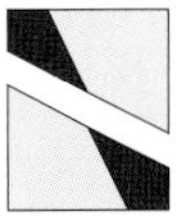

Sew Units C to Units D.

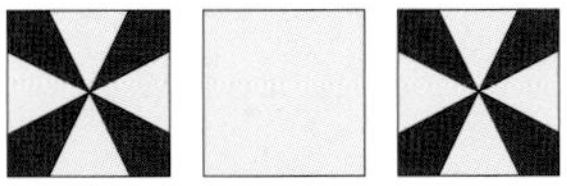

Sew Unit AB to each side of Unit E.

Sew Unit CD to each side of Unit AB. Make two.

Sew together as shown to complete the block.

The Colorado Quilt

JANUARY 1941 ★ 4" BLOCK

CUTTING INSTRUCTIONS

FROM THE BACKGROUND FABRIC, CUT:

★ 1 – 2" x 16" strip.
Cut the strip into 8 – 2" squares.
Cut the squares into half-square triangles.

FROM THE PRINT FABRIC, CUT:

★ 1 – 2 1/2" x 5" strip.
Cut the strip into 2 – 2 1/2" squares.
Cut the squares into half-square triangles.

★ 1 – 1 3/4" x 12" strips.
Cut the strip into 4 – 1 3/4" x 3" rectangles.

PATTERN ON PAGE 116.

POSITION CHART

FABRIC	POSITION	SIZE
UNIT A - MAKE 4		
Print	1	1¾" x 3"
Background	2,3,5,6	2" x 2"
Print	4	2½" x 2½"

ASSEMBLING THE BLOCK

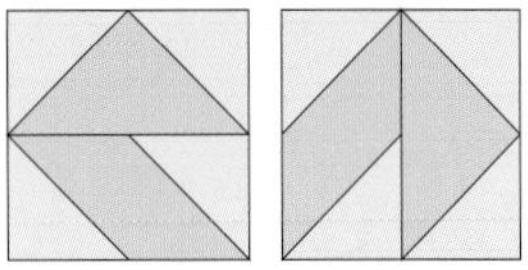

Sew two Units A together. Make two.

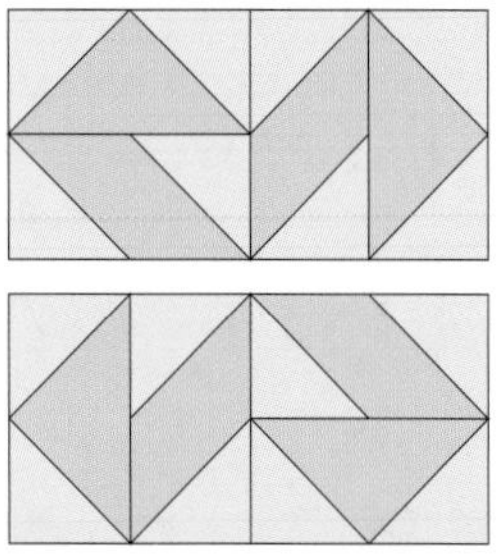

Sew the two halves together to complete the block.

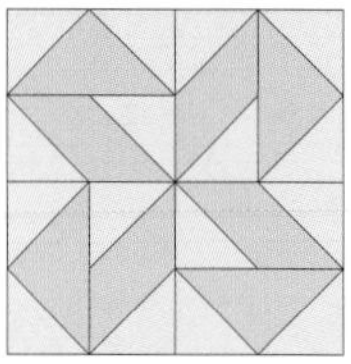

Anna's Choice

February 1941 ★ 4" Block

CUTTING INSTRUCTIONS

FROM THE DARK FABRIC, CUT:

★ 1 – 2 1/4" x 18" strip.
Cut the strip into 8 – 2 1/4" squares.
Cut the squares into half-square triangles.

FROM THE LIGHT FABRIC, CUT:

★ 1 – 2 1/4" x 18" strip.
Cut the strip into 8 – 2 1/4" squares.
Cut the squares into half-square triangles.

PATTERN ON PAGE 117.

POSITION CHART

FABRIC	POSITION	SIZE	
UNIT A – MAKE 2			
Dark	1,3,5,7	2¼"x 2¼"	◩
Light	2,4,6,8	2¼"x 2¼"	◩
UNIT B – MAKE 2			
Dark	1,4,6,7	2¼"x 2¼"	◩
Light	2,3,5,8	2¼"x 2¼"	◩

ASSEMBLING THE BLOCK

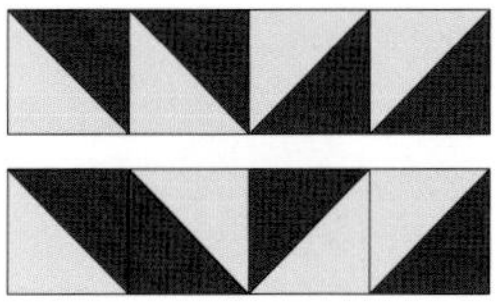

Sew each Unit A to each Unit B.

Sew the AB Units together as shown.

The 1941 Nine Patch

SEPTEMBER 1941 ★ 4" BLOCK

CUTTING INSTRUCTIONS

FROM THE DARK FABRIC, CUT:

★ 1 – 2 1/4" x 9" strip.
Cut the strip into 4 – 2 1/4" squares.

★ 1 – 1 1/4" x 9" strip.
Cut the strip into 4 1 1/4" x 2 1/4" rectangles.

FROM THE PRINT FABRIC, CUT:

★ 1 – 2 1/4" square.

★ 1 – 1 3/4" x 11" strip.
Cut the strip into 4 – 1 3/4" x 2 3/4" rectangles.

★ 1 – 1 1/2" x 7" strip.
Cut the strip into 4 – 1 1/2" x 1 3/4" rectangles.

PATTERN ON PAGE 118.

ASSEMBLING THE BLOCK

Sew Unit A to Unit B.

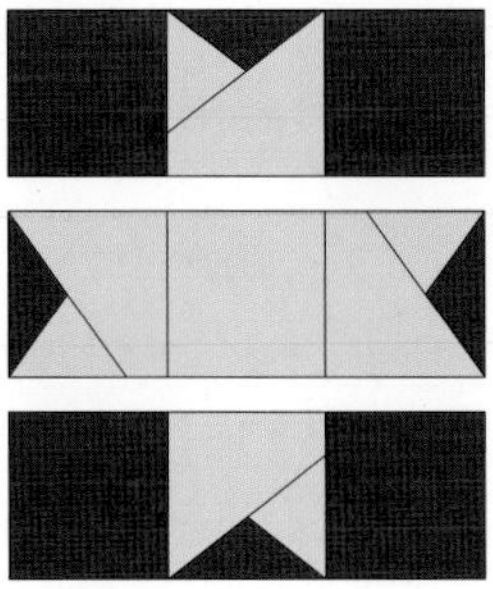

Sew Units C to Unit AB.

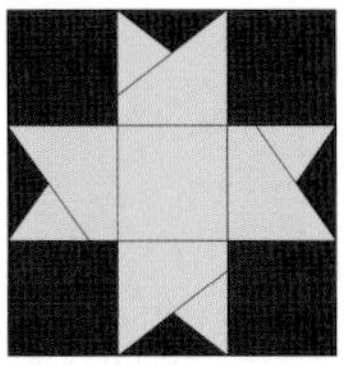

POSITION CHART

FABRIC	POSITION	SIZE
UNIT A – MAKE 1		
Dark	1	1¼" x 2¼"
Print	2	1½" x 1¾"
Print	3	1¾" x 2¾"
Print	4	2¼" x 2¼"
UNIT B –MAKE 1		
Dark	1	1¼" x 2¼"
Print	2	1½" x 1¾"
Print	3	1¾" x 2¾"
UNIT C – MAKE 2		
Dark	1	1¼" x 2¼"
Print	2	1½" x 1¾"
Print	3	1¾" x 2¾"
Dark	4,5	2¼" x 2¼"

Shepherd's Crossing

June 1942 ★ 4" Block

CUTTING INSTRUCTIONS

FROM THE PRINT FABRIC, CUT:

★ 1 – 1 3/4" x 7" strip.
Cut the strip into 4 – 1 3/4" squares.

FROM THE DARK FABRIC, CUT:

★ 1 – 1 3/4" x 10" strip.
Cut the strip into 1 – 1 3/4" x 5" rectangle and 2 – 1 3/4" x 2 1/2" rectangles.

FROM THE MEDIUM FABRIC, CUT:

★ 1 – 1 1/2" x 6" strip.
Cut the strip into 4 – 1 1/2" squares.
Cut the squares into half-square triangles.

★ 1 – 1 1/4" x 17" strip.
Cut the strip into 4 – 1 1/4" x 1 3/4" rectangles and 4 – 1 1/4" x 2 1/2" rectangles.

PATTERN ON PAGE 121.

POSITION CHART

FABRIC	POSITION	SIZE
UNIT A - MAKE 1		
Dark	1	1¾" x 5"
Medium	2,3,4,5	1½" x 1½"
UNIT B - MAKE 4		
Print	1	1¾"x 1¾"
Medium	2	1¼"x 1¾"
Medium	3	1¼"x 2½"
UNIT C - MAKE 2		
Dark	1	1¾"x 2½"
Medium	2,3	1½"x 1½"

ASSEMBLING THE BLOCK

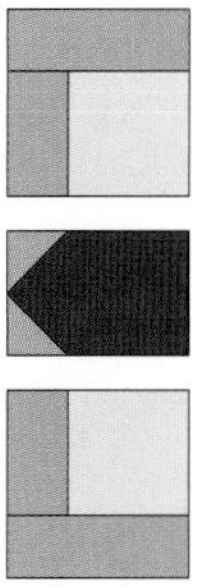

Sew Units B to Units C.

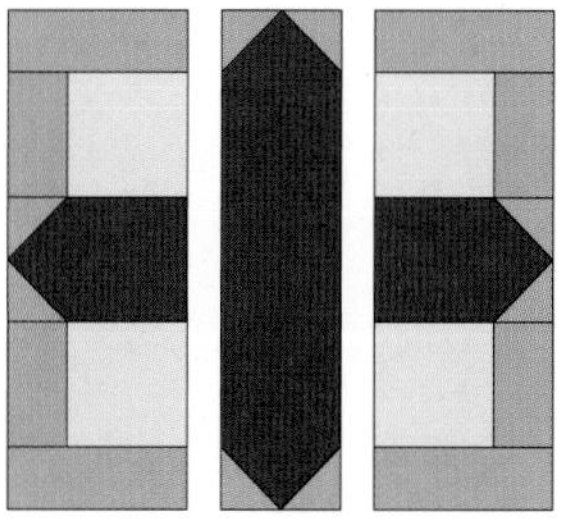

Sew Unit A to Units BCB.

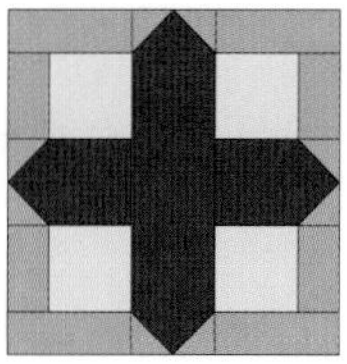

Sunlight and Shadows

January 1942 ★ 4" Block

CUTTING INSTRUCTIONS

FROM THE DARK FABRIC, CUT:

★ 1 – 2" x 4" strip.
Cut the strip into 2 – 2" squares.

★ 1 – 1 1/2" x 10" strip.
Cut the strip into 2 – 1 1/2" x 2" rectangles and 2 – 1 1/2" x 3" rectangles.

FROM THE PRINT FABRIC, CUT:

★ 1 – 2" x 8" strip.
Cut the strip into 4 – 2" squares.
Cut the squares into half-square triangles.

FROM THE BACKGROUND FABRIC, CUT:

★ 1 – 2" x 4" strip.
Cut the strip into 2 – 2" squares.

★ 1 – 1 1/2" x 10" strip.
Cut the strip into 2 – 1 1/2" x 2" rectangles and 2 – 1 1/2" x 3" rectangles.

PATTERN ON PAGE 119.

POSITION CHART

FABRIC	POSITION	SIZE
UNIT A - MAKE 2		
Dark	1	2" x 2"
Background	2	1½" x 2"
Background	3	1½" x 3"
Print	4,5	2" x 2"
UNIT B - MAKE 2		
Background	1	2" x 2"
Dark	2	1½"x 2"
Dark	3	1½"x 3"
Print	4,5	2" x 2"

ASSEMBLING THE BLOCK

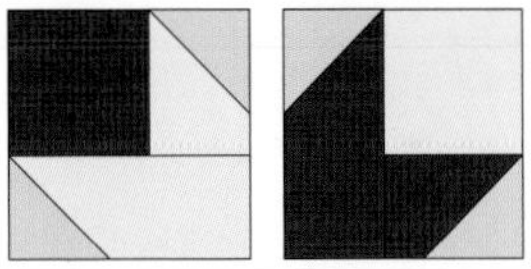

Sew Units A to Units B.

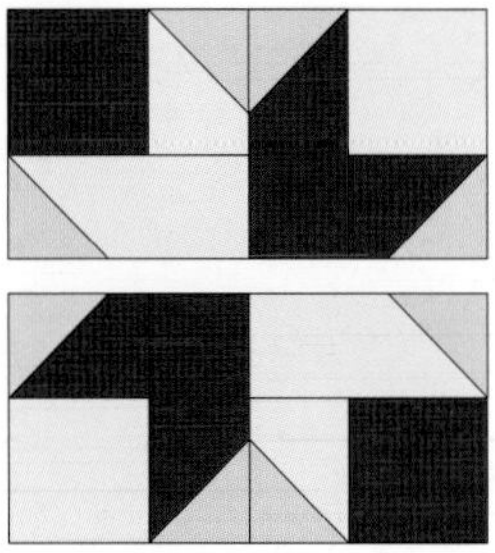

Sew the two halves together to complete the block.

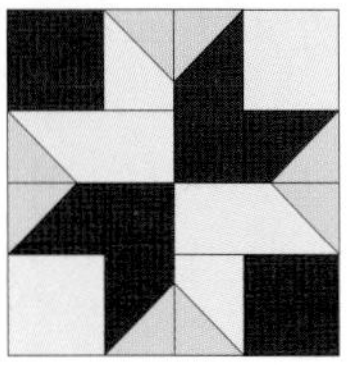

The Army Star

MAY 1943 ★ 4" BLOCK

CUTTING INSTRUCTIONS

FROM THE BACKGROUND FABRIC, CUT:

★ 1 – 2" x 4" strip. Cut the strip into 2 – 2" squares. Cut the squares into half-square triangles.

★ 1 – 1 3/4" x 10" strip. Cut the strip into 4 – 1 3/4" x 2 1/2" rectangles.

★ 1 – 1 1/4" x 5" strip. Cut the strip into 4 – 1 1/4" squares.

FROM THE DARK FABRIC, CUT:

★ 1 – 1 3/4" square.

★ 1 – 1 1/2" x 12" strip. Cut the strip into 8 – 1 1/2" squares. Cut the squares into half-square triangles.

FROM THE MEDIUM FABRIC, CUT:

★ 1 – 1 1/4" x 14" strip. Cut the strip into 8 – 1 1/4" x 1 3/4" rectangles.

★ 1 – 1" x 6" strip. Cut the strip into 4 – 1" x 1 1/2" rectangles.

PATTERN ON PAGE 123.

POSITION CHART

FABRIC	POSITION	SIZE
UNIT A - MAKE 1		
Background	1	1¾"x 2½"
Dark	2,3	1½"x 1½"
Dark	4	1¾"x 1¾"
UNIT B - MAKE 3		
Background	1	1¾"x 2½"
Dark	2,3	1½"x 1½"
UNIT C - MAKE 4		
Medium	1	1" x 1½"
Dark	2,3	1½"x 1½"
Background	4	2" x 2"
Medium	5	1¼"x 1¾"
UNIT D - MAKE 4		
Medium	1	1¼"x 1¾"
Background	2	1¼"x 1¼"

ASSEMBLING THE BLOCK

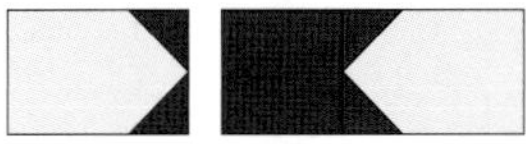

Sew Unit A to Unit B.

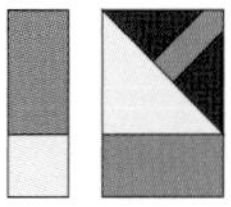

Sew Units C to Units D.

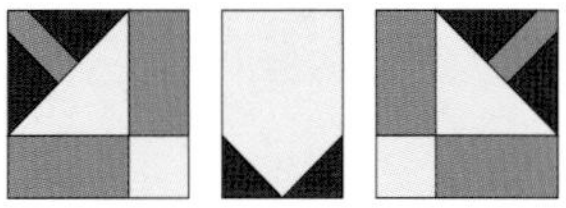

Sew a Unit CD to each side of a Unit B.

Sew together as shown.

A Salute to the Colors

MAY 1942 ★ 4" BLOCK

CUTTING INSTRUCTIONS

FROM THE BACKGROUND FABRIC, CUT:

★ 1 – 2" x 16" strip.
Cut the strip into 8 – 2" squares.
Cut the squares into half-square triangles.

FROM THE DARK FABRIC, CUT:

★ 1 – 1 3/4" x 7" strip.
Cut the strip into 4 – 1 3/4" squares.
Cut the squares into half-square triangles.

★ 1 – 1 1/2" x 3" strip.
Cut the strip into 2 – 1 1/2" squares.

★ 1 – 1 1/4" x 3" strip.*

FROM THE MEDIUM FABRIC, CUT:

★ 1 – 1 3/4" x 7" strip.
Cut the strip into 4 – 1 3/4" squares.
Cut the squares into half-square triangles.

★ 1 – 1 1/2" x 3" strip.
Cut the strip into 2 – 1 1/2" squares.

★ 1 – 1 1/4" x 3" strip.*

* Sew the medium 1 1/4" x 3" strip to the dark 1 1/4" x 3" strip using a 1/4" seam allowance. Press towards the dark fabric. Cut the strip into 2 – 1 1/2" pieces.

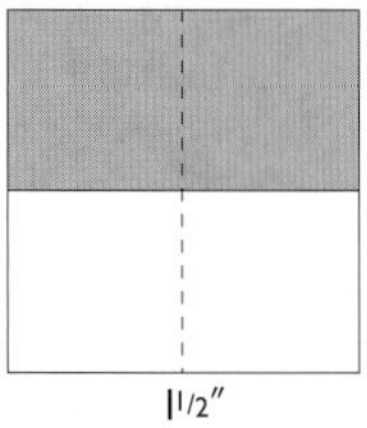

PATTERN ON PAGE 120.

ASSEMBLING THE BLOCK

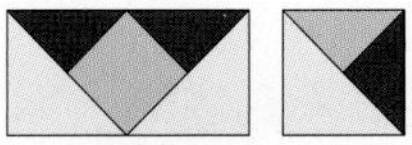

Sew Units A to Units B.

Sew Units AB to Units C.

Sew one Unit E to each side of Unit D.

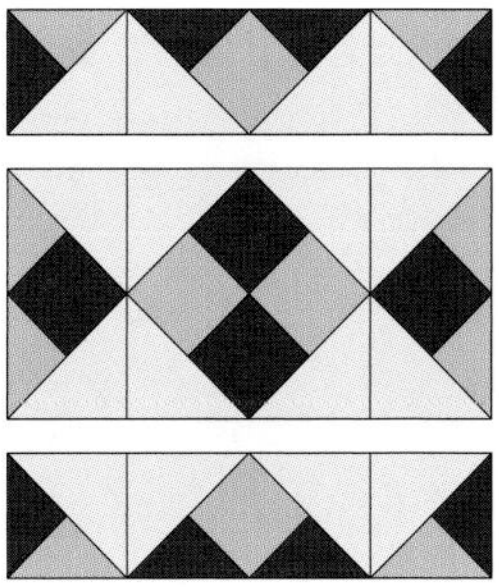

Sew together as shown.

POSITION CHART

FABRIC	POSITION	SIZE
UNIT A - MAKE 2		
Medium	1	1½"x 1½"
Dark	2,3	1¾"x 1¾"
Background	4,5	2" x 2"
UNIT B - MAKE 2		
Dark	1	1¾"x 1¾"
Medium	2	1¾"x 1¾"
Background	3	2" x 2"
UNIT C - MAKE 2		
Dark	1	1¾"x 1¾"
Medium	2	1¾"x 1¾"
Background	3	2" x 2"
UNIT D - MAKE 1		
Medium/Dark	1,2	*
Background	3,4,5,6	2" x 2"
UNIT E - MAKE 2		
Dark	1	1½"x 1½"
Medium	2,3	1¾"x 1¾"
Background	4,5	2" x 2"

**See cutting instructions.*

A Basket Quilt in Triangles

December 1942 ★ 4" Block

CUTTING INSTRUCTIONS

FROM THE BACKGROUND FABRIC, CUT:

★ 1 – 4 1/4" square.
Cut the square into half-square triangles.
You will have one half-square triangle left over.

★ 1 – 2 3/4" square.
Cut the square into half-square triangles.
You will have one half-square triangle left over.

★ 1 – 1 3/4" x 12 1/4" strip.
Cut the strip into 7 – 1 3/4" squares.
Cut the squares into half-square triangles.

★ 1 – 1 1/2" x 8 1/2" strip.
Cut the strip into 1 – 1 1/2" square
and 2 – 1 1/2" x 3 1/2" rectangles.

FROM THE DARK FABRIC, CUT:

★ 1 – 1 3/4" x 17 1/2" strip.
Cut the strip into 10 – 1 3/4" squares.
Cut the squares into half-square triangles.

PATTERN ON PAGE 122.

ASSEMBLING THE BLOCK

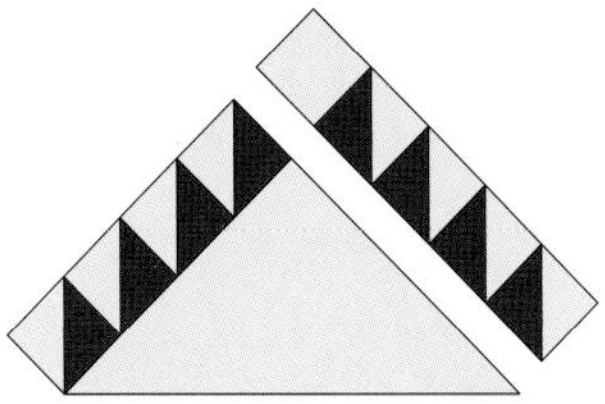

Sew Unit A to Unit B.

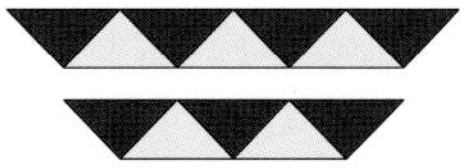

Sew Unit C to Unit D.

Sew Unit E to Unit CD.

Sew Unit AB to Unit CDE.

ASSEMBLING THE BLOCK, CONTINUED

Sew Units F and G to Unit ABCDE.

Add Unit H as shown to complete the block.

POSITION CHART

FABRIC	POSITION	SIZE
UNIT A - MAKE 1		
Background	1	1½" x 1½"
Dark	2,4,6,8	1¾" x 1¾" ◩
Background	3,5,7,9	1¾" x 1¾" ◩
UNIT B - MAKE 1		
Background	1,3,5,7	1¾" x 1¾" ◩
Dark	2,4,6,8	1¾" x 1¾" ◩
Background	9	4¼" x 4¼" ◩
UNIT C - MAKE 1		
Dark	1,3,5,7	1¾" x 1¾" ◩
Background	2,4,6	1¾" x 1¾" ◩
UNIT D - MAKE 1		
Dark	1,3,5	1¾" x 1¾" ◩
Background	2,4	1¾" x 1¾" ◩
UNIT E - MAKE 1		
Dark	1,3,4	1¾" x 1¾" ◩
Background	2	1¾" x 1¾" ◩
UNIT F & G - MAKE 1 EACH		
Background	1	1½" x 3½"
Dark	2	1¾" x 1¾" ◩
UNIT H - MAKE 1		
Background	1	2¾" x 2¾" ◩

The New Four Pointer

May 1944 ★ 4" Block

CUTTING INSTRUCTIONS

FROM THE BACKGROUND FABRIC, CUT:

★ 1 – 2 1/4" x 2 1/2" rectangle.

★ 1 – 1 1/4" x 20" strip.
Cut the strip into 8 – 1 1/4" x 2 1/2" rectangles.

★ 1 – 1" x 4 1/2" strip.
Cut the strip into 2 – 1" x 2 1/4" rectangles.

FROM THE DARK FABRIC, CUT:

★ 1 – 2 1/2" x 5" strip.
Cut the strip into 2 – 2 1/2" squares.
Cut the squares into half-square triangles.

FROM THE MEDIUM FABRIC, CUT:

★ 1 – 2 1/2" x 5" strip.
Cut the strip into 2 – 2 1/2" squares.
Cut the squares into half-square triangles.

FROM THE PRINT FABRIC, CUT:

★ 1 – 1 3/4" x 8" strip.
Cut the strip into 4 – 1 3/4" x 2" rectangles.

★ 1 – 1" x 5" strip.
Cut the strip into 4 – 1" x 1 1/4" rectangles.

PATTERN ON PAGE 124.

ASSEMBLING THE BLOCK

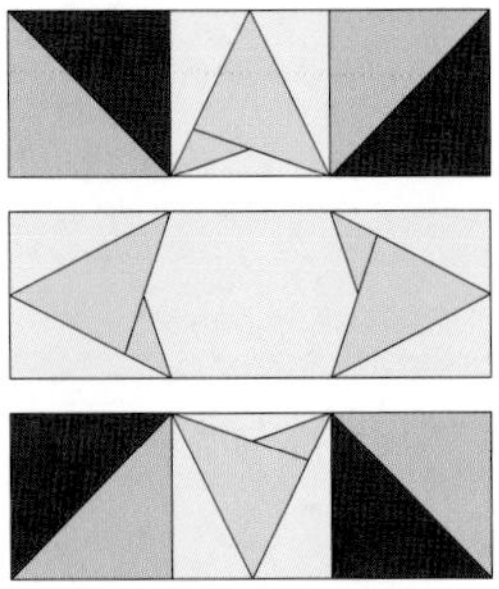

Sew Unit A to Units B.

POSITION CHART

FABRIC	POSITION	SIZE
UNIT A - MAKE 1		
Background	1	2¼" x 2½"
Print	2,3	1" x 1¼"
Print	4,5	1¾" x 2"
Background	6,7,8,9	1¼" x 2½"
UNIT B - MAKE 2		
Background	1	1" x 2¼"
Print	2	1" x 1¼"
Print	3	1¾" x 2"
Background	4,5	1¼" x 2½"
Dark	6,9	2½" x 2½"
Medium	7,8	2½" x 2½"

A Quilt Mosaic

SEPTEMBER 1945 ★ 4" BLOCK

CUTTING INSTRUCTIONS

FROM THE BACKGROUND FABRIC, CUT:

★ 1 – 1 3/4" x 24 1/2" strip.
Cut the strip into 14 – 1 3/4" squares.
Cut 10 squares into half-square triangles.

FROM THE DARK FABRIC, CUT:

★ 1 – 1 3/4" x 5 1/4" strip.
Cut the strip into 3 – 1 3/4" squares.
Cut 2 of the squares into half-square triangles.

★ 1 – 1 1/4" x 27" strip.
Cut the strip into 4 – 1 1/4" x 1 3/4" rectangles and 8 – 1 1/4" x 2 1/2" rectangles.

PATTERN ON PAGE 125.

POSITION CHART

FABRIC	POSITION	SIZE
UNIT A - MAKE 1		
Dark	1	1¾" x 1¾"
Background	2,3	1¾" x 1¾"
Dark	4,5	1¾" x 1¾"
Dark	6,7	1¼" x 2½"
Background	8,9,10,11	1¾" x 1¾"
UNIT B - MAKE 2		
Background	1	1¾" x 1¾"
Dark	2	1¾" x 1¾"
Dark	3	1¼" x 2½"
Background	4,5	1¾" x 1¾"
UNIT C - MAKE 4		
Background	1	1¾" x 1¾"
Dark	2	1¼" x 1¾"
Dark	3	1¼" x 2½"
Background	4,5	1¾" x 1¾"

ASSEMBLING THE BLOCK

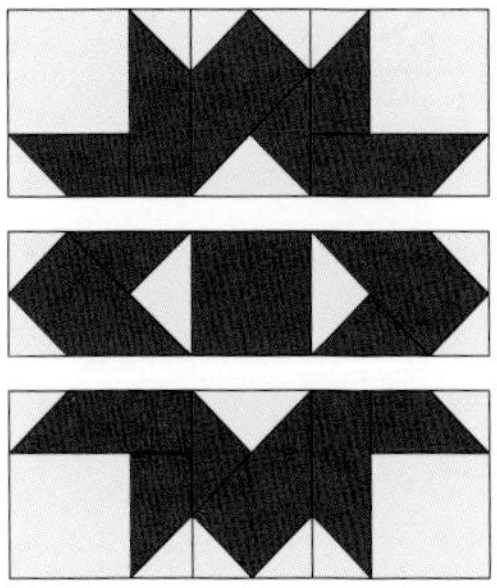

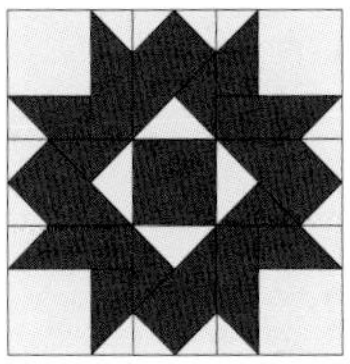

Sew Unit A to Units BC.

Return of the Swallows

OCTOBER 1946 ★ 4" BLOCK

CUTTING INSTRUCTIONS

FROM THE BACKGROUND FABRIC, CUT:

★ 1 – 2" x 16" strip.
  Cut the strip into 8 – 2" squares.
  Cut the squares into half-square triangles.

FROM THE PRINT FABRICS, CUT:

★ 4 – 2 1/2" squares.
  Cut the squares into half-square triangles.

PATTERN ON PAGE 126.

ASSEMBLING THE BLOCK

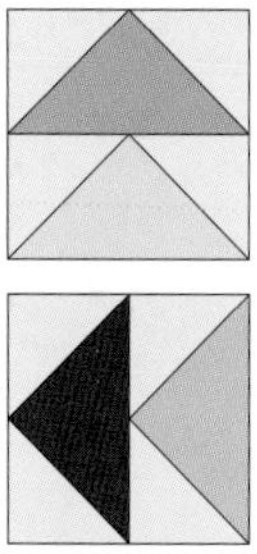

Sew Unit B to Unit C.

Sew Unit A to Unit BC.

POSITION CHART

FABRIC	POSITION	SIZE
UNIT A - MAKE 1		
Various Prints	1,4,7,10	2½" x 2½"
Background	2,3,5,6,8,9,	2" x 2"
	11,12	2" x 2"
UNIT B - MAKE 1		
Various Prints	1,4	2½" x 2½"
Background	2,3,5,6	2" x 2"
UNIT C - MAKE 1		
Various Prints	1,4	2½" x 2½"
Background	2,3,5,6	2" x 2"

The North Star

MARCH 1949 ★ 4" BLOCK

CUTTING INSTRUCTIONS

FROM THE BACKGROUND FABRIC, CUT:

★ 1 – 1 1/4" x 20" strip.
Cut the strip into 8 – 1 1/4" x 2 1/2" rectangles.

FROM THE PRINT FABRIC, CUT:

★ 1 – 2" x 10" strip.
Cut the strip into 4 – 2" x 2 1/2" rectangles.

FROM THE DARK FABRIC, CUT:

★ 1 – 1 3/4" x 3 1/2" strip.
Cut the strip into 2 – 1 3/4" squares.
Cut the squares into half-square triangles.

★ 1 – 1 1/4" x 36" strip.
Cut the strip into 8 – 1 1/4" x 1 1/2" rectangles
and 8 – 1 1/4" x 3" rectangles.

PATTERN ON PAGE 129.

POSITION CHART

FABRIC	POSITION	SIZE
UNIT A - MAKE 4		
Dark	1	1¼"x 3"
Background	2	1¼"x 2½"
Dark	3	1¼"x 1½"
Print	4	2" x 2½"
Dark	5	1¾"x 1¾"
JNIT B - MAKE 4		
Dark	1	1¼"x 3"
Background	2	1¼"x 2½"
Dark	3	1¼"x 1½"

ASSEMBLING THE BLOCK

Sew Units AB together.

Sew Units A to Units B.

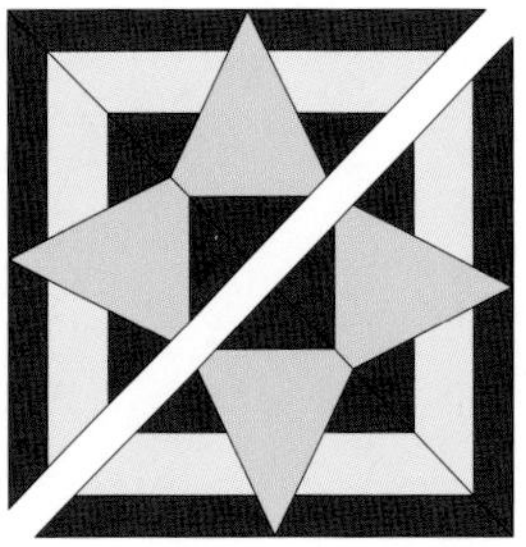

Sew the two halves together
to complete the block.

The Christmas Star

DECEMBER 1947 ★ 4" BLOCK

CUTTING INSTRUCTIONS

FROM THE BACKGROUND FABRIC, CUT:

★ 1 – 2 1/2" x 15" strip.
Cut the strip into 6 – 2 1/2" squares.
Cut the squares into half-square triangles.

★ 1 – 1 1/4" x 10" strip.
Cut the strip into 8 – 1 1/4" squares.
Cut the squares into half-square triangles.

FROM THE PRINT FABRIC, CUT:

★ 1 – 1" x 24" strip.
Cut the strip into 16 – 1" x 1 1/2" rectangles.

FROM THE DARK FABRIC, CUT:

★ 1 – 1" x 24" strip.
Cut the strip into 16 – 1" x 1 1/2" rectangles.

FROM THE MEDIUM FABRIC, CUT:

★ 1 – 1" x 36" strip.
Cut the strip into 24 – 1" x 1 1/2" rectangles.

PATTERN ON PAGE 127.

ASSEMBLING THE BLOCK

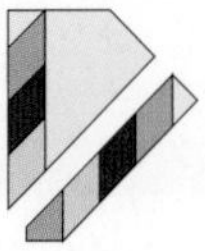

Sew Units A to Units B.

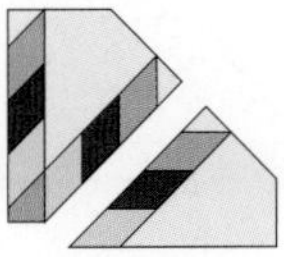

Sew Units C to Units AB.

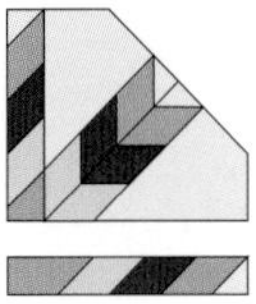

Sew Units D to Units ABC.

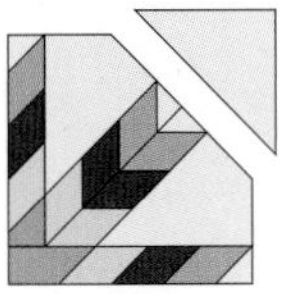

Add Units E to Units ABCD.

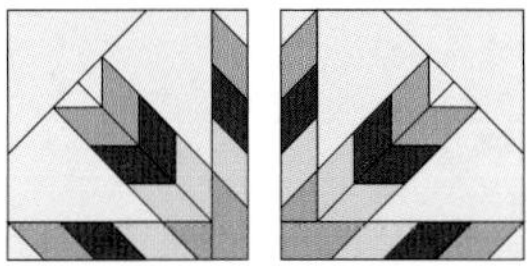

Sew 2 Units ABCDE together.

Sew the two halves together to complete the block.

POSITION CHART

FABRIC	POSITION	SIZE
UNITS A AND C - MAKE 4 EACH		
Print	1	1" x 1½"
Dark	2	1" x 1½"
Medium	3	1" x 1½"
Background	4	1¼"x 1¼"
Background	5	2½" x 2½"
UNIT B - MAKE 4		
Medium	1	1" x 1½"
Print	2	1" x 1½"
Dark	3	1 x 1½"
Medium	4	1" x 1½"
Background	5	1¼" x 1¼"
UNIT D - MAKE 4		
Medium	1	1" x 1½"
Print	2	1" x 1½"
Dark	3	1" x 1½"
Medium	4	1" x 1½"
Background	5	1¼" x 1¼"
UNIT E - MAKE 4		
Background	1	2½" x 2½"

The Spider Web

JUNE 1943 ★ 4" BLOCK

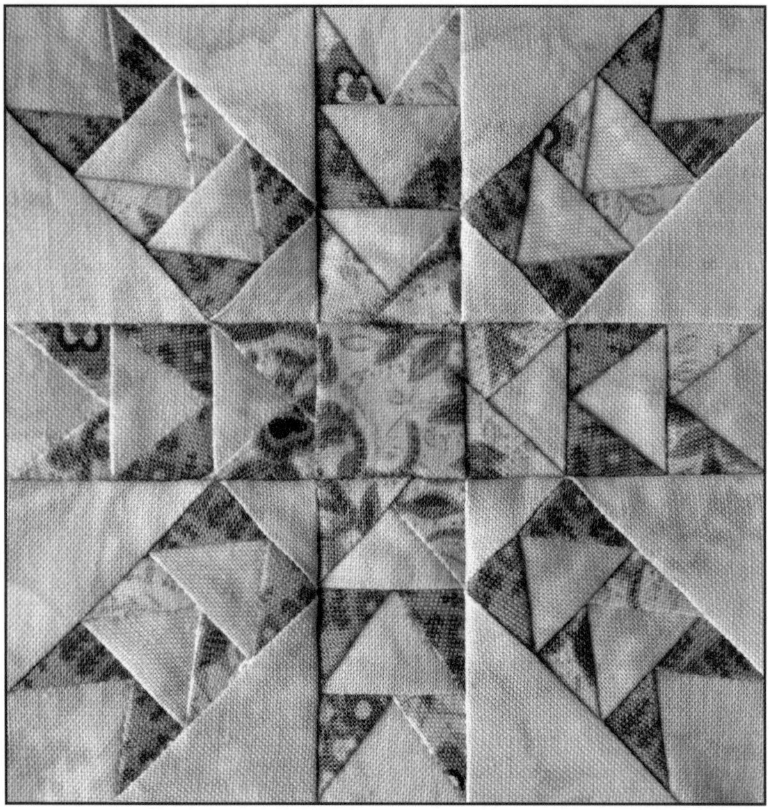

CUTTING INSTRUCTIONS

FROM THE BACKGROUND FABRIC, CUT:

★ 1 – 2 1/4" x 9" strip.
Cut the strip into 4 – 2 1/4" squares.
Cut the squares into half-square triangles.

★ 1 – 1 1/2" x 3" strip.
Cut the strip into 2 – 1 1/2" squares.
Cut the squares into half-square triangles.

★ 1 – 1 1/4" x 36" strip.
Cut the strip into 24 – 1 1/4" x 1 1/2" rectangles.

FROM THE PRINT FABRIC, CUT:

★ 1 – 1 1/2" x 7 1/2" strip.
Cut the strip into 5 – 1 1/2" squares.
Cut 4 of the squares into half-square triangles.

1 – 1" x 20" strips.
Cut the strips into 16 – 1" x 1 1/4" rectangles.

FROM THE MEDIUM FABRIC, CUT:

★ 1 – 1"x 30" strip.
Cut the strip into 24 – 1"x 1 1/4" rectangles.

PATTERN ON PAGE 128.

ASSEMBLING THE BLOCK

Sew Unit A to Unit B.

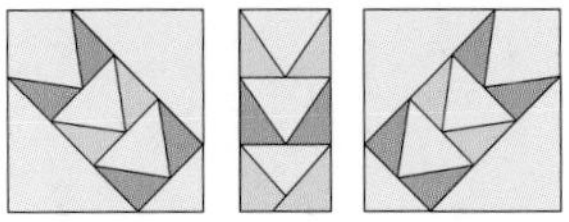

Sew Units B to Units C.

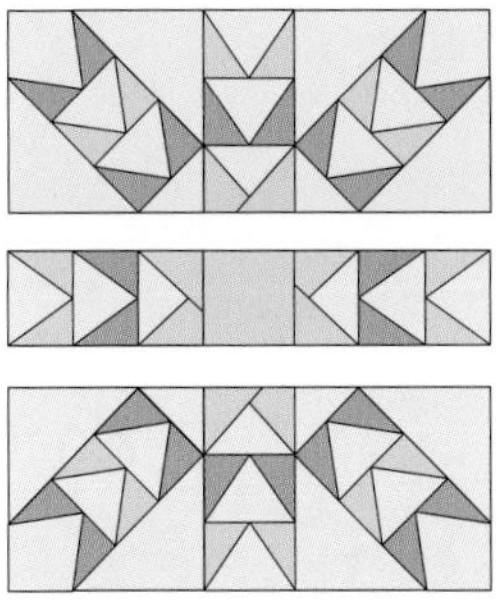

Sew together as shown.

POSITION CHART

FABRIC	POSITION	SIZE
UNIT A- MAKE 1		
Background	1,4,7	1¼" x 1½"
Print	2,3	1" x 1¼"
Medium	5,6	1" x 1¼"
Print	8,9	1½" x 1½"
Print	10	1½" x 1½"
UNIT B - MAKE 3		
Background	1,4,7	1¼" x 1½"
Print	2,3	1" x 1¼"
Medium	5,6	1" x 1¼"
Print	8,9	1½" x 1½"
UNIT C - MAKE 4		
Background	1,4,7	1¼" x 1½"
Medium	2,3	1" x 1¼"
Print	5,6	1" x 1¼"
Medium	8,9	1" x 1¼"
Background	10	1½" x 1½"
Background	11,12	2¼" x 2¼"

A Flash of Diamonds

APRIL 1949 ★ 4" BLOCK

CUTTING INSTRUCTIONS

FROM THE BACKGROUND FABRIC, CUT:

★ 1 – 1 3/4" x 10 1/2" strip.
Cut the strip into 6 – 1 3/4" squares.
Cut the squares into half-square triangles.

★ 1 – 1 1/2" x 12" strip.
Cut the strip into 8– 1 1/2" squares.
Cut the squares into half-square triangles.

★ 1 – 1 1/4" x 10" strip.
Cut the strip into 8 – 1 1/4" squares.

FROM THE DARK FABRIC, CUT:

★ 1 – 1 3/4" square.

★ 1 – 1 1/2" x 6" strip.
Cut the strip into 4 – 1 1/2" squares.
Cut the squares into half-square triangles.

★ 1 – 1" x 14" strip.
Cut the strip into 8 – 1" x 1 3/4" rectangles.

FROM THE MEDIUM FABRIC, CUT:

★ 1 – 1 1/2" x 3" strip.
Cut the strip into 2 – 1 1/2" squares.
Cut the squares into half-square triangles.

★ 1 – 1" x 7" strip.
Cut the strip into 4 – 1" x 1 3/4" rectangles.

FROM THE LIGHT FABRIC, CUT:

★ 1 – 2 3/4" x 5 1/2" strip.
Cut the strip into 2 – 2 3/4" squares.
Cut the squares into half-square triangles.

PATTERN ON PAGE 130.

ASSEMBLING THE BLOCK

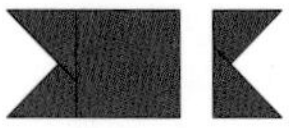

Sew Unit A to Unit B.

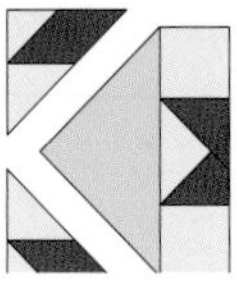

Sew Units D and E to Units C.

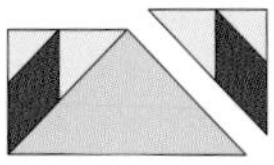

Sew Units D to Units G.

Sew Units CDE to Unit AB.

ASSEMBLING THE BLOCK, CONTINUED

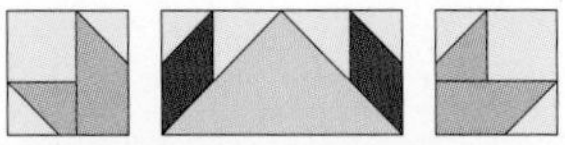

Sew Units F to Units DG.

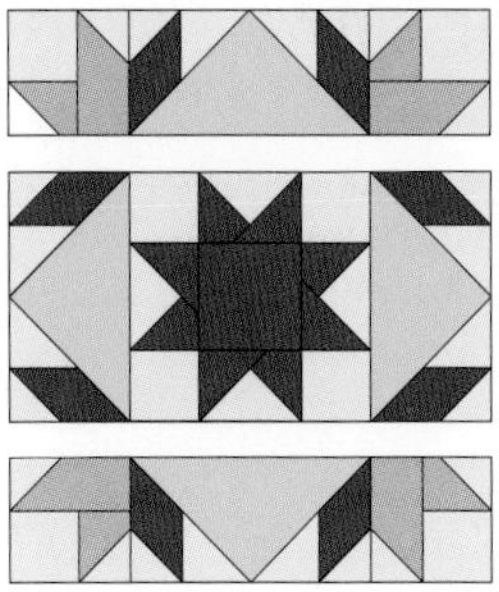

Sew together as shown to complete the block.

POSITION CHART

FABRIC	POSITION	SIZE	
UNIT A - MAKE 1			
Background	1	1¾" x 1¾"	◩
Dark	2,3	1½" x 1½"	◩
Dark	4	1¾" x 1¾"	
UNIT B - MAKE 1			
Background	1	1¾" x 1¾"	◩
Dark	2,3	1½" x 1½"	◩
UNIT C - MAKE 2			
Background	1	1¾" x 1¾"	◩
Dark	2,3	1½" x 1½"	◩
Background	4,5	1¼" x 1¼"	
Light	6	2¾" x 2¾"	◩
UNITS D - MAKE 4			
Dark	1	1" x 1¾"	
Background	2	1½" x 1½"	◩
Background	3	1¾" x 1¾"	◩
UNIT E - MAKE 2			
Dark	1	1" x 1¾"	
Background	2	1½" x 1½"	◩
Background	3	1¾" x 1¾"	◩
UNIT F - MAKE 4			
Background	1	1¼" x 1¼"	
Medium	2	1½" x 1½"	◩
Medium	3	1" x 1¾"	
Background	4,5	1½" x 1½"	◩
UNIT G - MAKE 2			
Dark	1	1" x 1¾"	
Background	2	1½" x 1½"	◩
Background	3	1¾" x 1¾"	◩
Light	4	2¾" x 2¾"	◩

The Kansas Star

May 1949 ★ 4" Block

CUTTING INSTRUCTIONS

FROM THE BACKGROUND FABRIC, CUT:

★ 1 – 1 3/4" x 10 1/2" strip.
Cut the strip into 6 – 1 3/4" squares.
Cut the squares into half-square triangles.

FROM THE DARK FABRIC, CUT:

★ 1 – 1 3/4" x 7" strip.
Cut the strip into 4 – 1 3/4" squares.
Cut the squares into half-square triangles.

FROM THE PRINT FABRIC, CUT:

★ 1 – 1 3/4" x 8 3/4" strip.
Cut the strip into 5 – 1 3/4" squares.

FROM THE LIGHT FABRIC, CUT:

★ 1 – 1 3/4" x 14" strip.
Cut the strip into 8 – 1 3/4" squares.
Cut 4 squares into half-square triangles.

FROM THE MEDIUM FABRIC, CUT:

★ 1 – 1 3/4" x 7" strip.
Cut the strip into 4 – 1 3/4" squares.
Cut the squares into half-square triangles.

PATTERN ON PAGE 131.

ASSEMBLING THE BLOCK

Sew one Unit A to either side of Unit B. Make two.

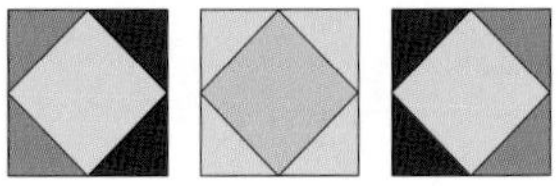

Sew one Unit B to either side of Unit C.

Sew together as shown.

POSITION CHART

FABRIC	POSITION	SIZE
UNIT A - MAKE 4		
Print	1	1¾" x 1¾"
Light	2	1¾" x 1¾"
Background	3,4,5	1¾" x 1¾"
UNIT B - MAKE 4		
Light	1	1¾" x 1¾"
Dark	2,4	1¾" x 1¾"
Medium	3,5	1¾" x 1¾"
UNIT C - MAKE 1		
Print	1	1¾" x 1¾"
Light	2,3,4,5	1¾" x 1¾"

Crazy Anne

JUNE 1949 ★ 4" BLOCK

CUTTING INSTRUCTIONS

FROM THE BACKGROUND FABRIC, CUT:

★ 1 – 1 3/4" x 10" strip.
Cut the strip into 4 – 1 3/4" x 2 1/2" rectangles.

★ 1 – 1 1/2" x 10" strip.
Cut the strip into 4 – 1 1/2" x 2 1/2" rectangles.

★ 1 – 1 1/4" x 12" strip.
Cut the strip into 8 – 1 1/4" x 1 1/2" rectangles.

FROM THE PRINT FABRICS, CUT:

★ 4 – 2 1/4" squares.
Cut the squares into half-square triangles.

★ 8 – 1" x 2" rectangles.

PATTERN ON PAGE 132.

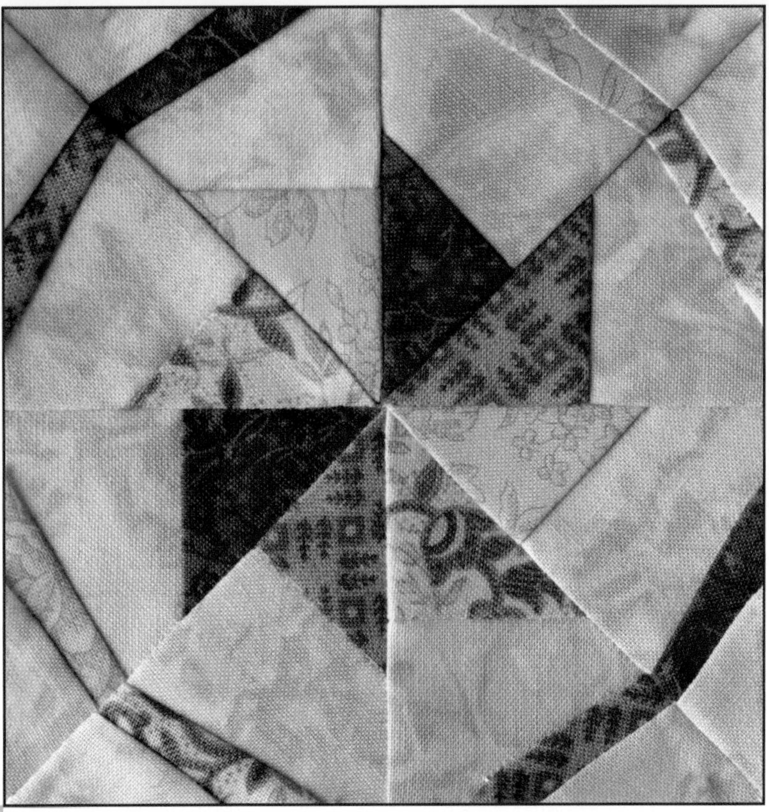

POSITION CHART

FABRIC	POSITION	SIZE
UNIT A - MAKE 4		
Background	1	1½"x 2½"
Prints	2	2¼" x 2¼"
Prints	3	1" x 2"
Background	4	1¼"x 1½"
UNIT B - MAKE 4		
Background	1	1¾" x 2½"
Prints	2	2¼" x 2¼"
Prints	3	1" x 2"
Background	4	1¼"x 1½"

ASSEMBLING THE BLOCK

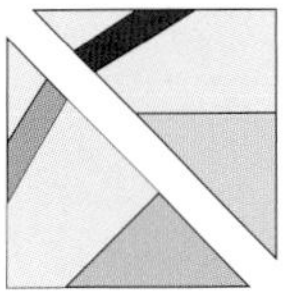

Sew Units A to Unit Bs.

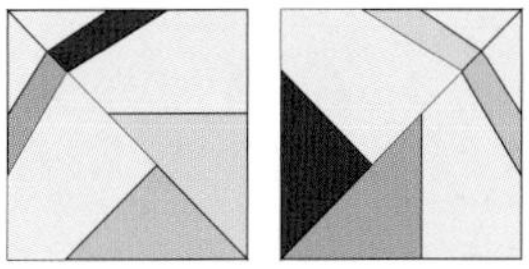

Sew two AB Units together. Make two.

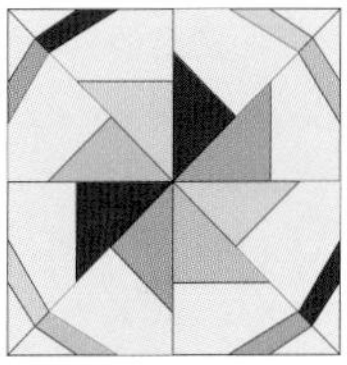

Sew the two halves together.

The Bright Jewel

September 1949 ★ 4" Block

CUTTING INSTRUCTIONS

FROM THE BACKGROUND FABRIC, CUT:

★ 1 – 2" x 16" strip.
Cut the strip into 8 – 2" square.
Cut the squares into half-square triangles.

★ 1 – 1 1/2" square.

FROM THE MEDIUM FABRIC, CUT:

★ 1 – 2" x 16" strip.
Cut the strip into 8 – 2" squares.
Cut the squares into half-square triangles.

★ 1 – 1 1/2" x 10" strip.
Cut the strip into 4 – 1 1/2" x 2 1/2" rectangles.

PATTERN ON PAGE 114.

ASSEMBLING THE BLOCK

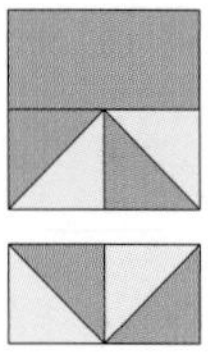

Sew Units A to Units B.

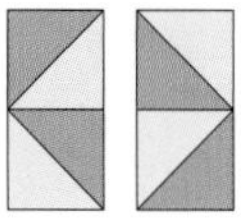

Sew Units C to Units D.

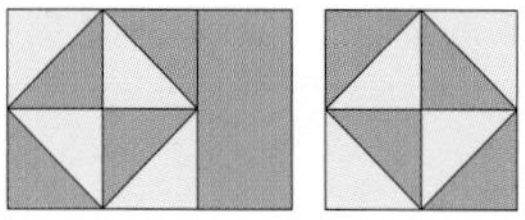

Sew Units AB to Units CD. Make two.

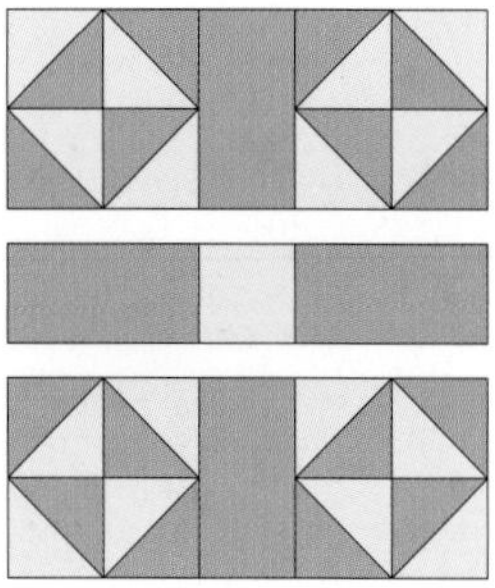

Sew Units ABCD to Unit E.

POSITION CHART

FABRIC	POSITION	SIZE
UNIT A - MAKE 2		
Medium	1,3	2" x 2"
Background	2,4	2" x 2"
Medium	5	1½"x 2½"
UNITS B AND C- MAKE 2 EACH		
Medium	1,3	2" x 2"
Background	2,4	2" x 2"
UNIT D - MAKE 2		
Background	1,3	2" x 2"
Medium	2,4	2" x 2"
UNIT E - MAKE 1		
Background	1	1½"x 1½"
Medium	2,3	1½"x 2½"

Gallery

It's All About Pat by Kelly Green Collins, Littleton, Colorado.

Emerson's Chocolate Creams made by Carolyn Cullinan McCormick, quilted by Carol Willey, Castle Rock, Colorado.

Above: This eye-catching black, white and red sampler was made and quilted by Sandra Reinke, Lakewood, Colorado. Below: The North Star quilt was made and quilted by Megan McCormick, Parker, Colorado.

Above: The Christmas Star table runner was made by Diane Donnelly, Bozeman, Montana, and quilted by Tracy Yadon, Manhattan, Montana.

Above: 4" Sampler Quilt made and quilted by Carol Netwal, Castle Rock, Colorado. Opposite: Army Star quilt made by Carolyn Cullinan McCormick, Franktown, Colorado, and quilted by Jan Korytkowski, Castle Rock, Colorado.

The Spider Web was made and quilted by Carolyn Cullinan McCormick, Franktown, Colorado.

The Christmas Star

Pattern for 10" Block on Page 30.

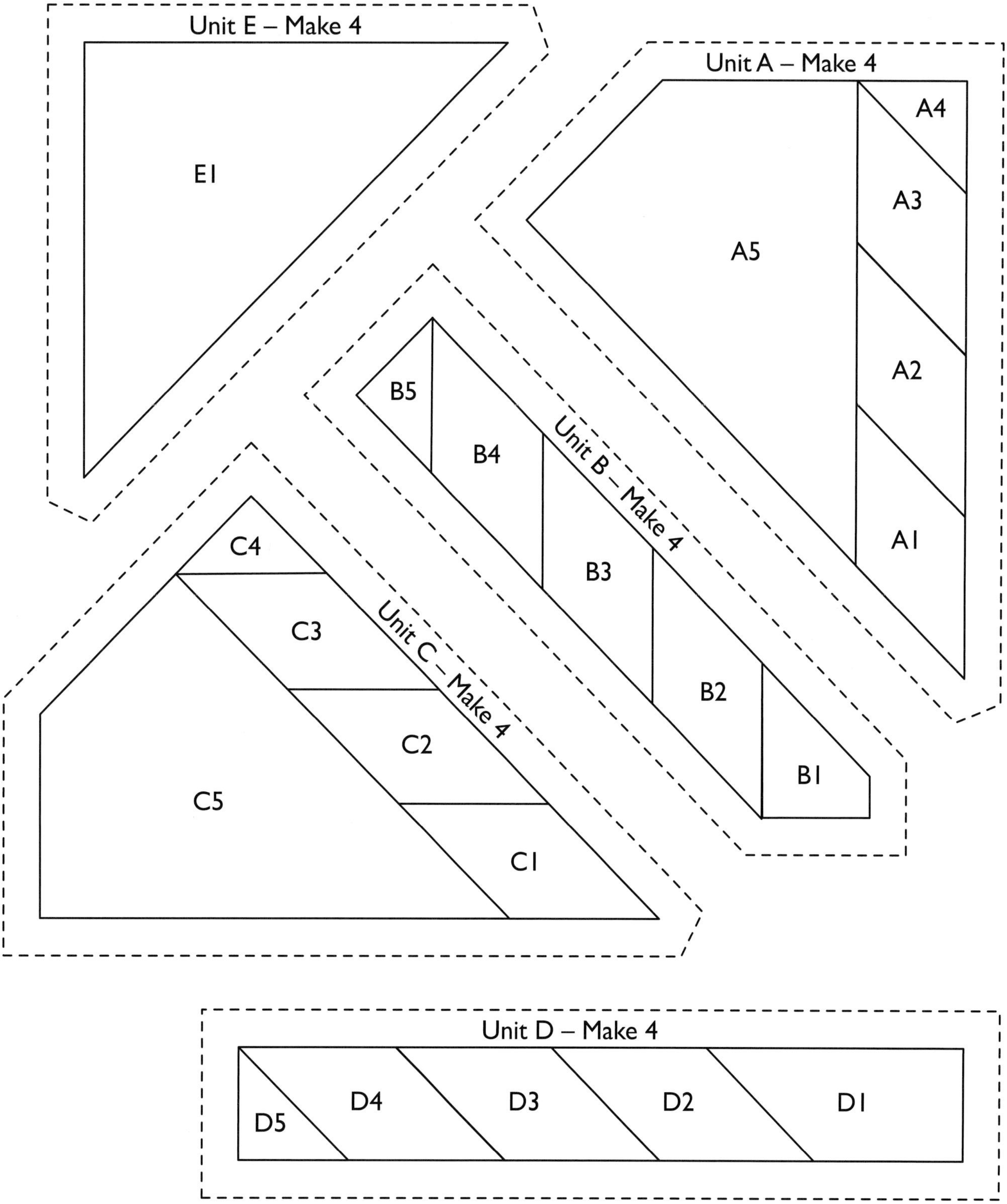

Mother's Favorite Star

Patterns for 10" Block on Page 14.

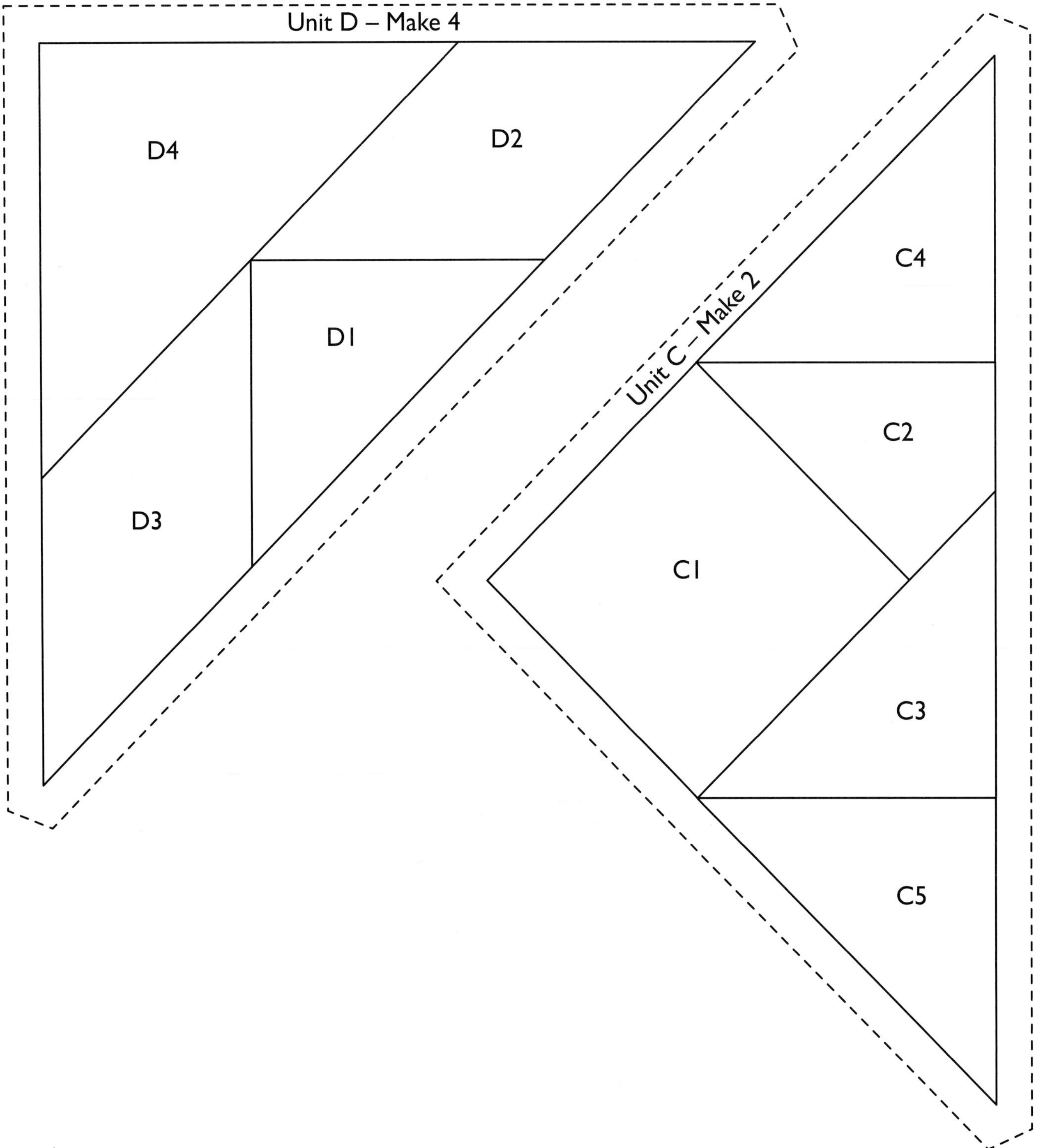

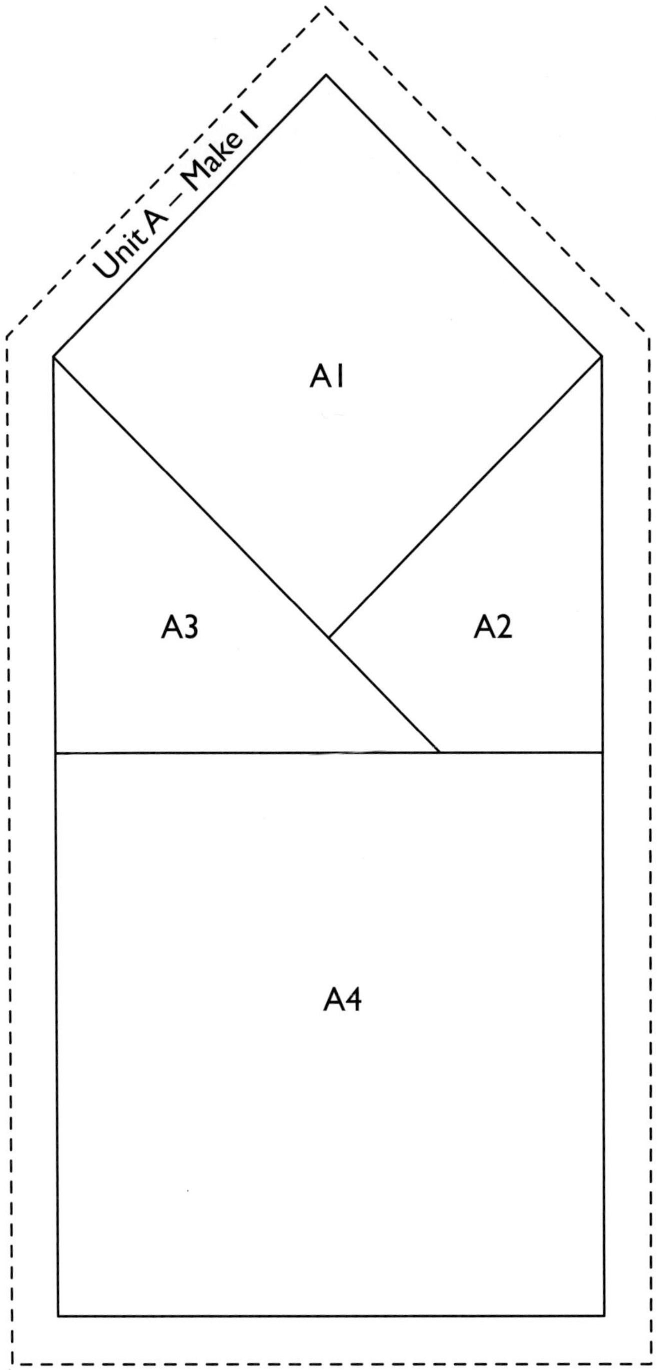
Unit A – Make 1
A1
A3
A2
A4

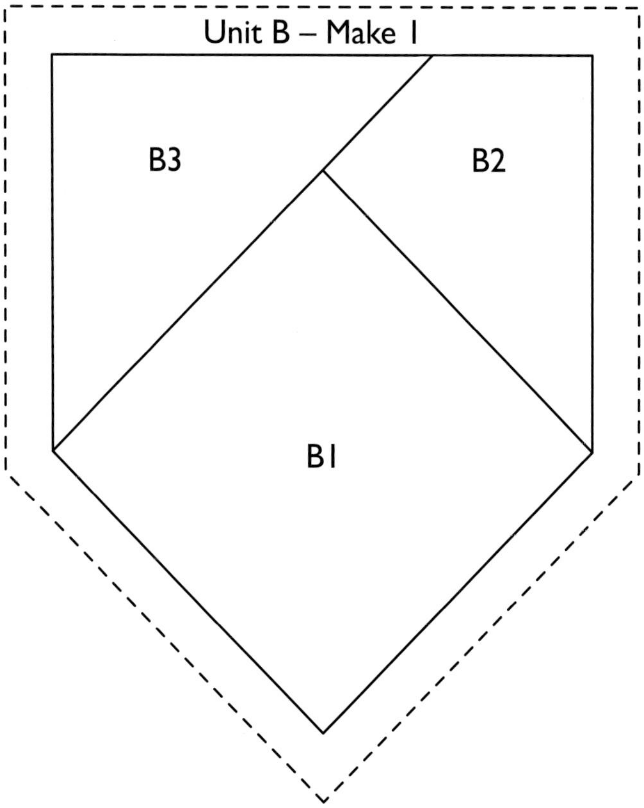
Unit B – Make 1
B3
B2
B1

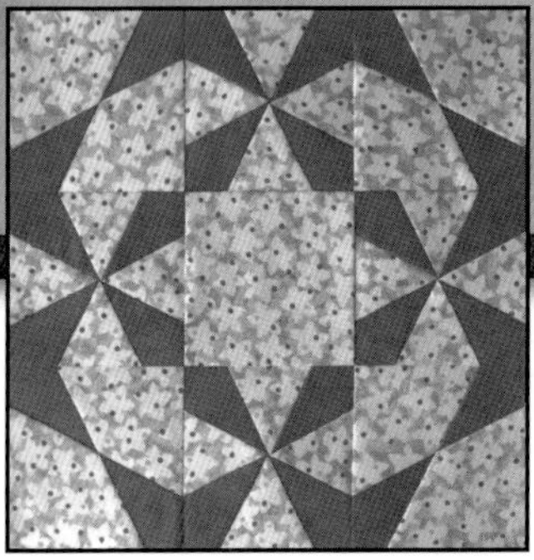

Mona's Choice

Patterns for 10" Block on Page 15.

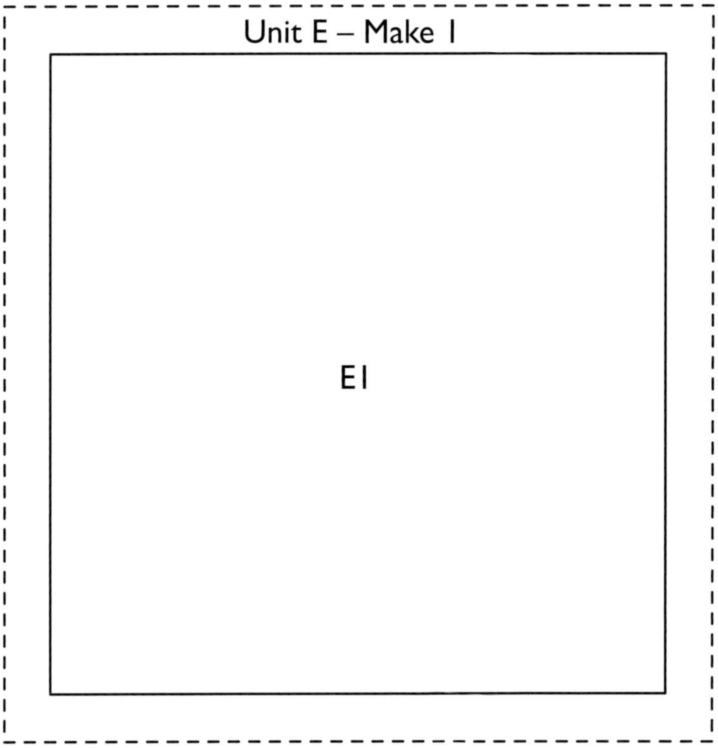

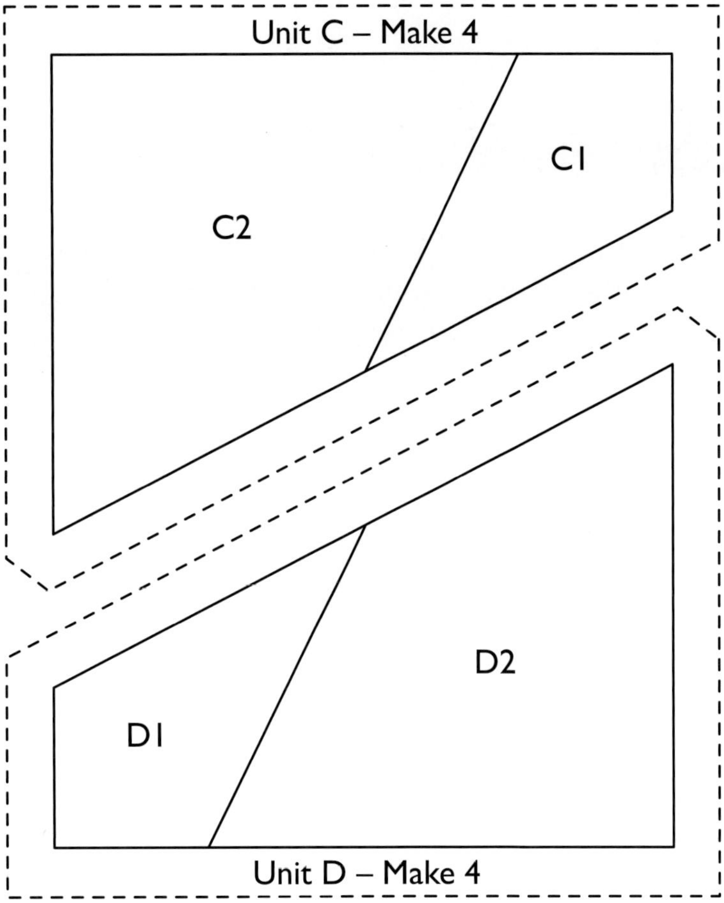
Unit C – Make 4
C1
C2
D2
D1
Unit D – Make 4

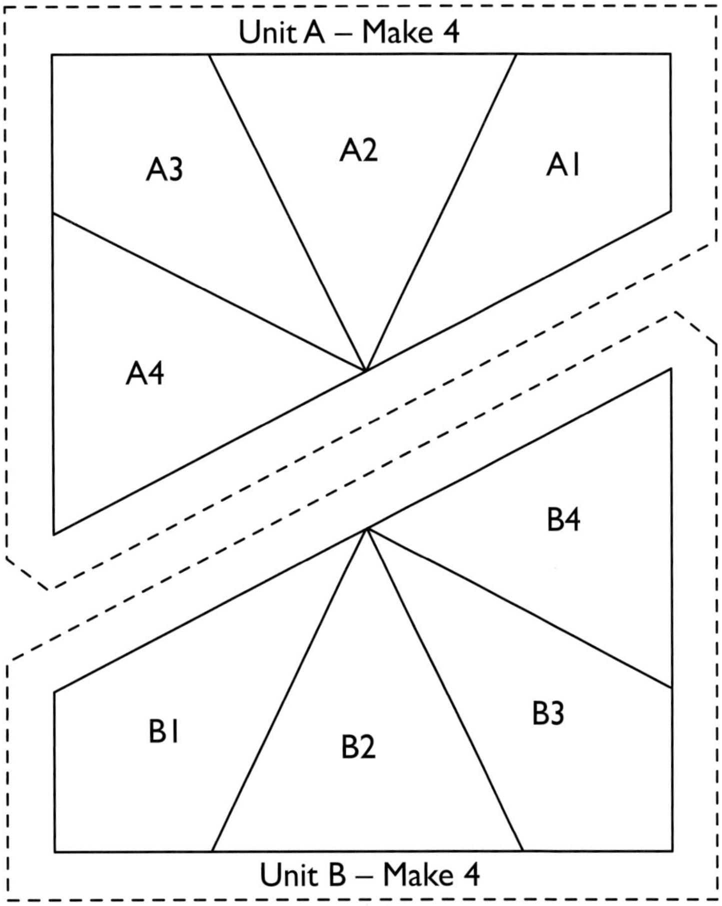
Unit A – Make 4
A3
A2
A1
A4
B4
B1
B2
B3
Unit B – Make 4

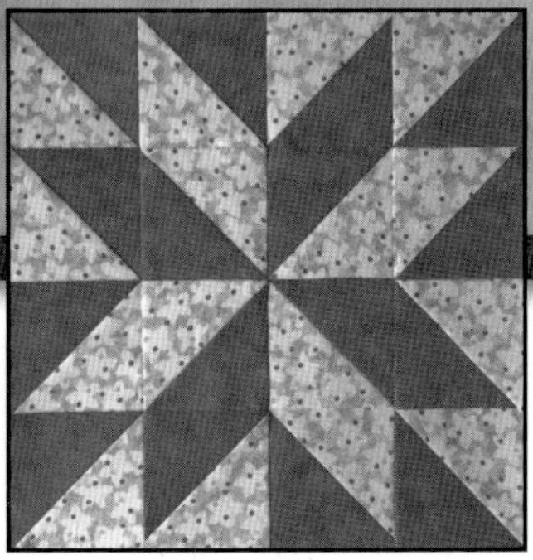

Anna's Choice

Patterns for 10" Block on Page 17.

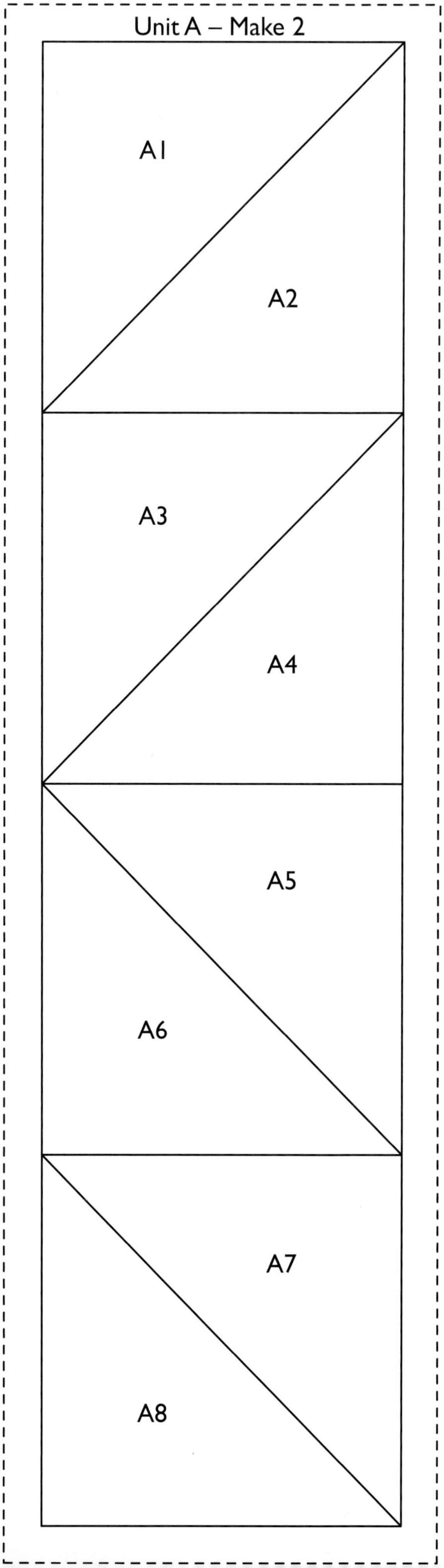

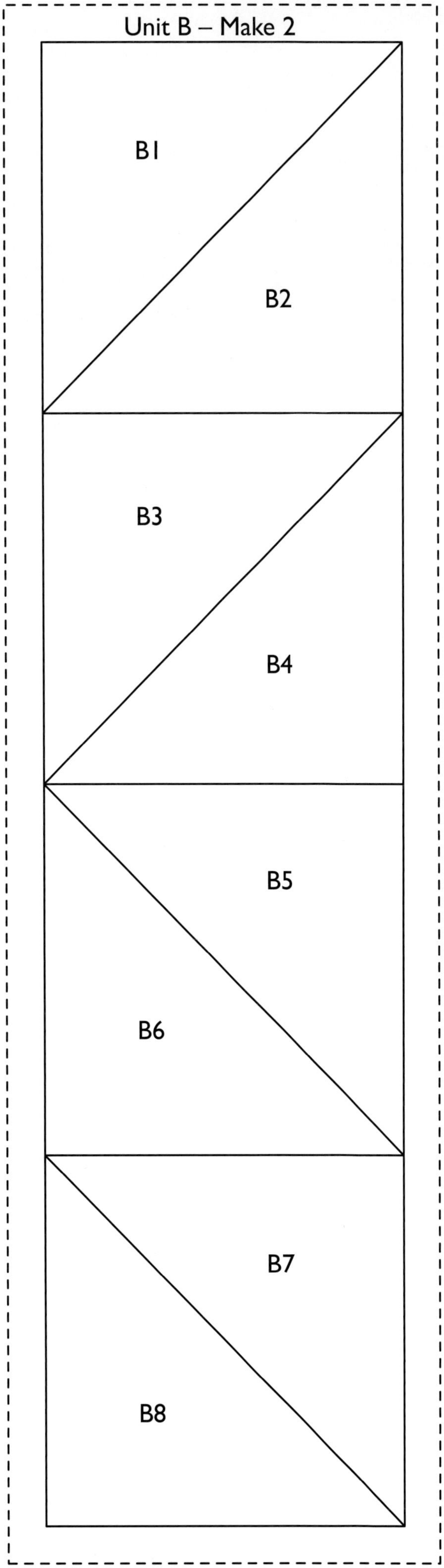
Unit B – Make 2
B1
B2
B3
B4
B5
B6
B7
B8

The Colorado Quilt

Pattern for 10" Block on Page 16.

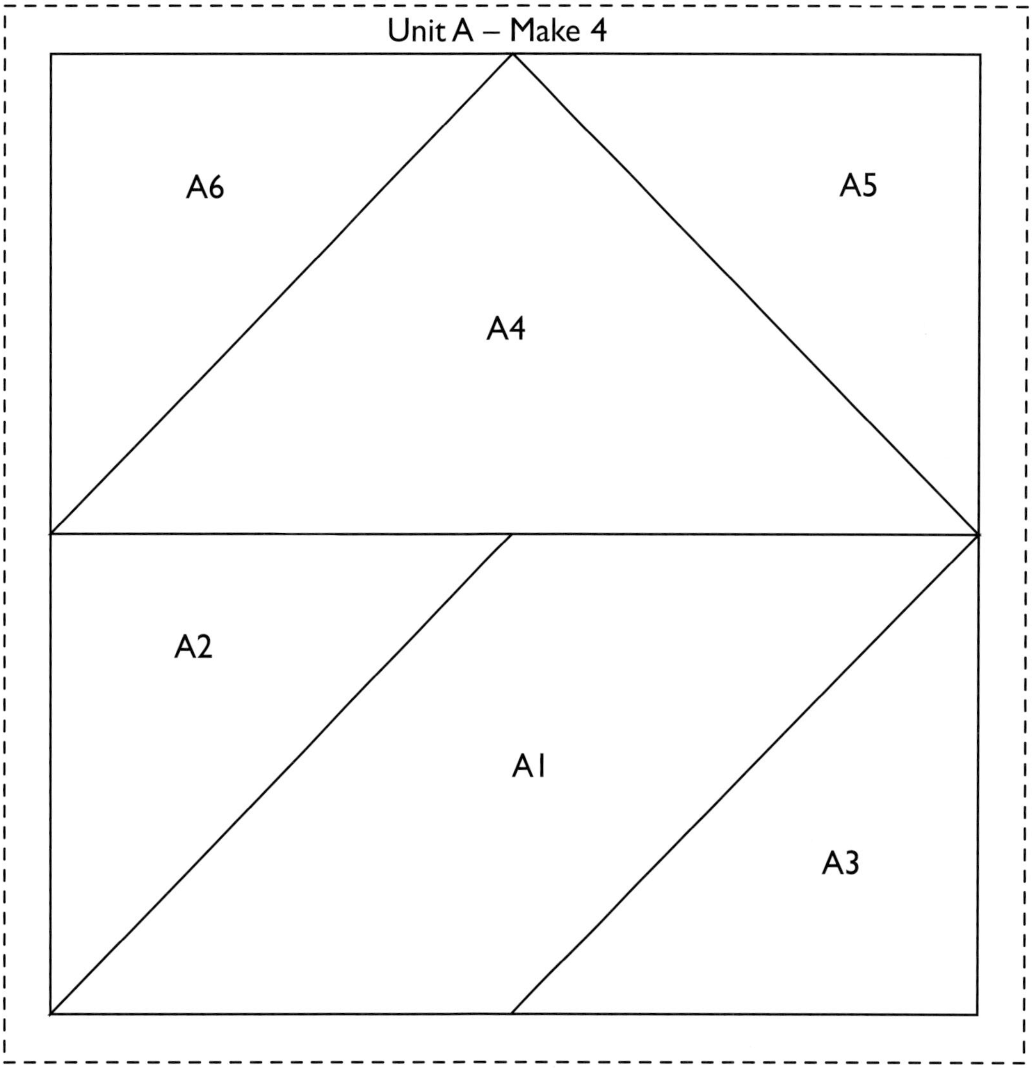

The 1941 Nine Patch

Patterns for 10" Block on Page 18.

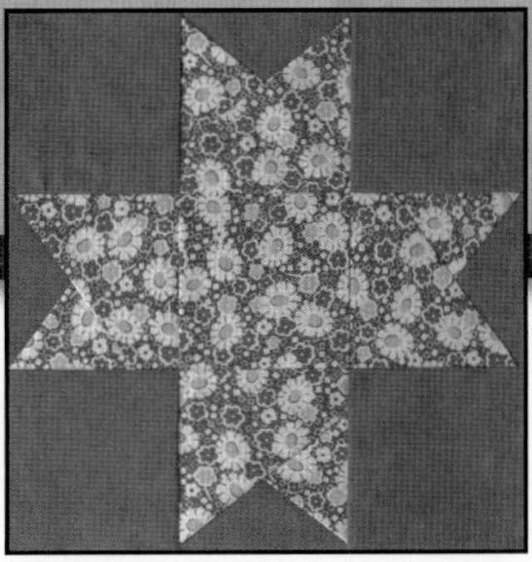

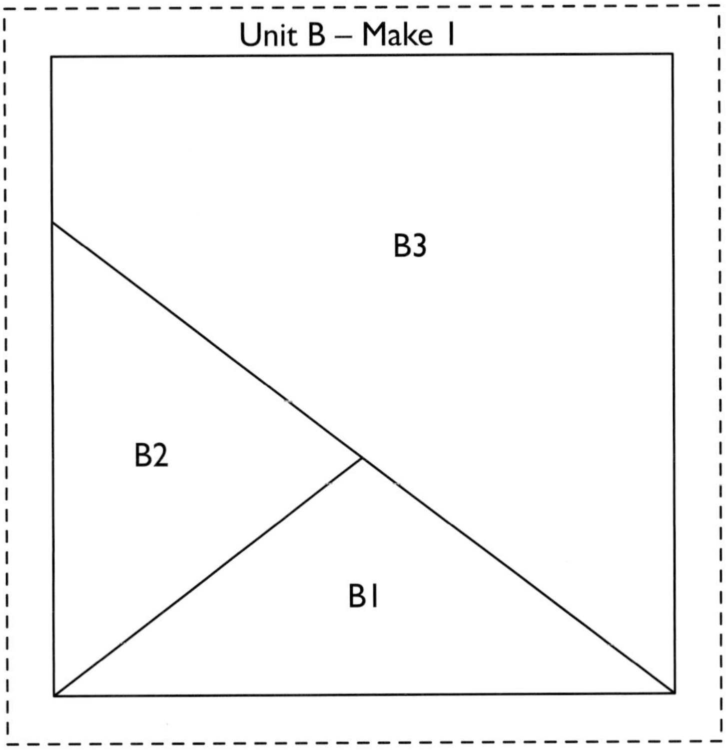

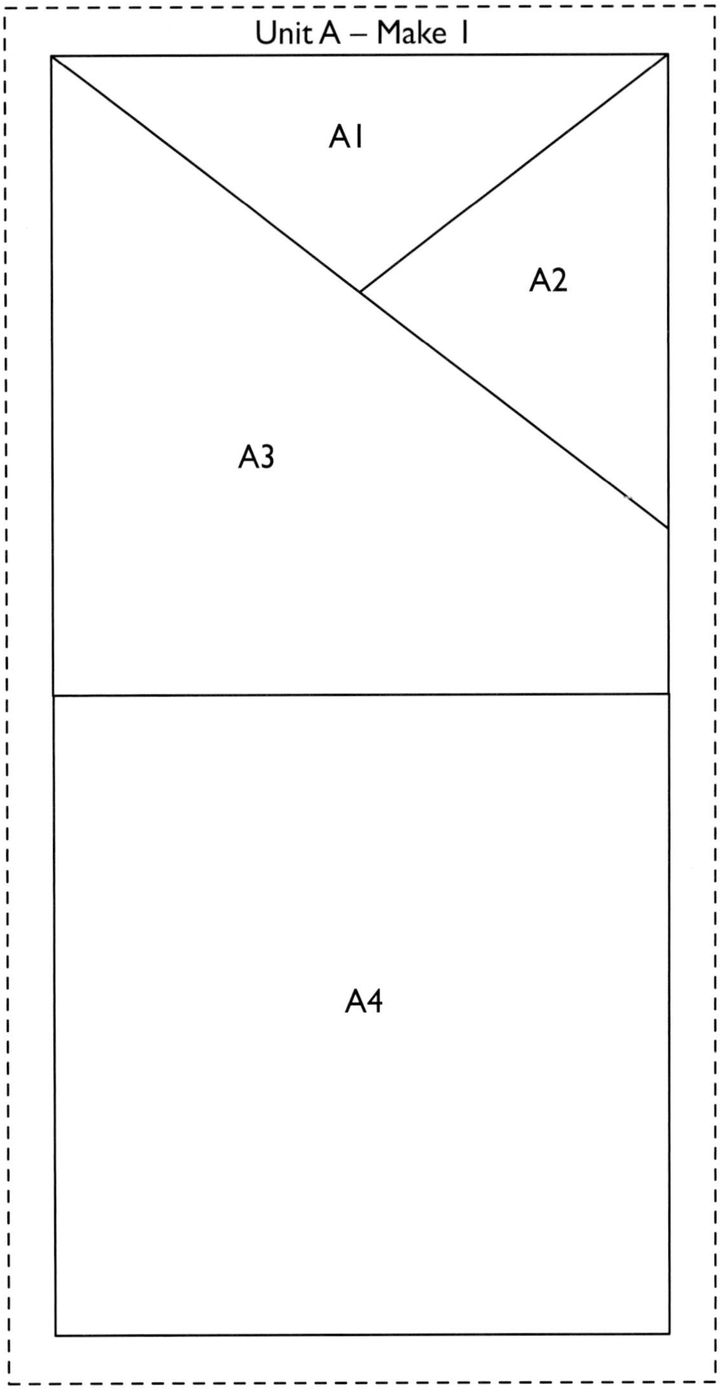

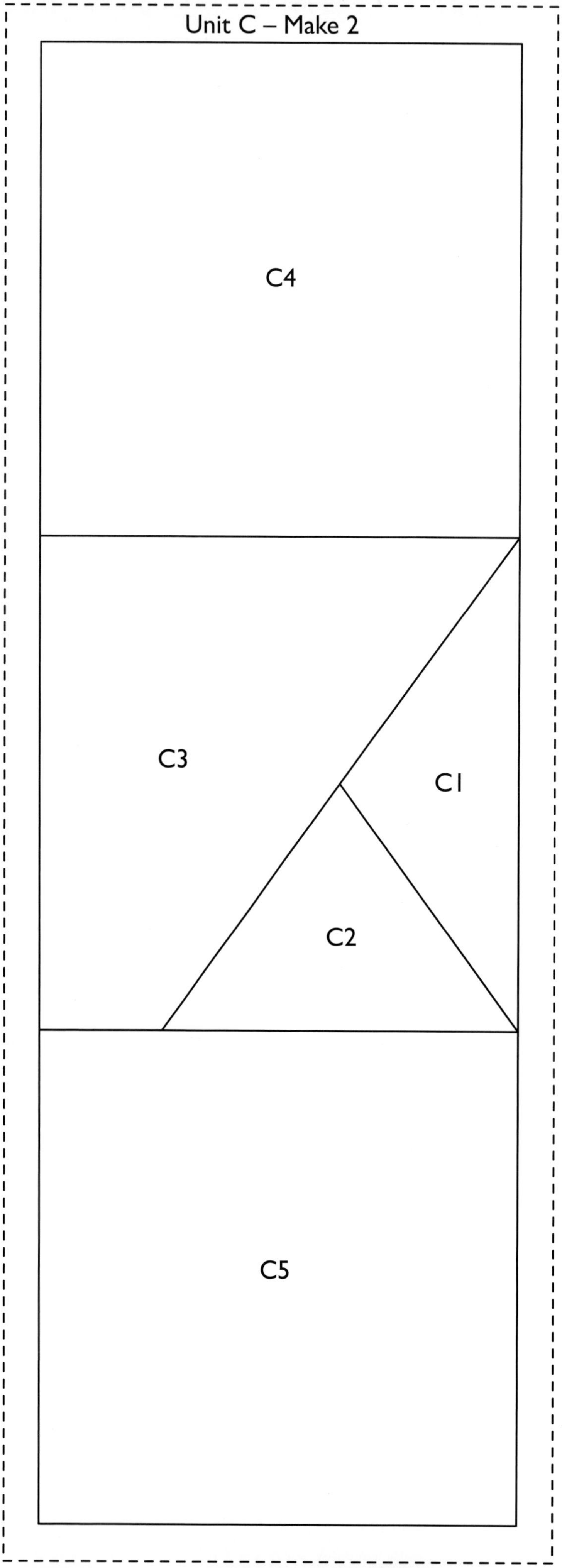
Unit C – Make 2
C4
C3
C1
C2
C5

Sunlight and Shadows

Patterns for 10" Block on Page 19.

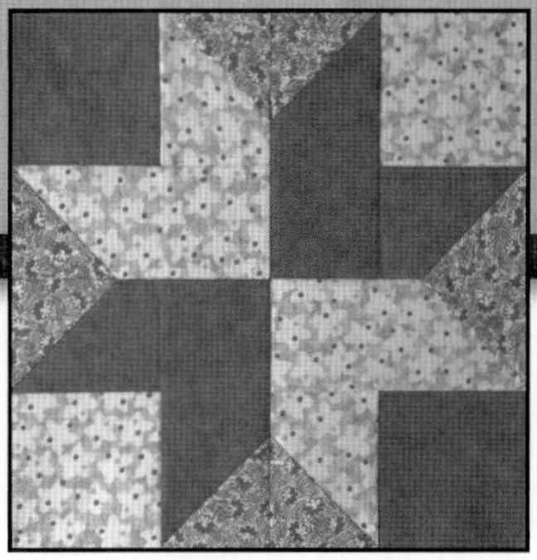

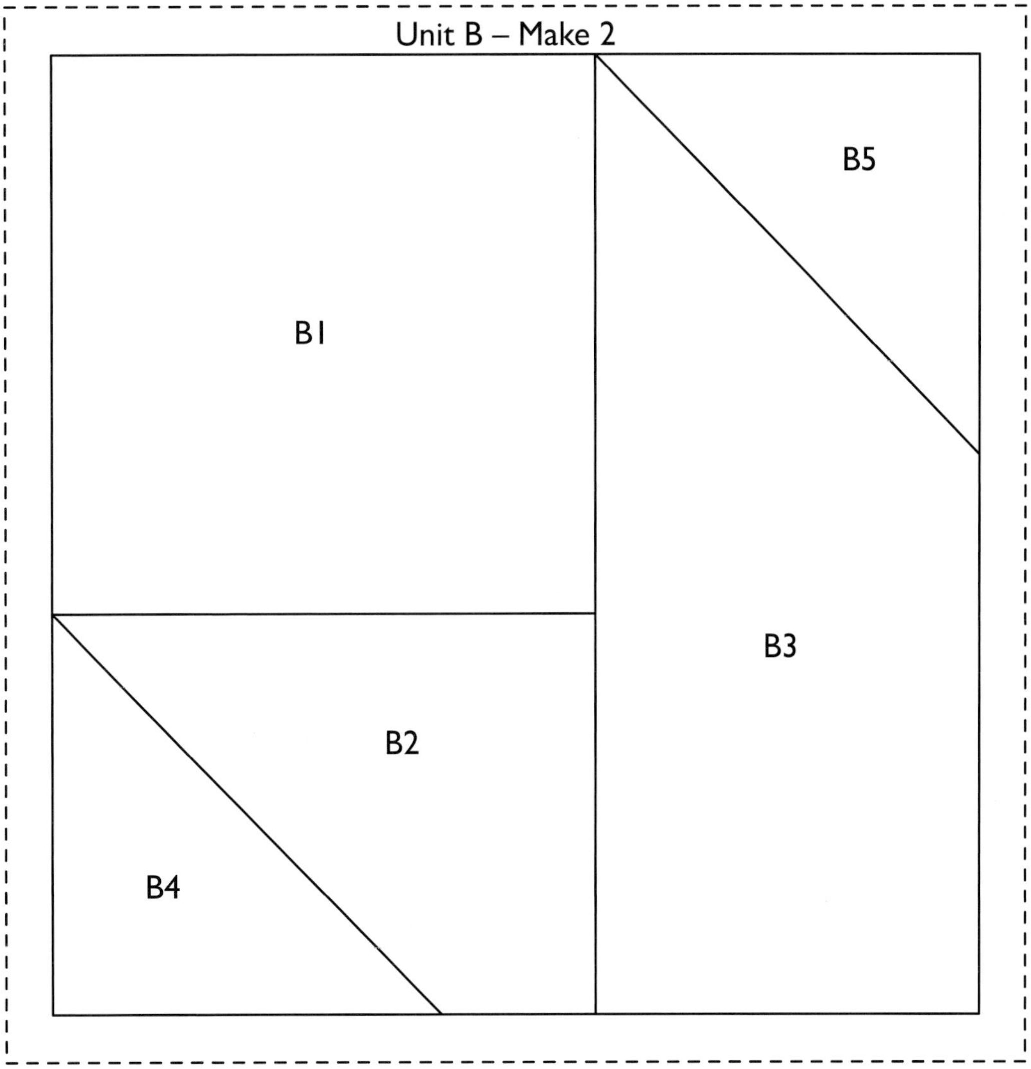

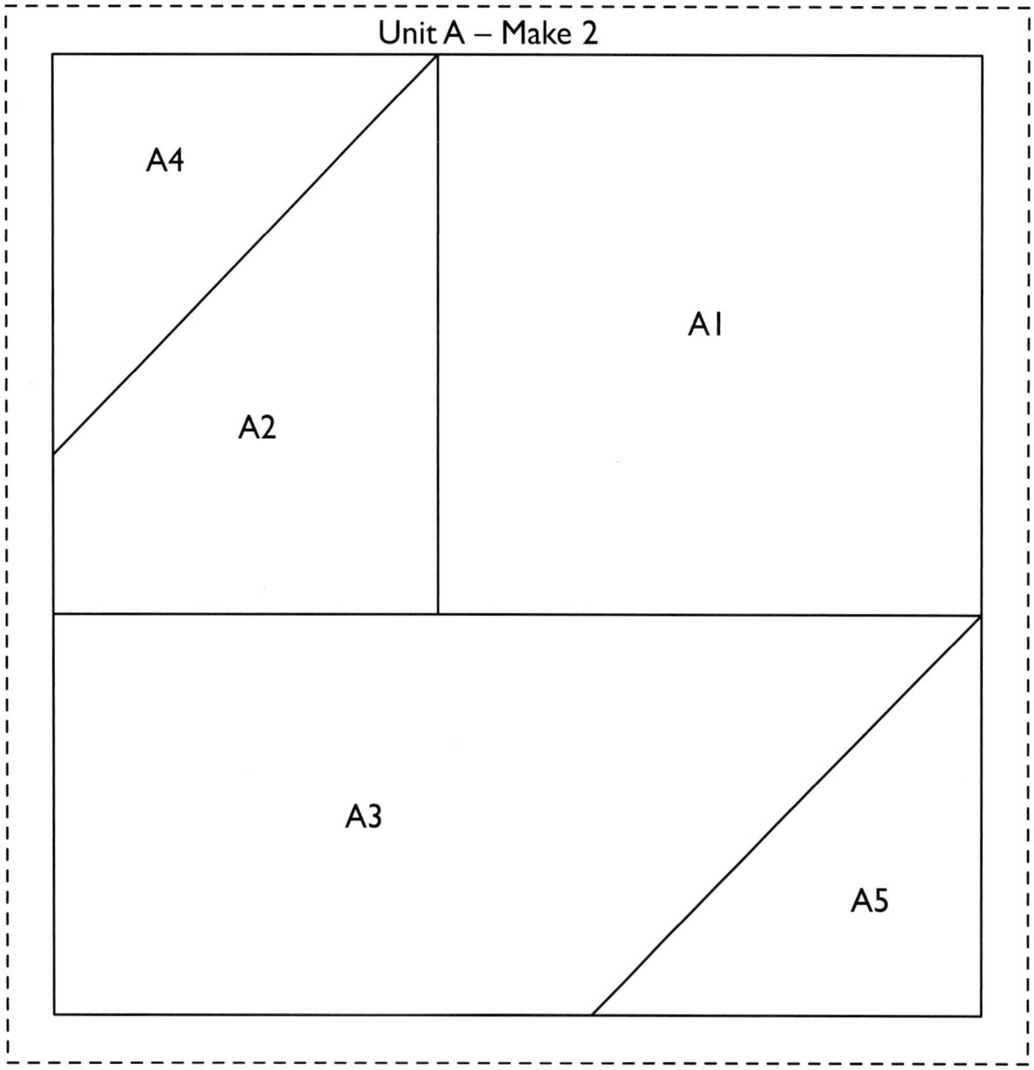
Unit A – Make 2
A4
A1
A2
A3
A5

A Salute to the Colors

PATTERNS FOR 10" BLOCK ON PAGE 20.

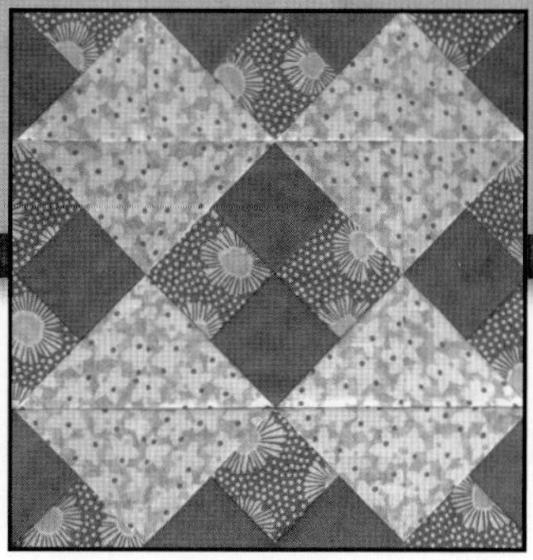

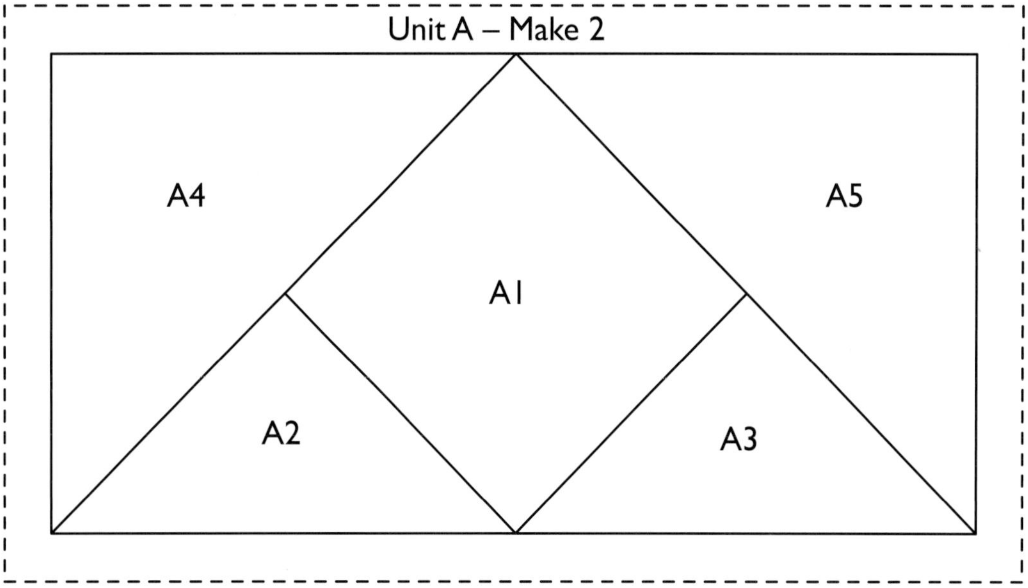

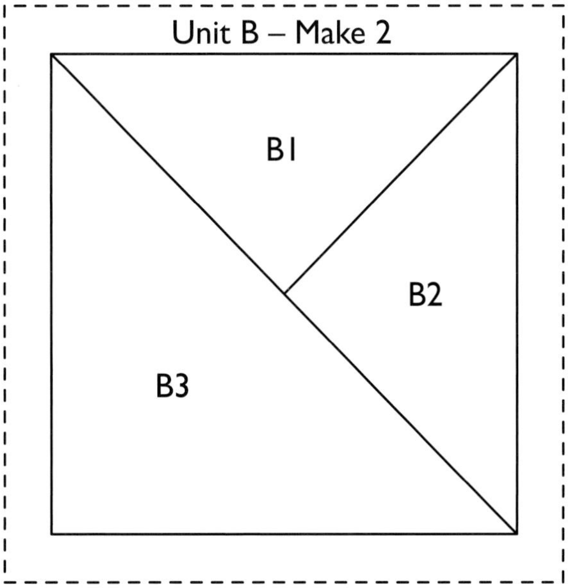

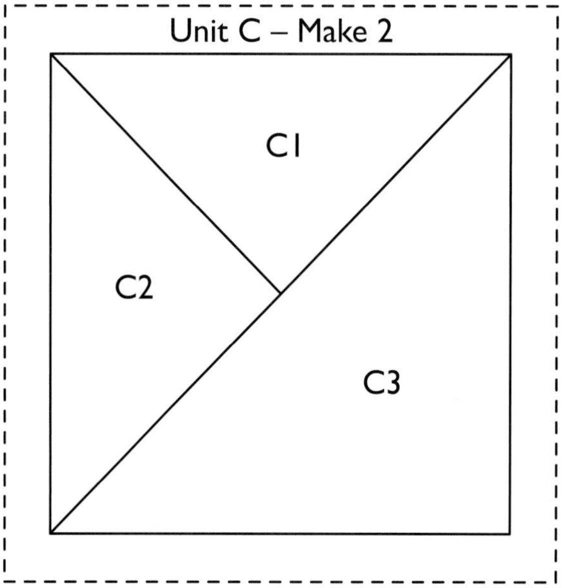

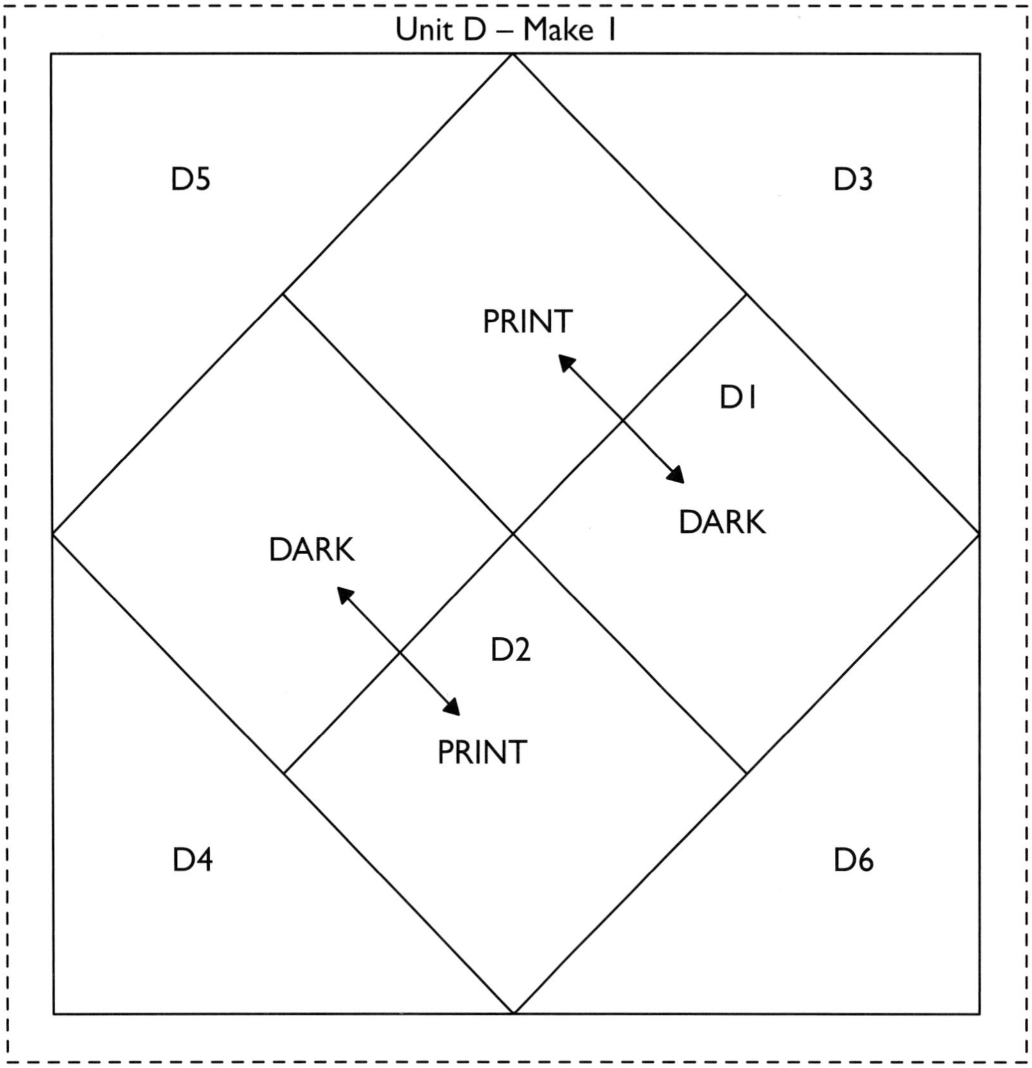
Unit D – Make 1
D5
D3
PRINT
D1
DARK
DARK
D2
PRINT
D4
D6

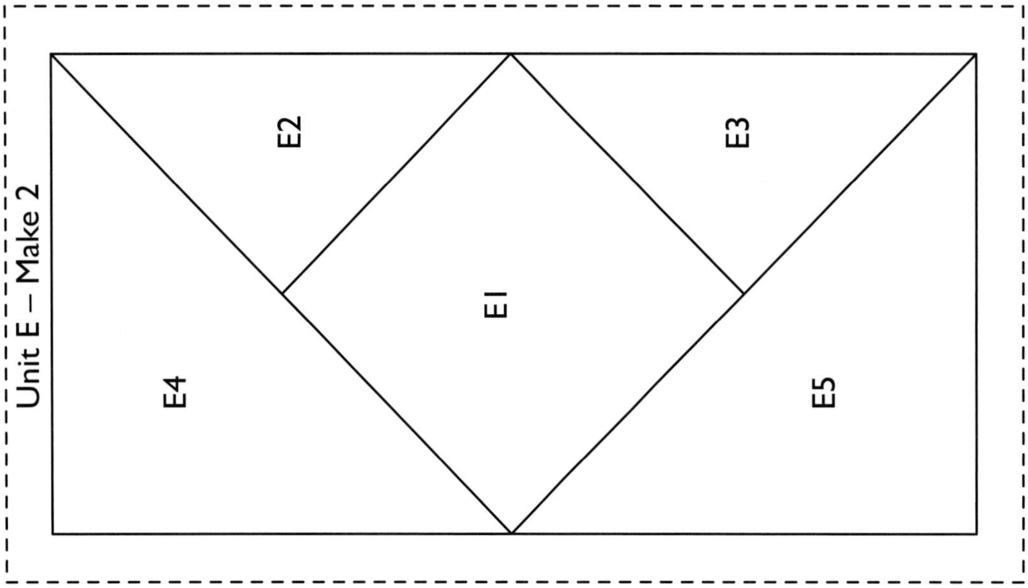
Unit E – Make 2
E2
E3
E1
E4
E5

Shepherd's Crossing

Patterns for 10" Block on Page 22.

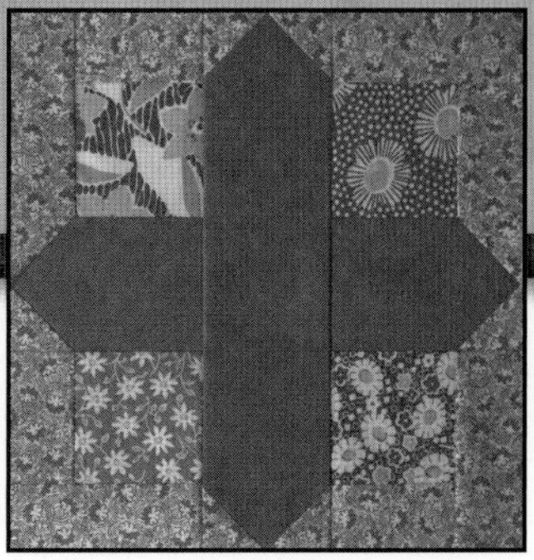

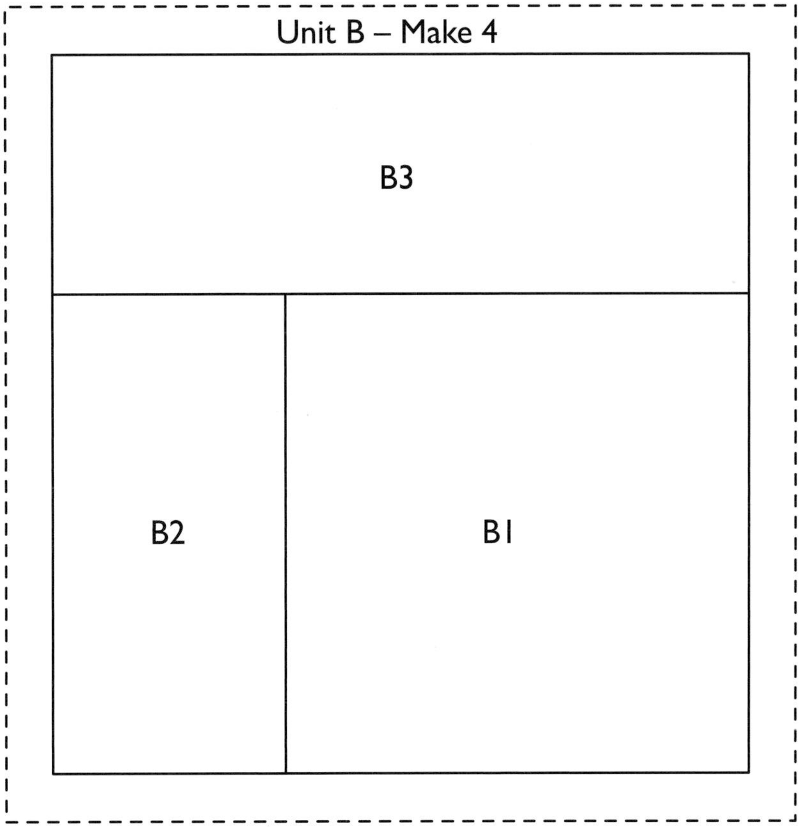

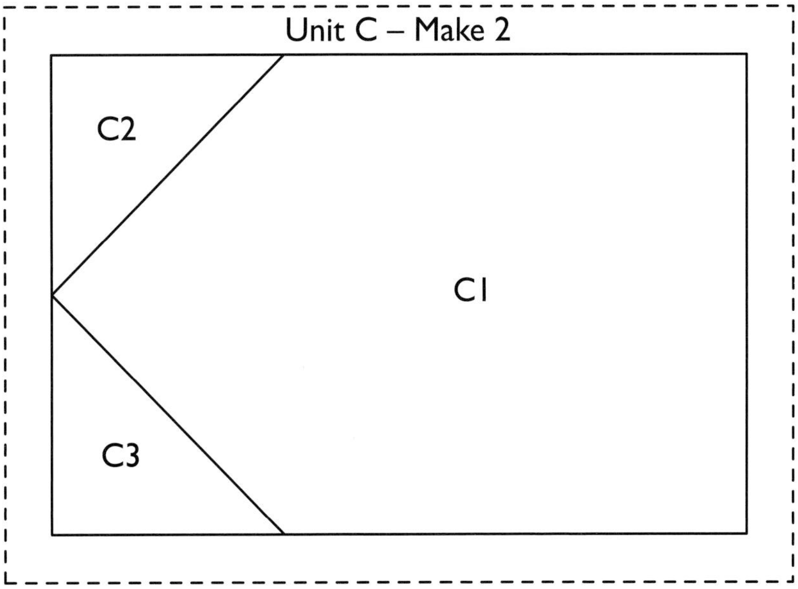

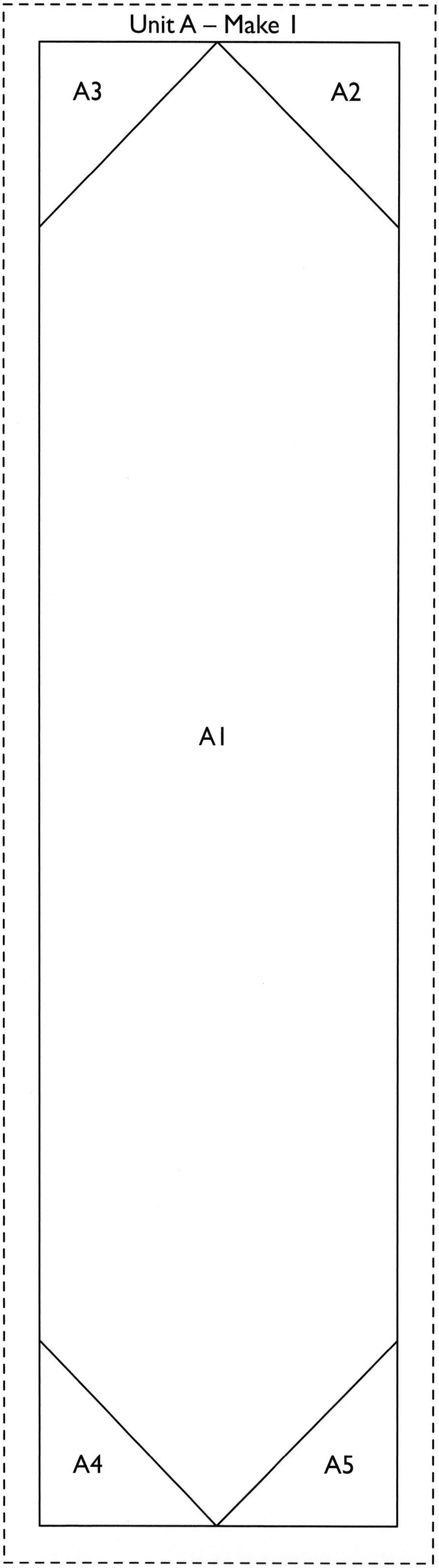
Unit A – Make 1
A3
A2
A1
A4
A5

A Basket Quilt in Triangles

PATTERNS FOR 10" BLOCK ON PAGE 24.

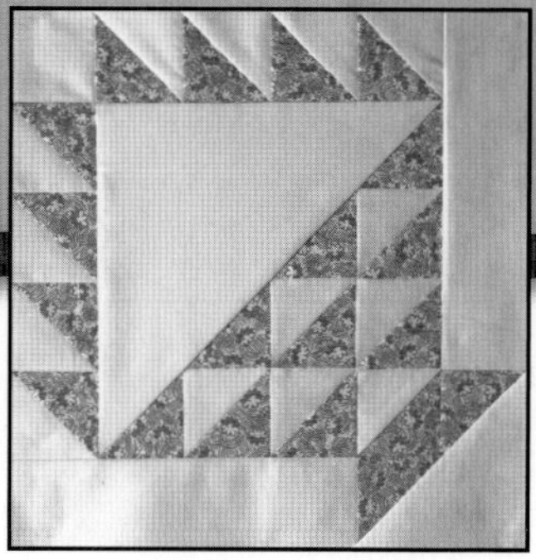

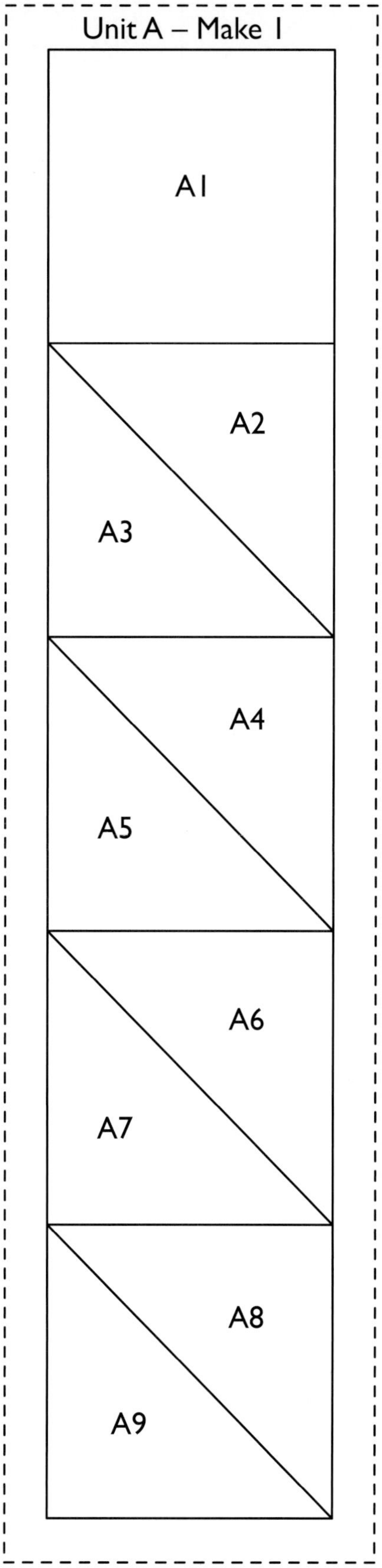

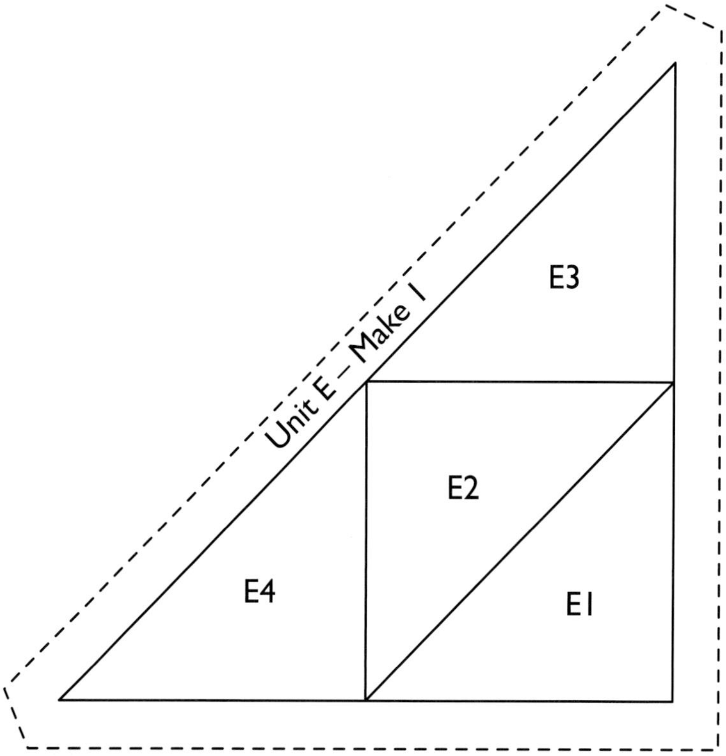

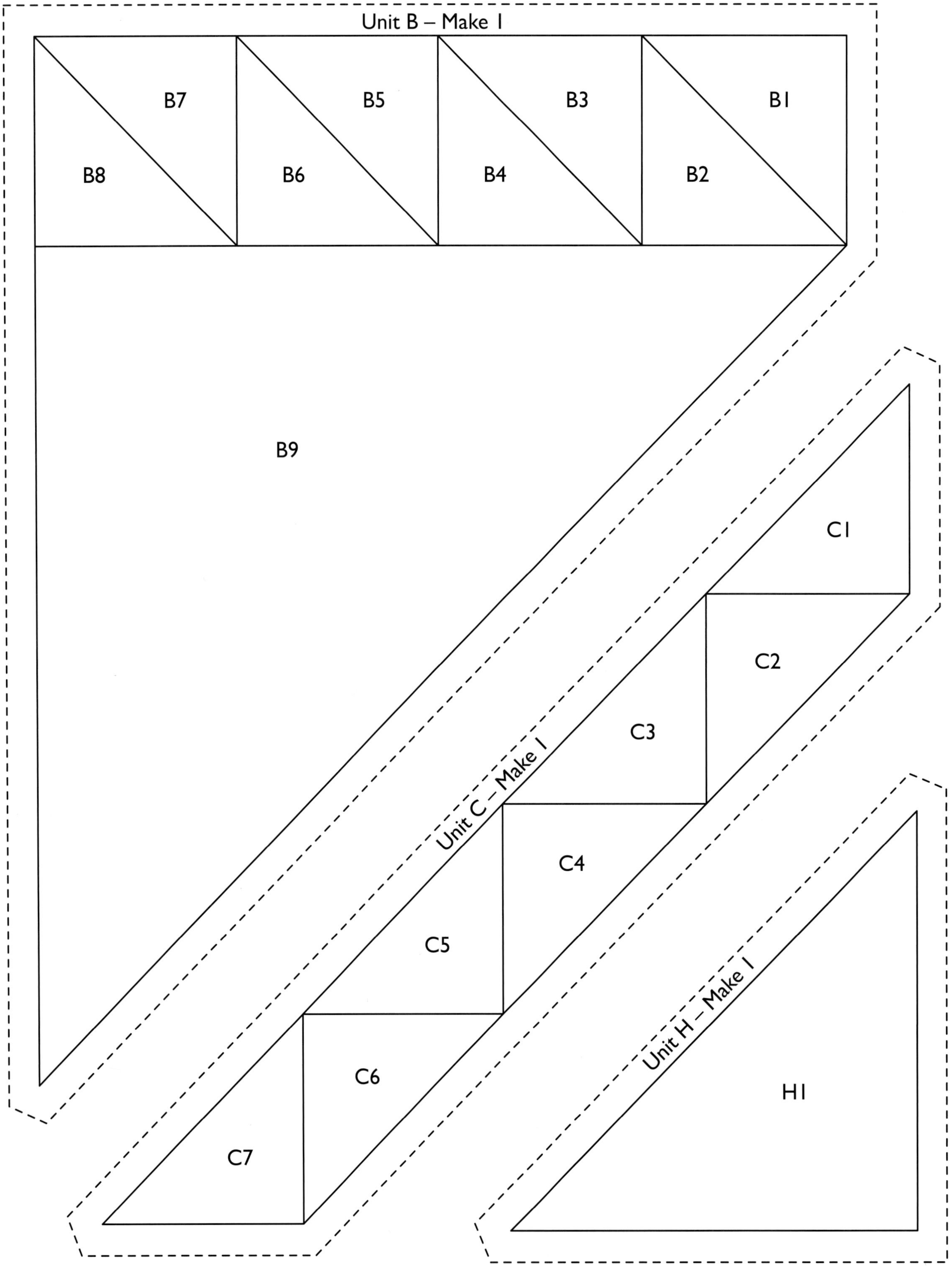
Unit B – Make 1
B7
B5
B3
B1
B8
B6
B4
B2
B9
C1
C2
C3
Unit C – Make 1
C4
C5
C6
C7
Unit H – Make 1
H1

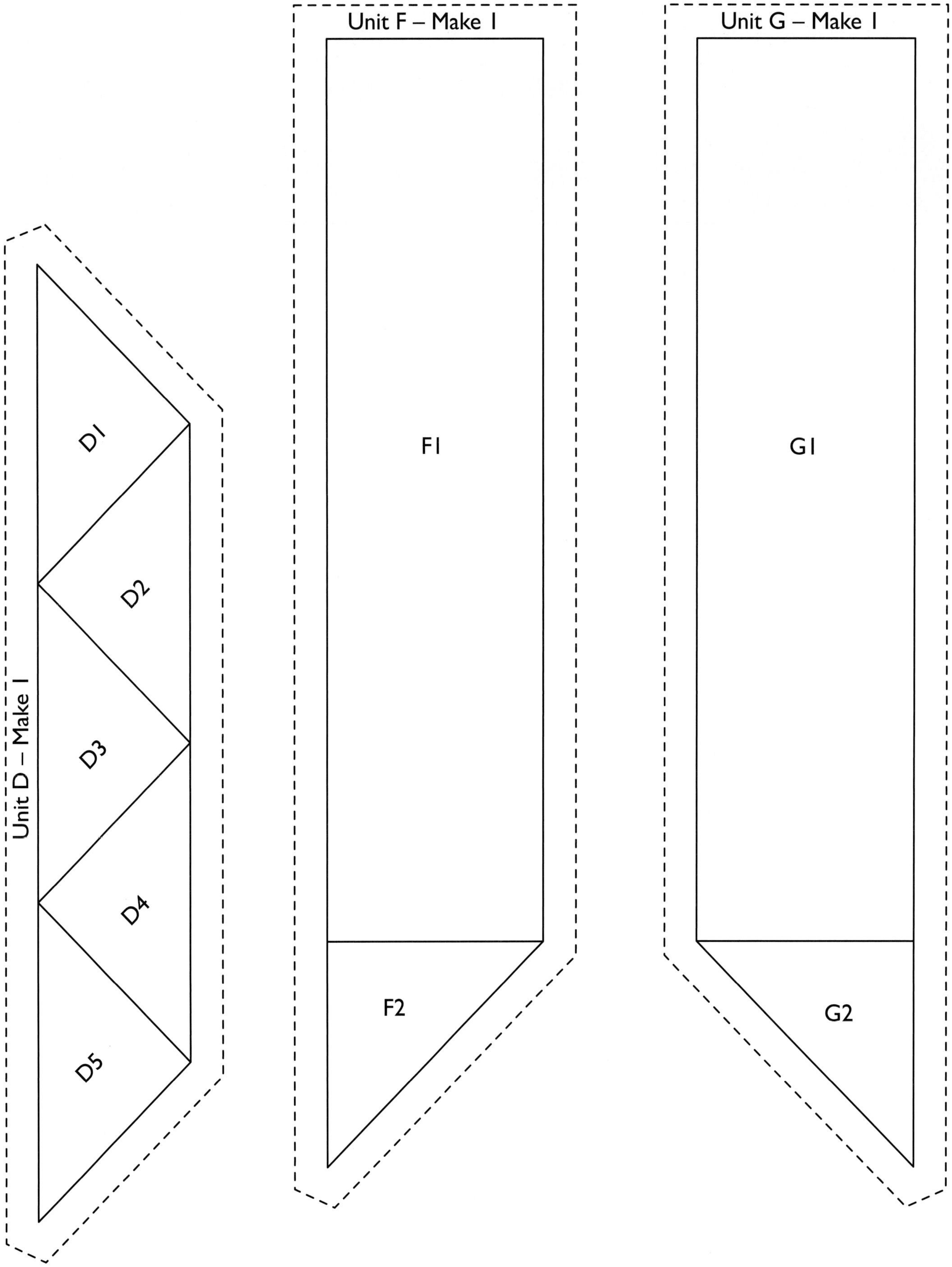
Unit D – Make 1
D1
D2
D3
D4
D5
Unit F – Make 1
F1
F2
Unit G – Make 1
G1
G2

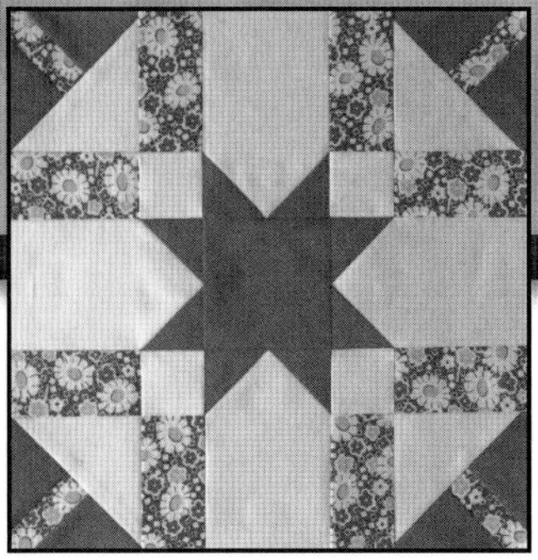

The Army Star

PATTERNS FOR 10" BLOCK ON PAGE 23.

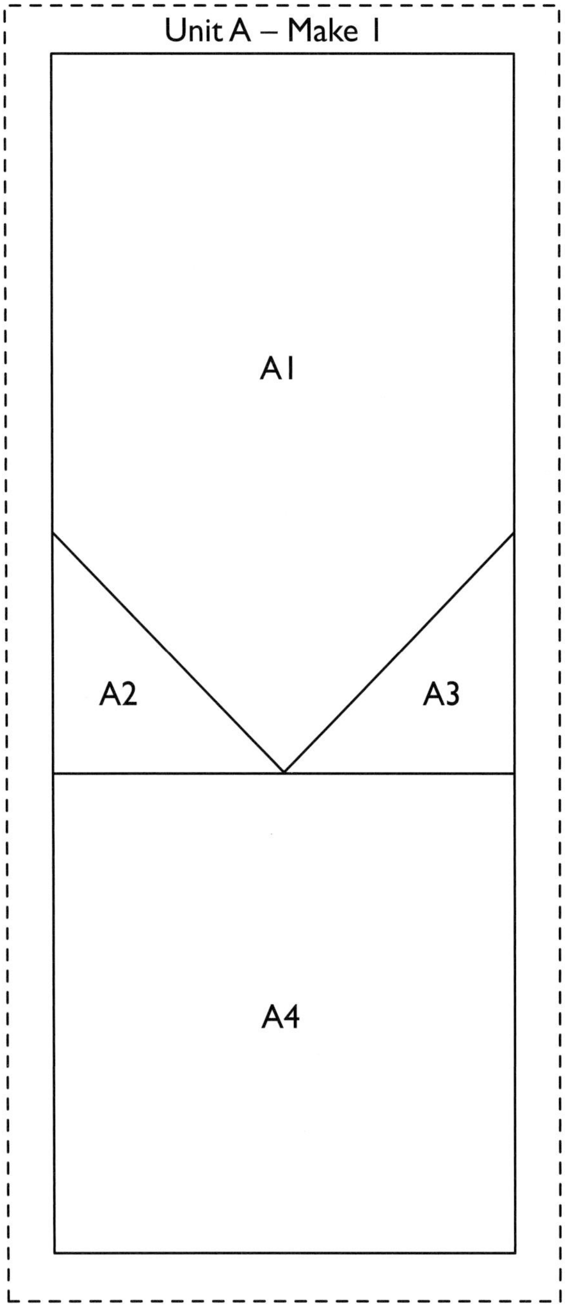

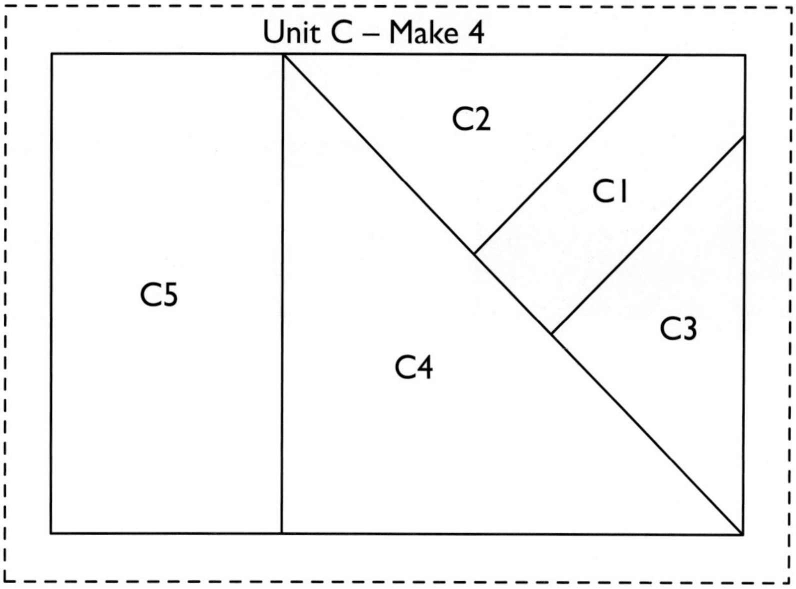
Unit C – Make 4
C2
C1
C5
C3
C4

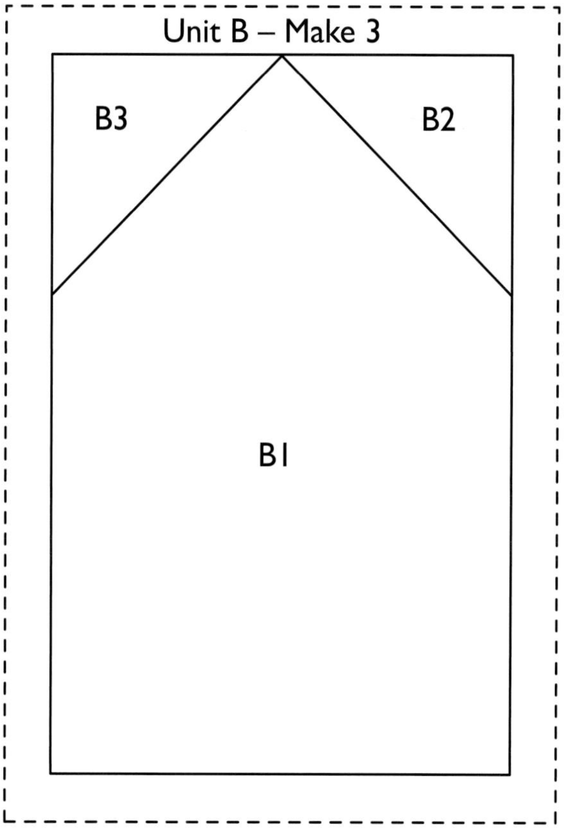
Unit B – Make 3
B3
B2
B1

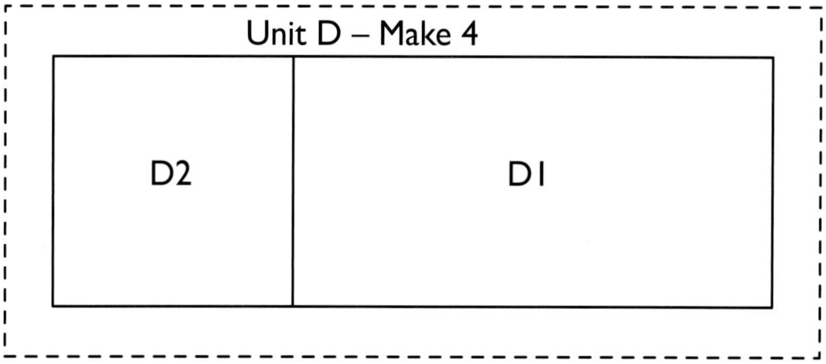
Unit D – Make 4
D2
D1

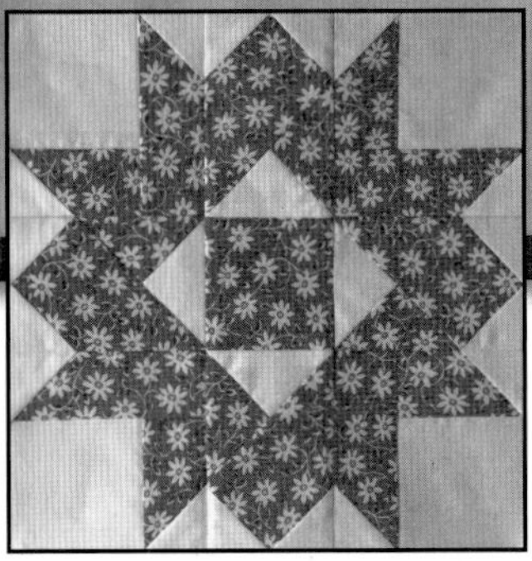

A Quilt Mosaic

Patterns for 10" Block on Page 27.

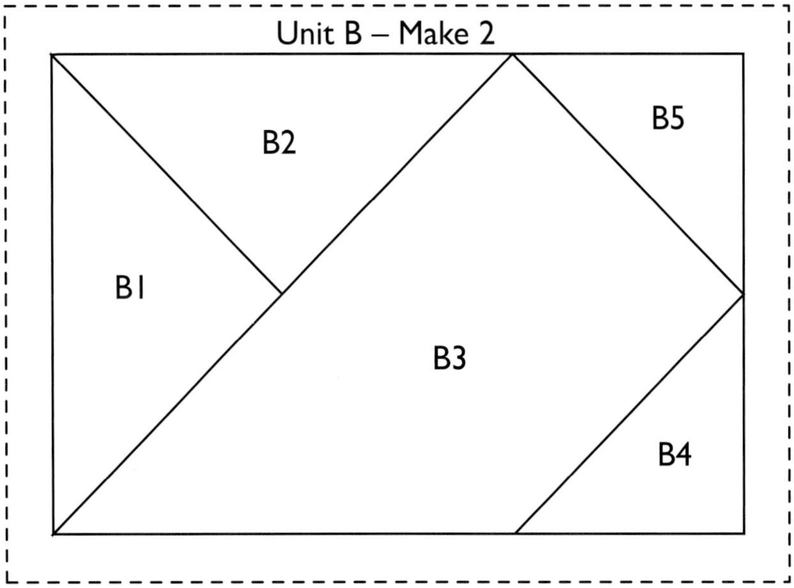

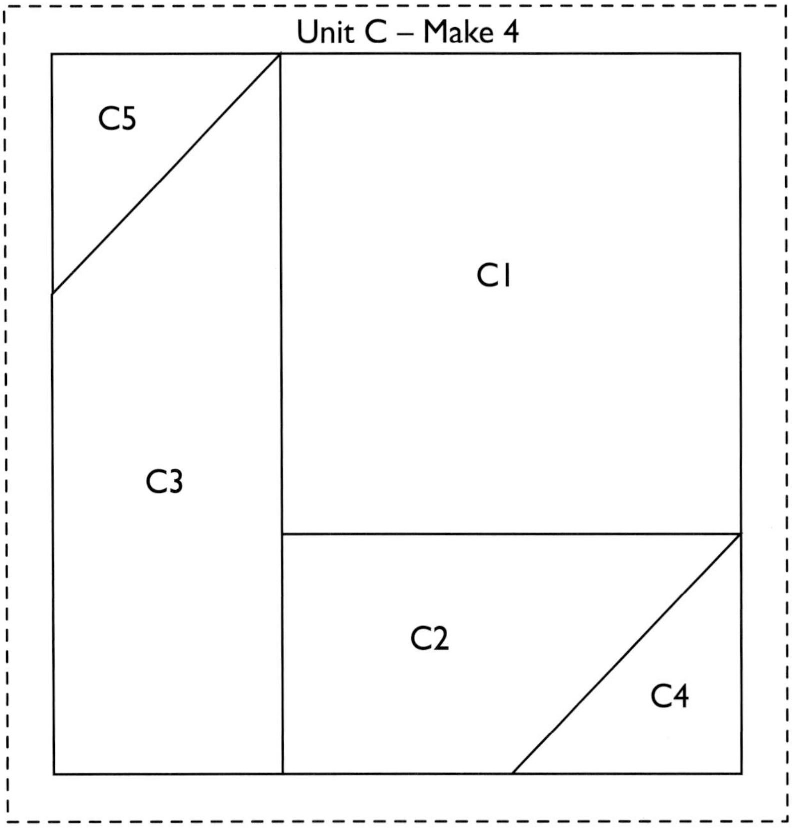

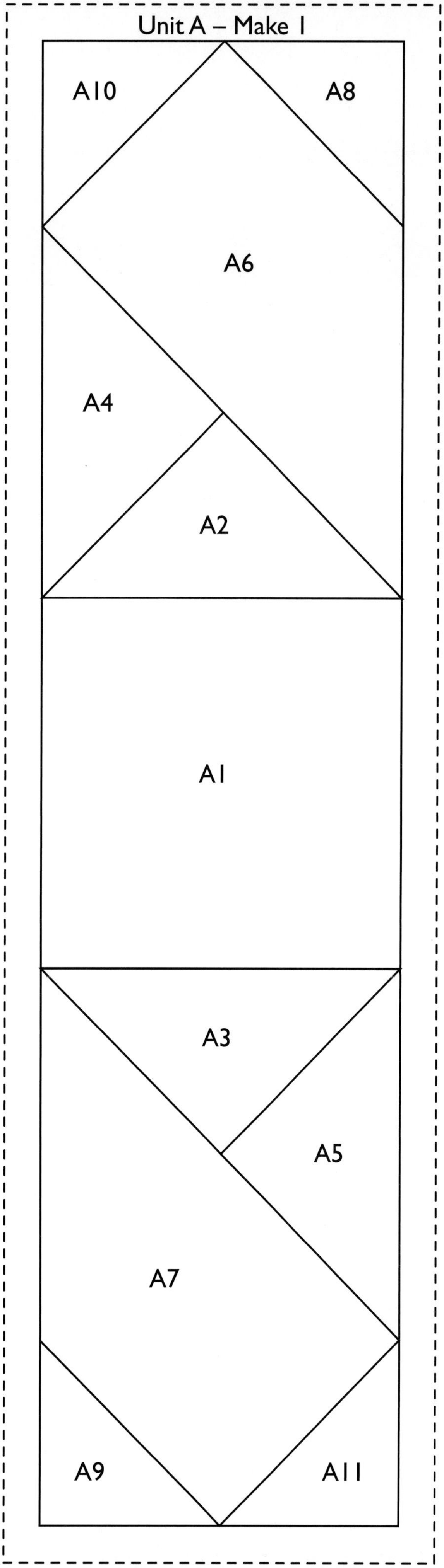
Unit A – Make 1
A10
A8
A6
A4
A2
A1
A3
A5
A7
A9
A11

Return of the Swallows

PATTERNS FOR 10" BLOCK ON PAGE 28.

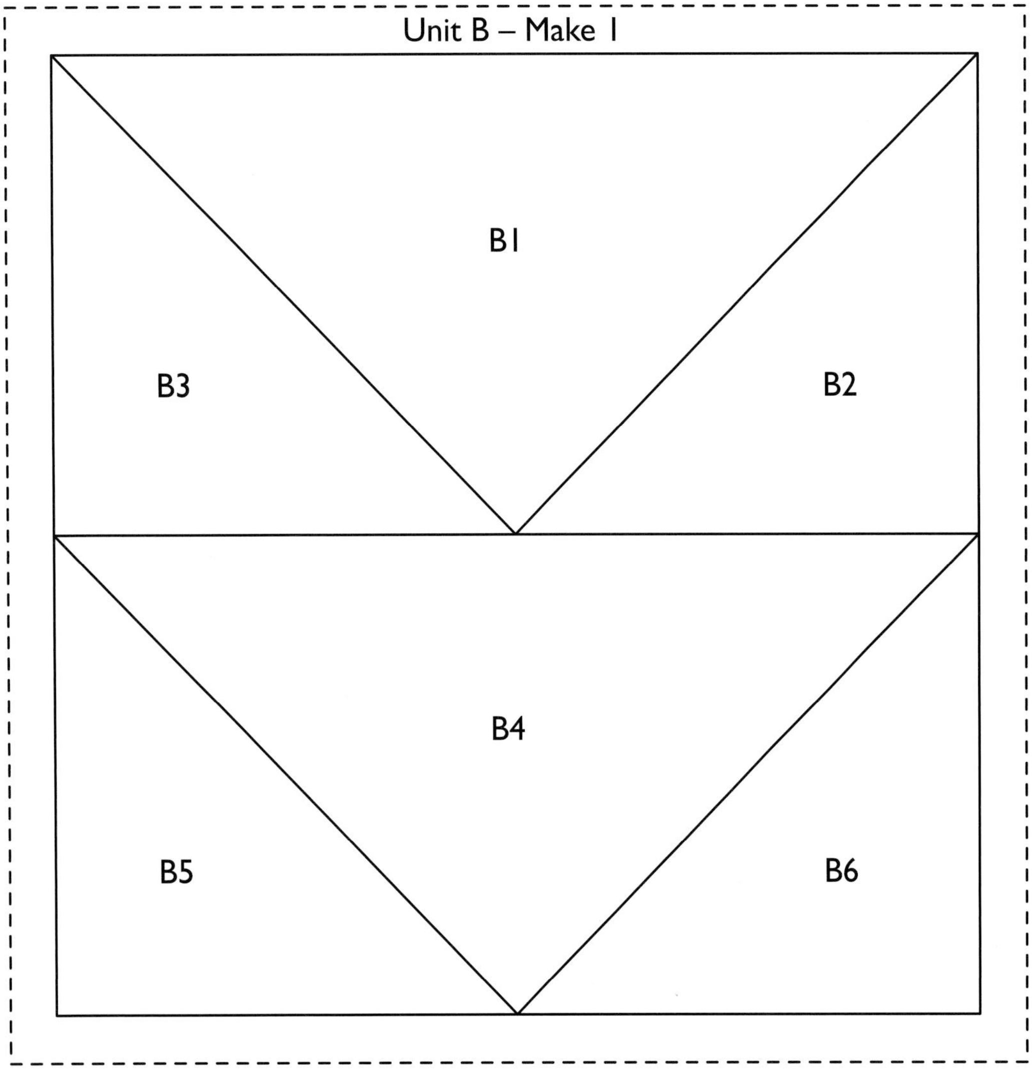

Unit A – Make 1

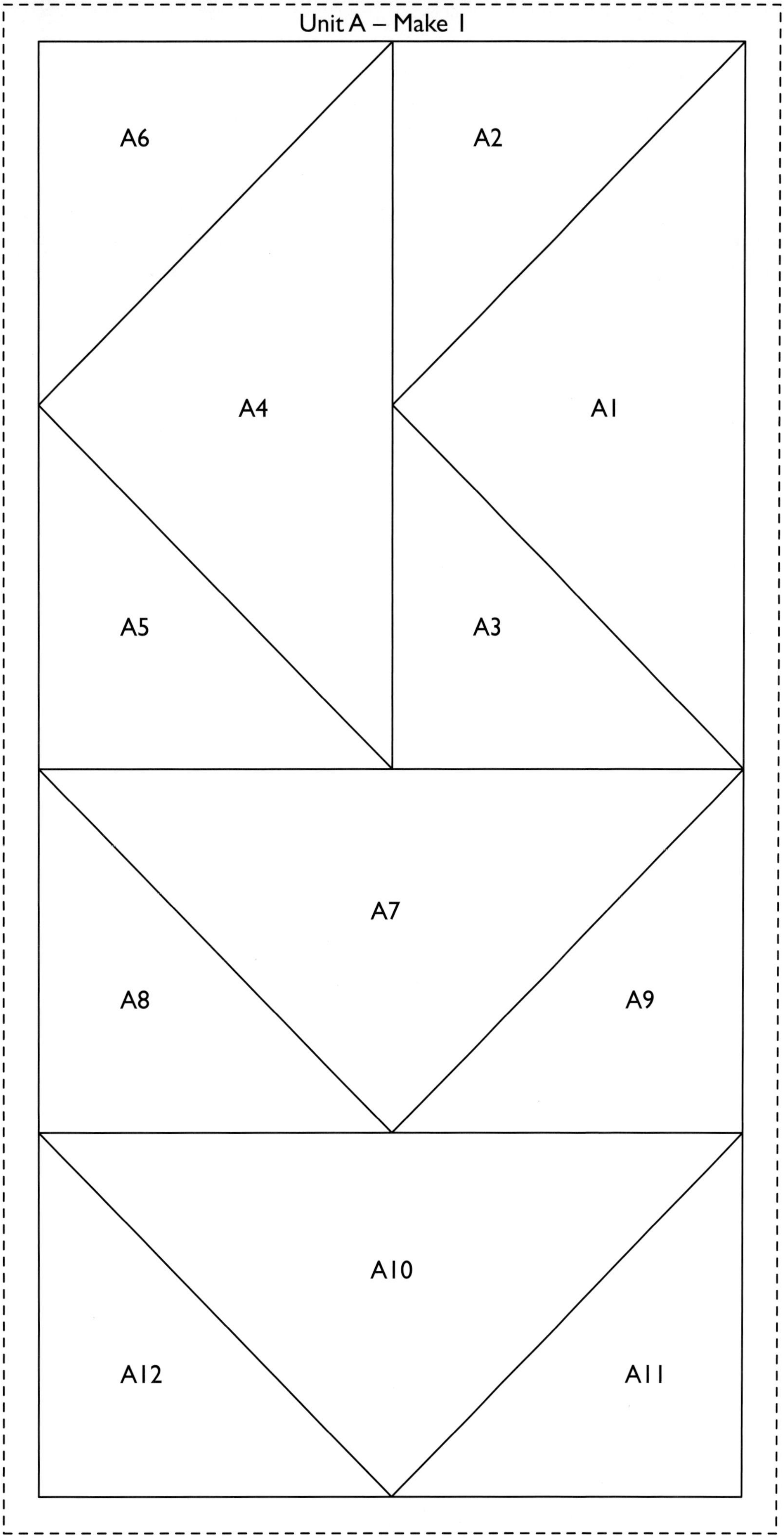

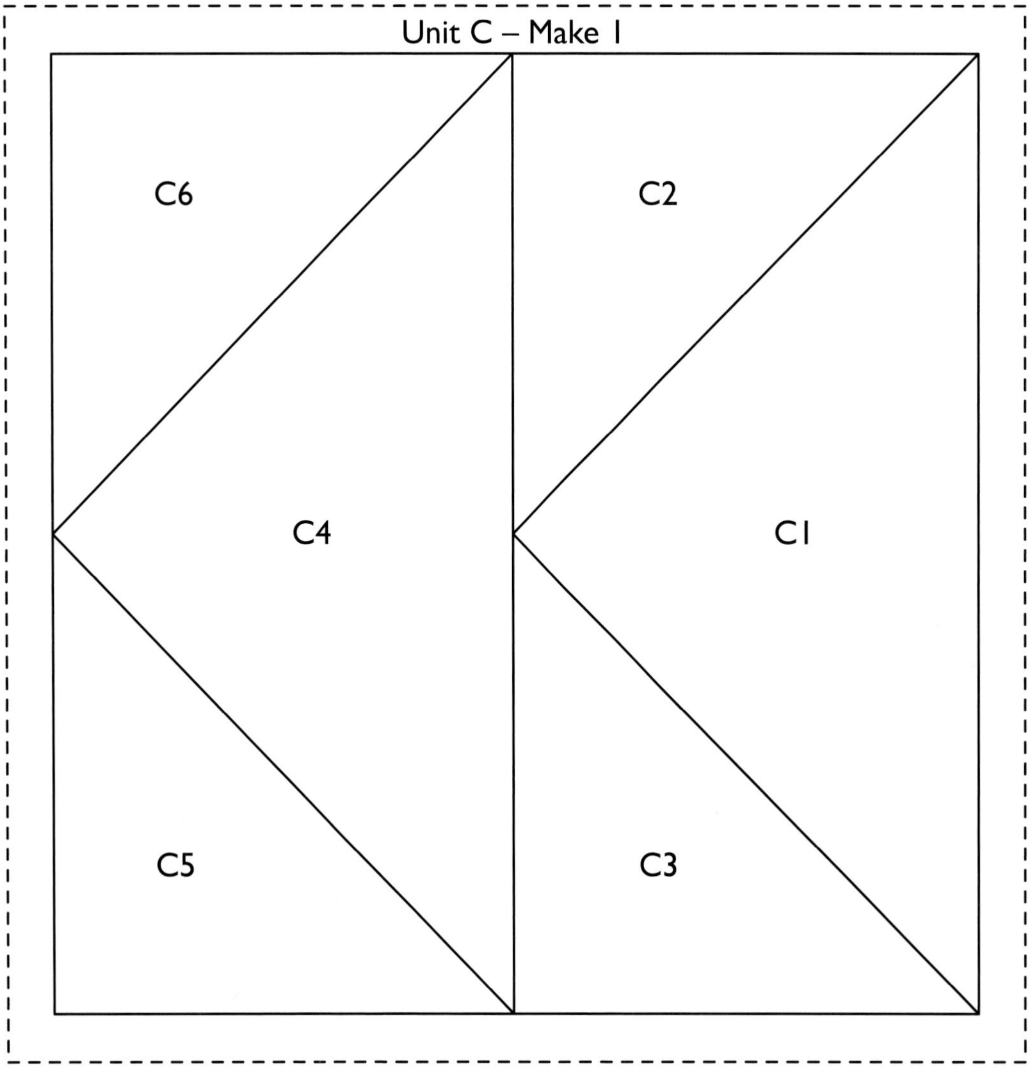
Unit C – Make 1
C6
C2
C4
C1
C5
C3

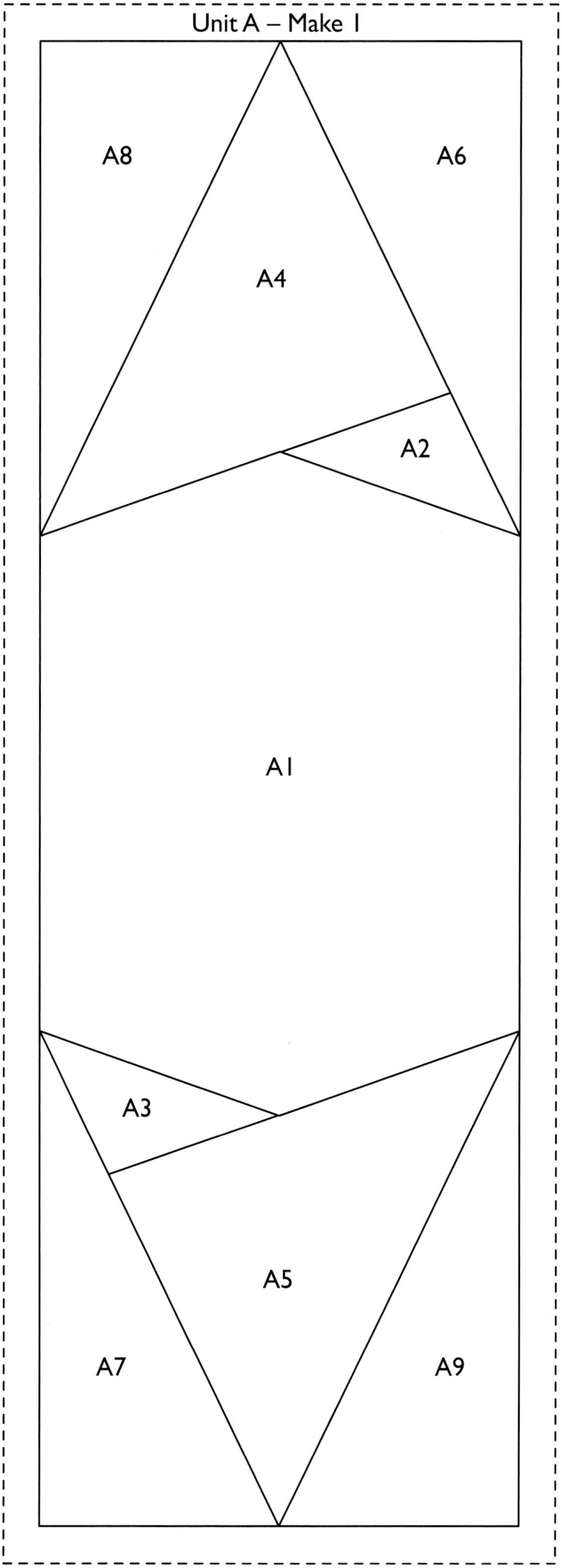

The New Four Pointer

PATTERNS FOR 10" BLOCK ON PAGE 26.

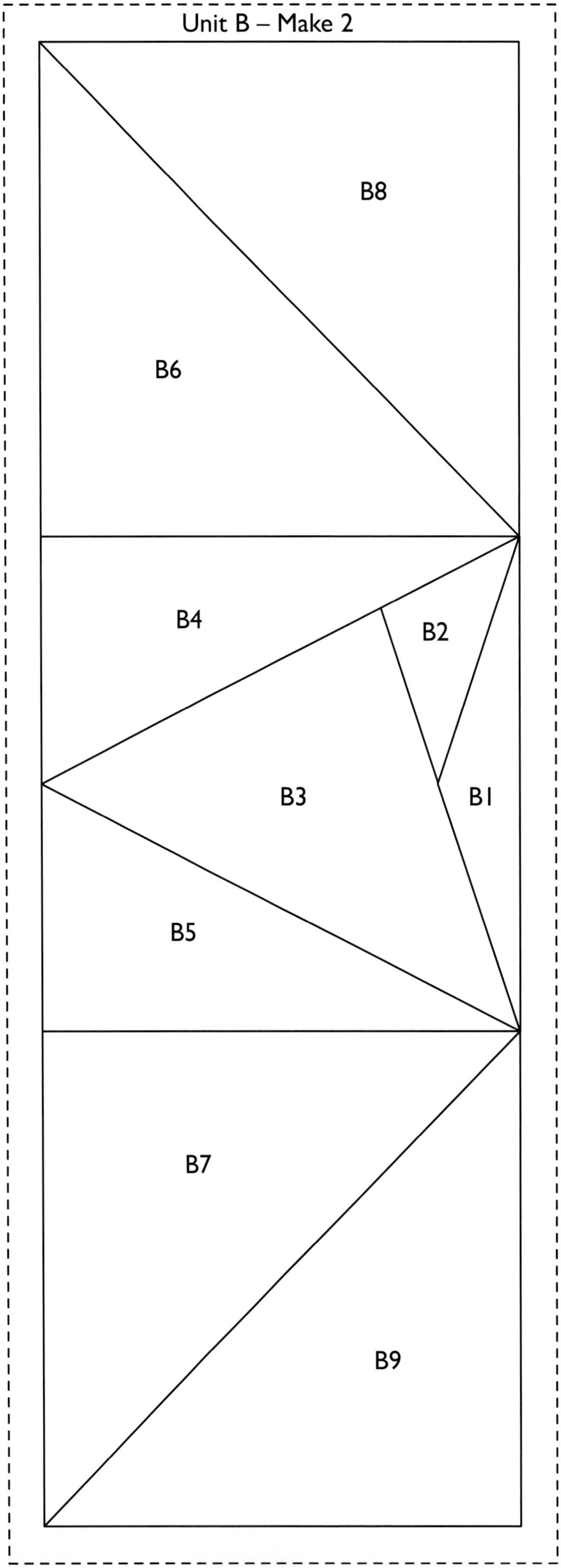
Unit B – Make 2
B8
B6
B4
B2
B3
B1
B5
B7
B9

The North Star

PATTERN FOR 10" BLOCK ON PAGE 29.

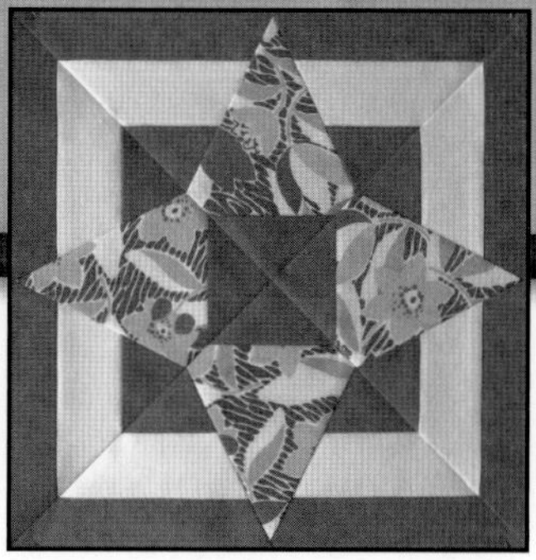

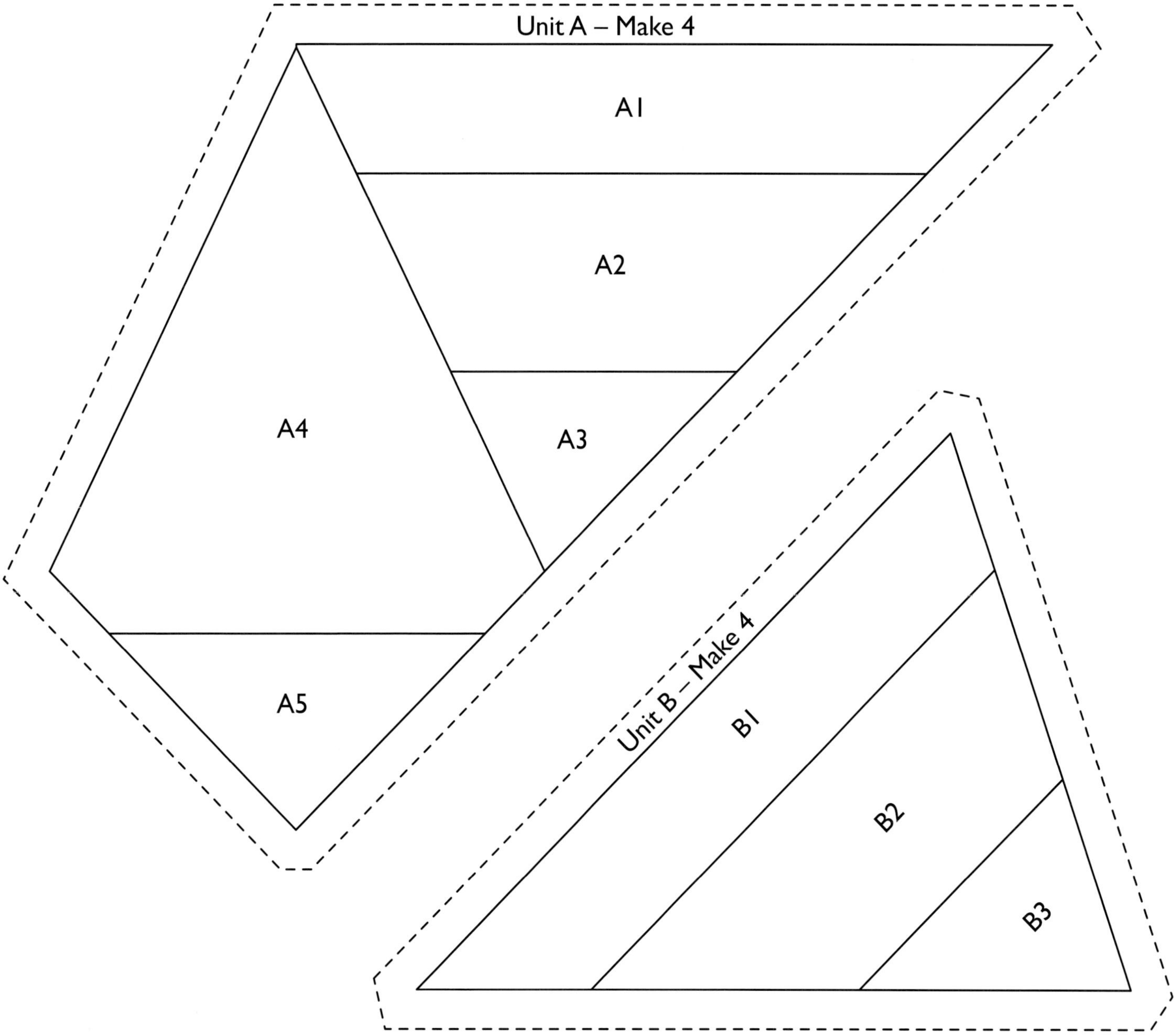

The Spider Web

Pattern for 10" Block on Page 32.

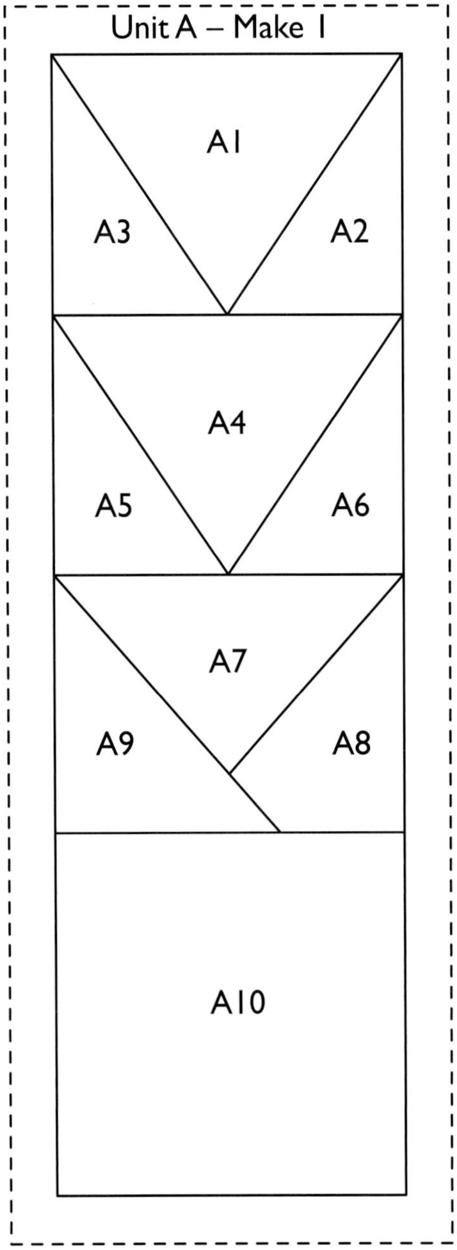

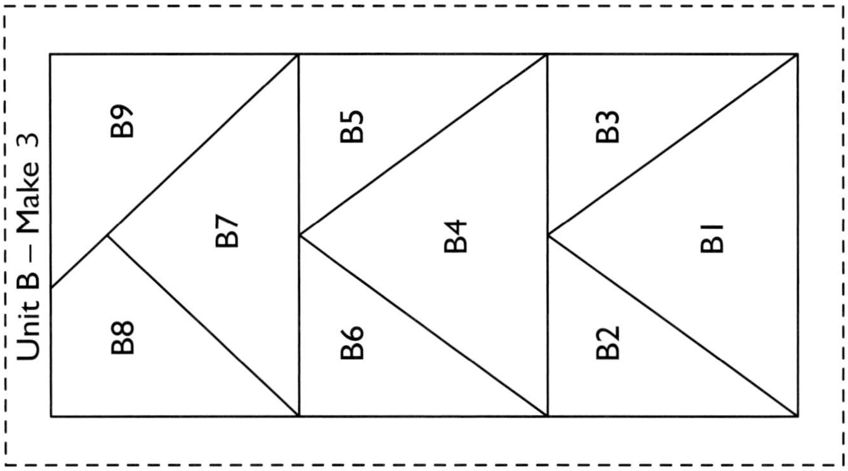

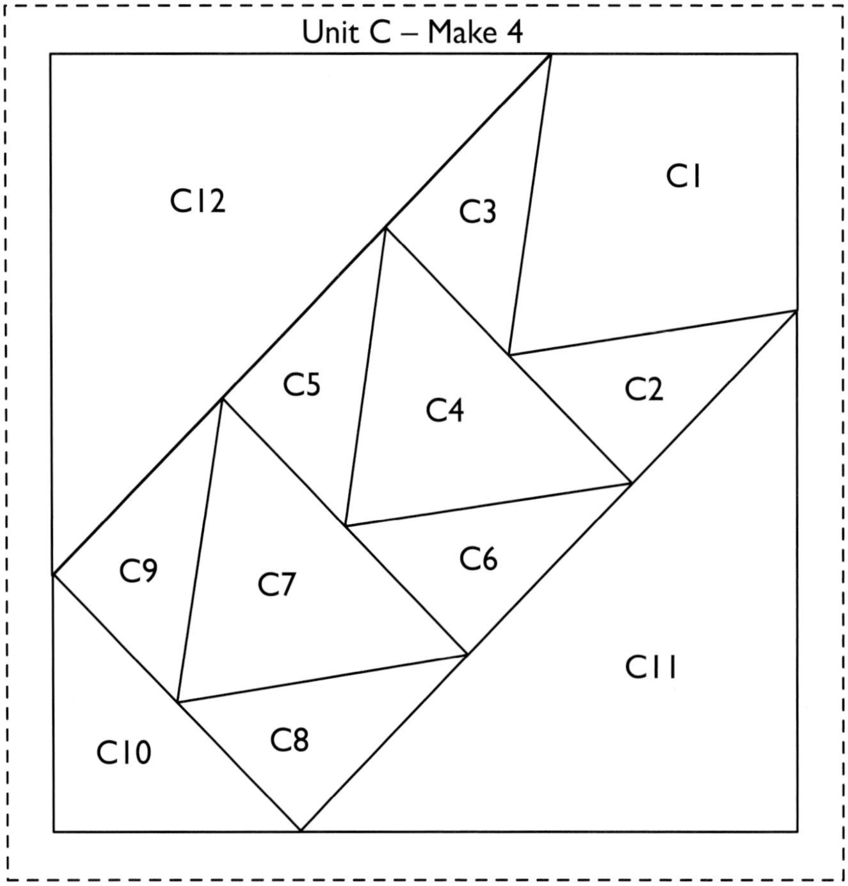

Crazy Anne

Pattern for 10" Block on Page 37.

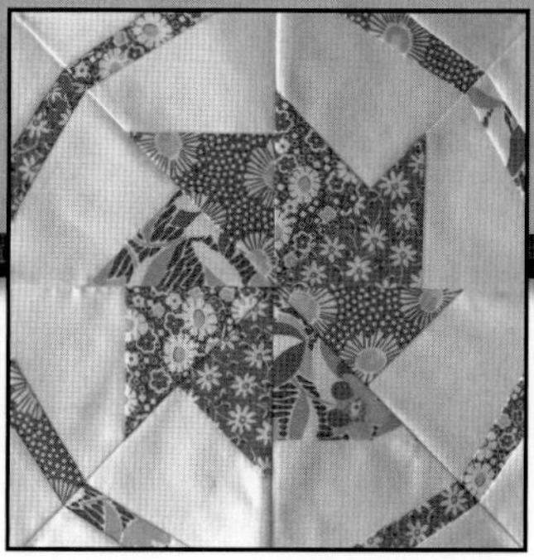

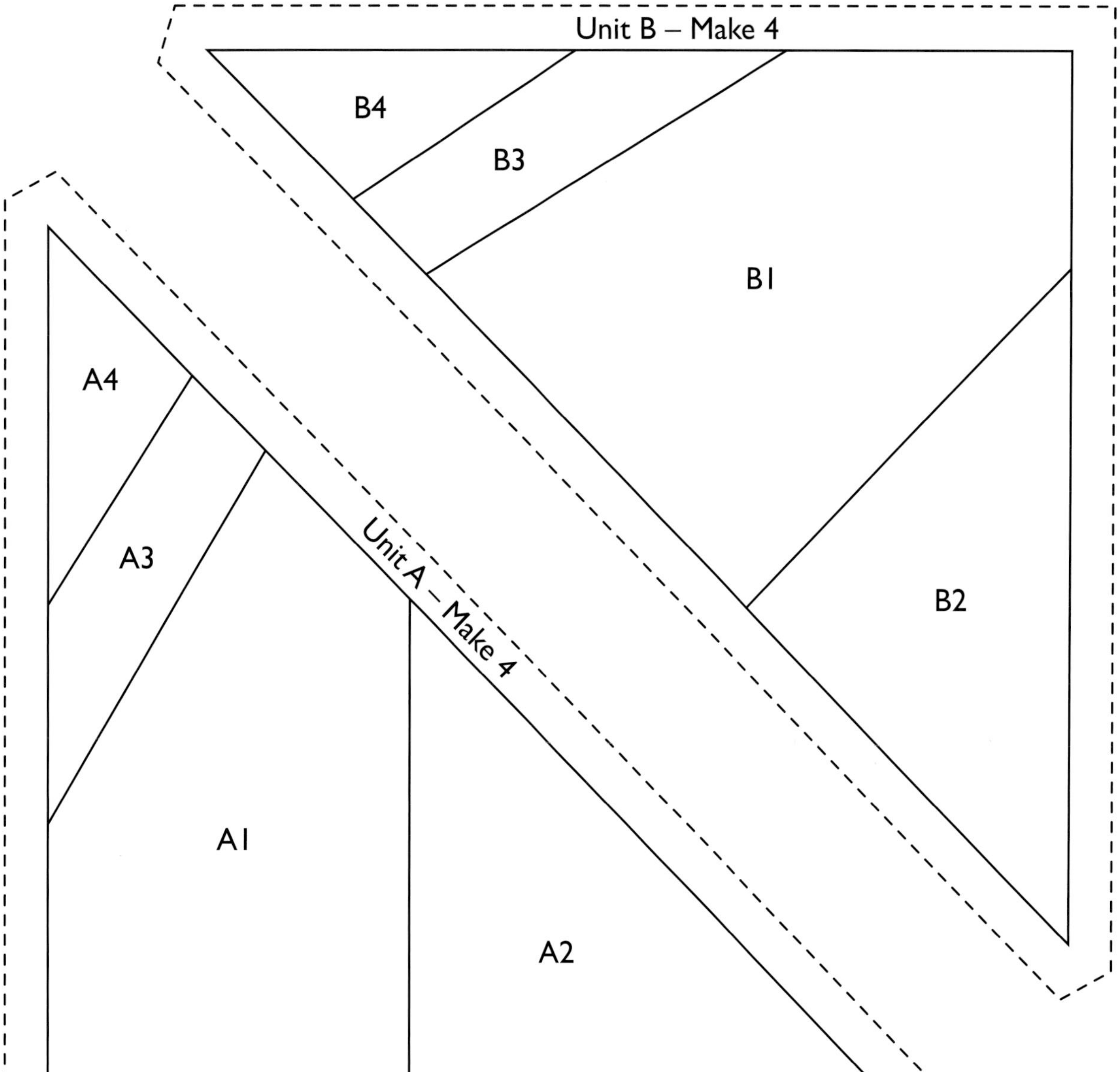

A Flash of Diamonds

Patterns for 10" Block on Page 34.

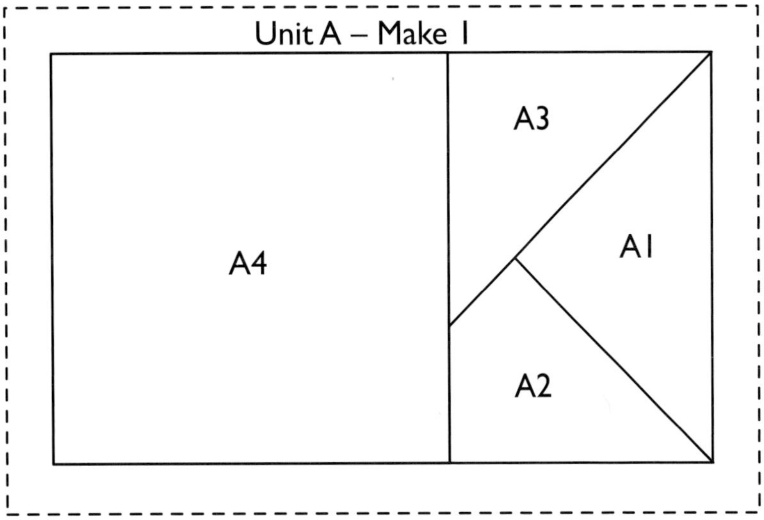

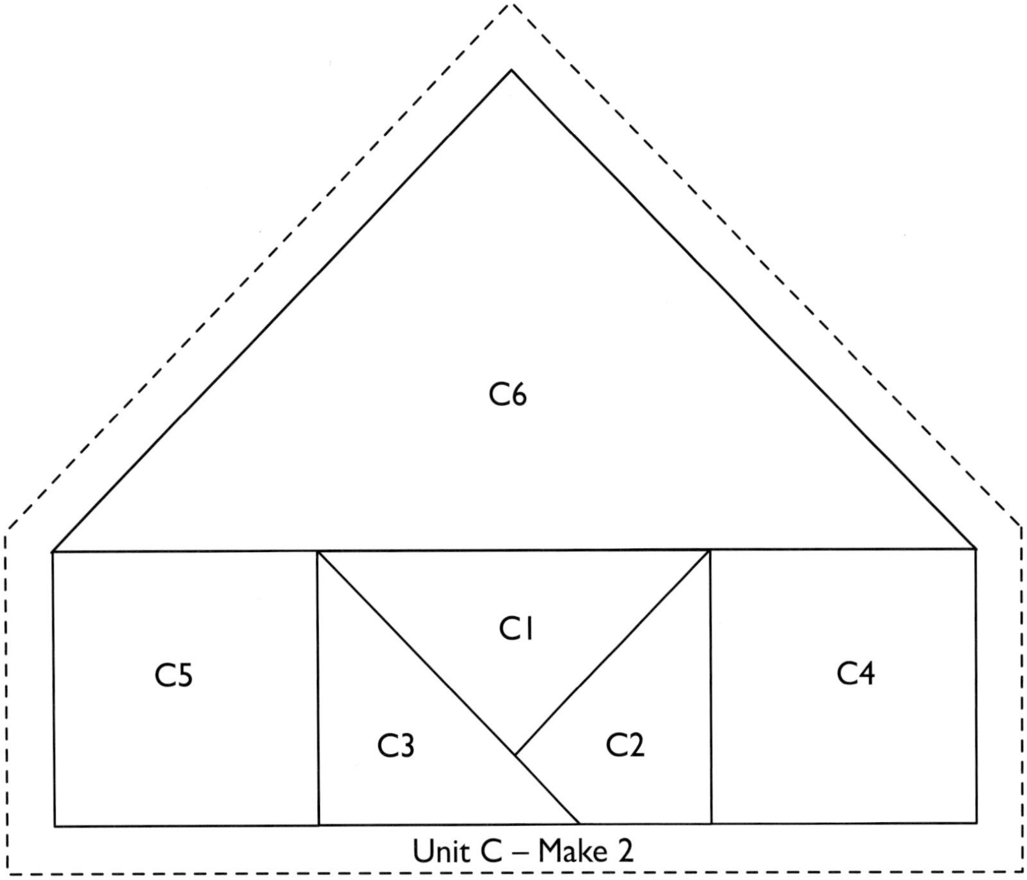

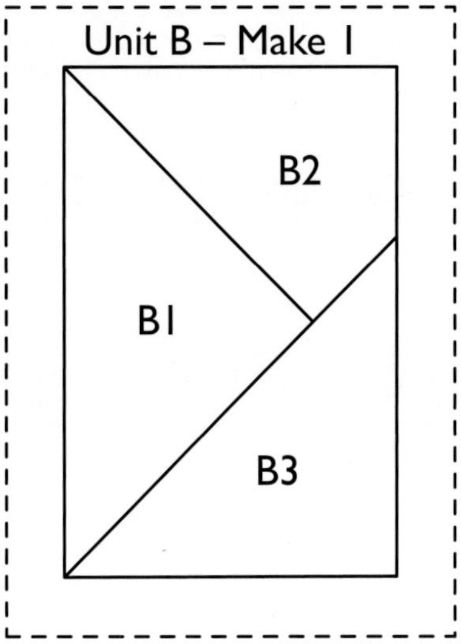
Unit B – Make 1
B2
B1
B3

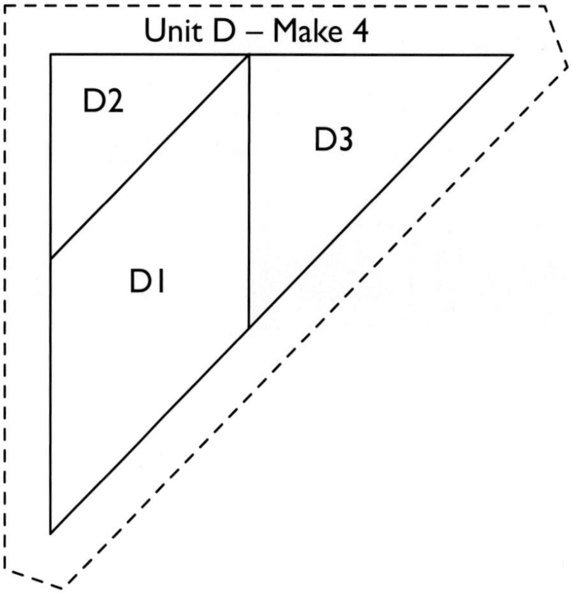
Unit D – Make 4
D2
D3
D1

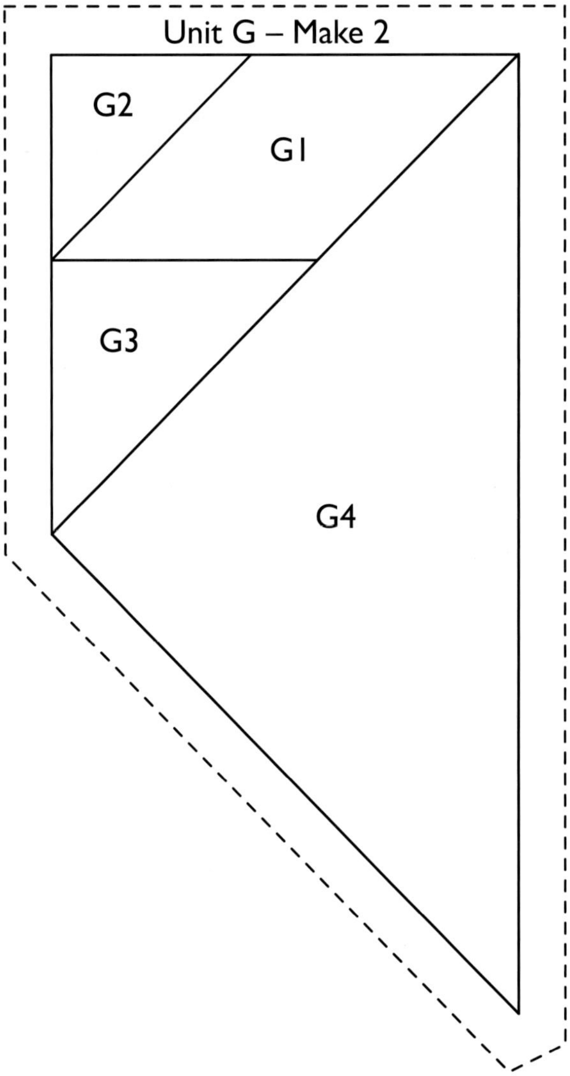
Unit G – Make 2
G2
G1
G3
G4

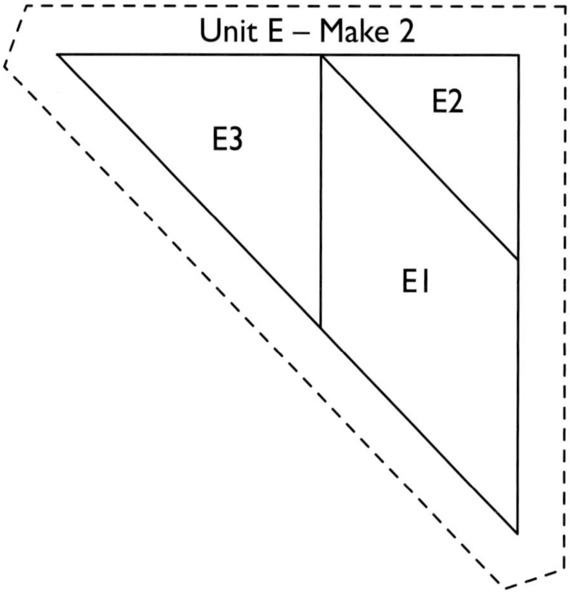
Unit E – Make 2
E3
E2
E1

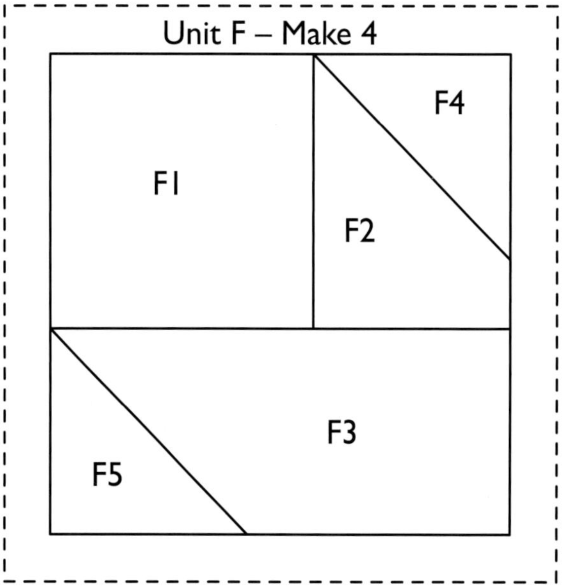
Unit F – Make 4
F4
F1
F2
F3
F5

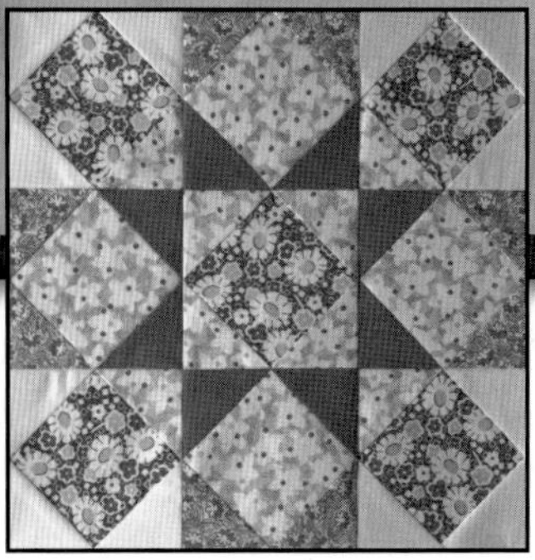

The Kansas Star

Pattern for 10" Block on Page 36.

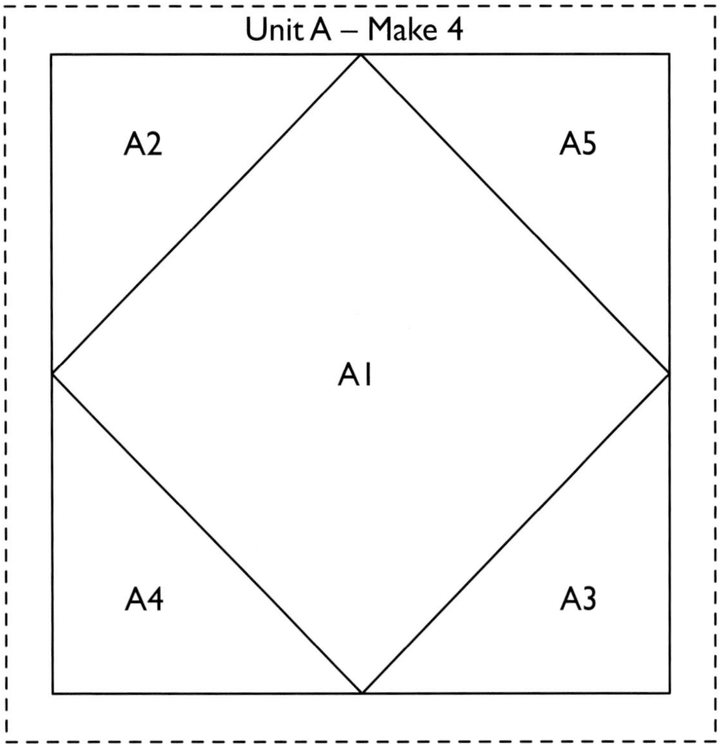

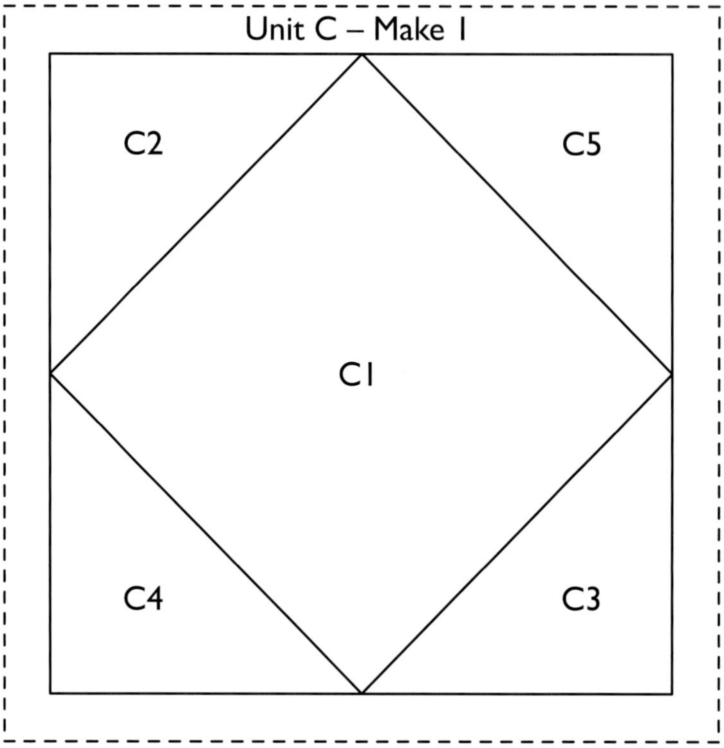

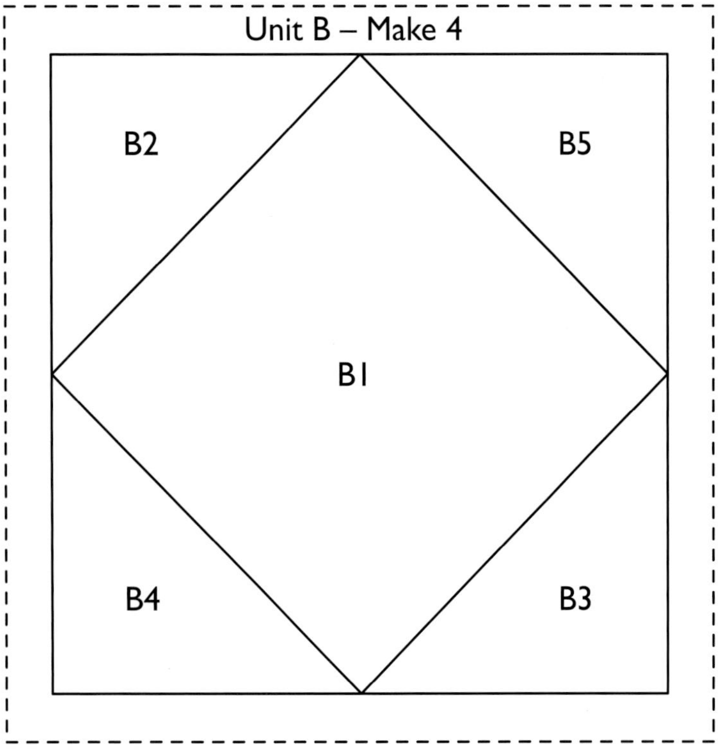

The Bright Jewel

Patterns for 10" Block on Page 38.

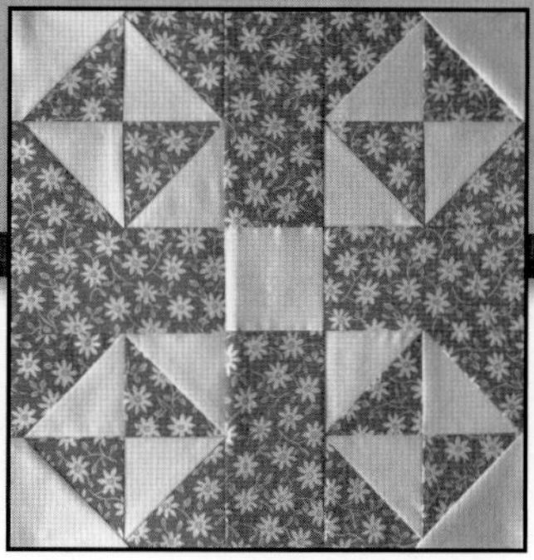

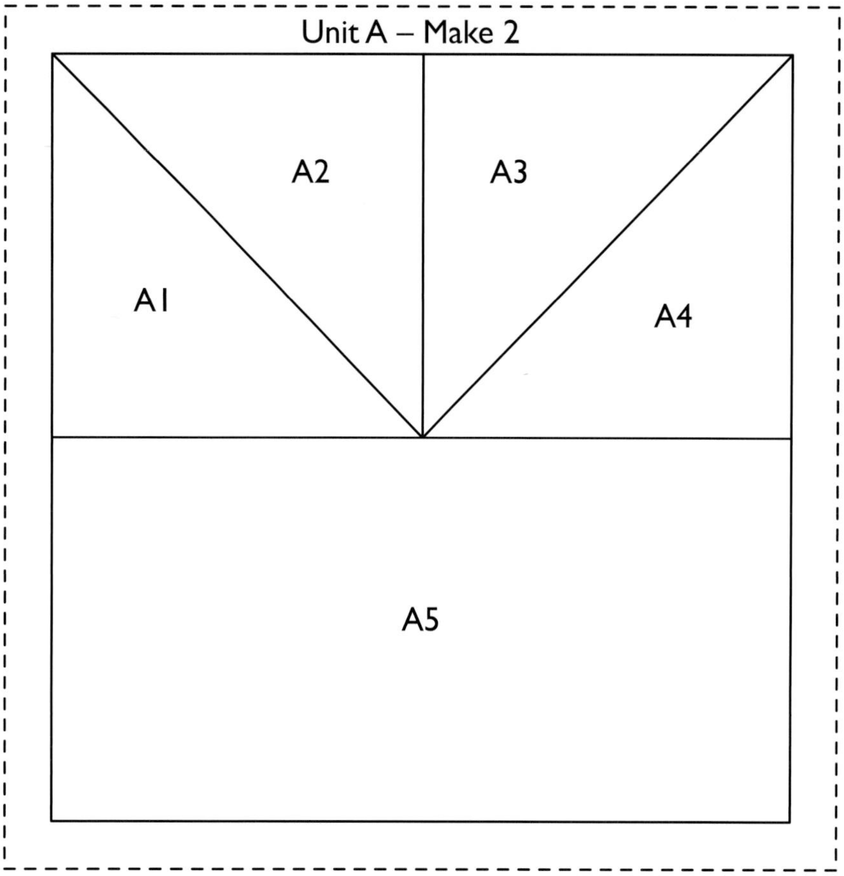

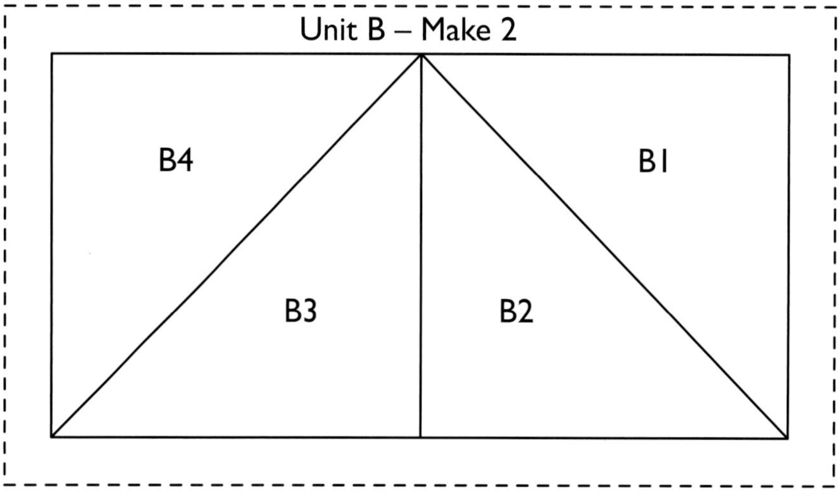

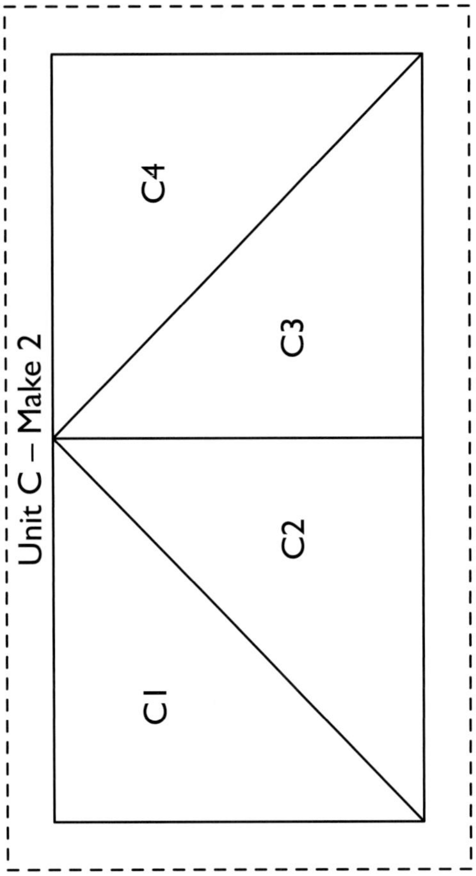
Unit C – Make 2
C4
C3
C2
C1

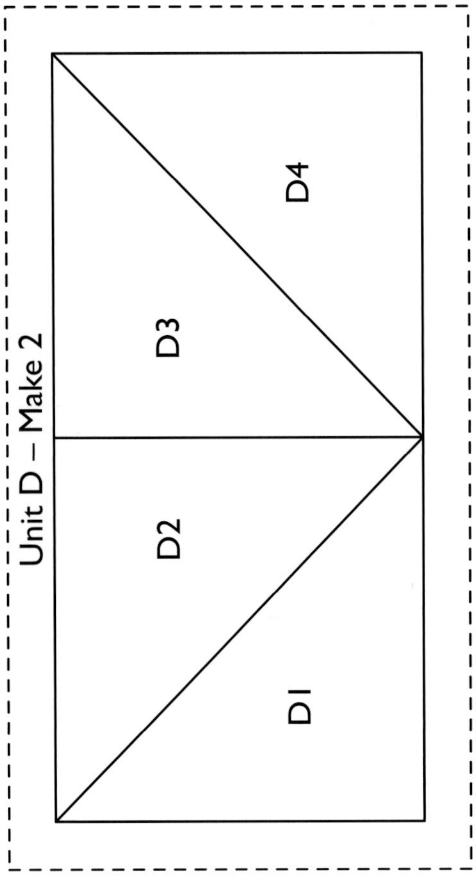
Unit D – Make 2
D4
D3
D2
D1

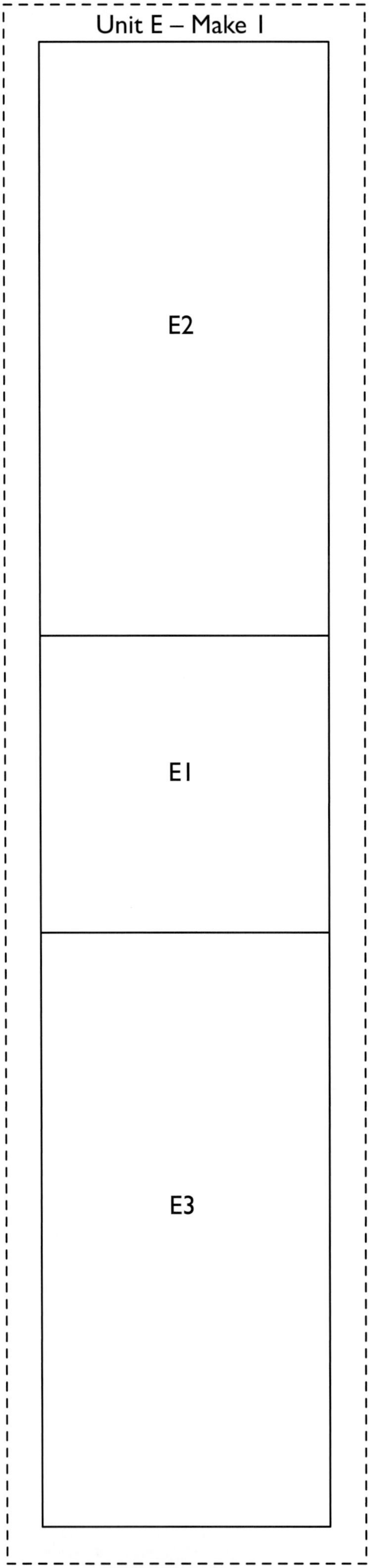
Unit E – Make 1
E2
E1
E3

Mother's Favorite Star

Pattern for 4" Block on Page 46.

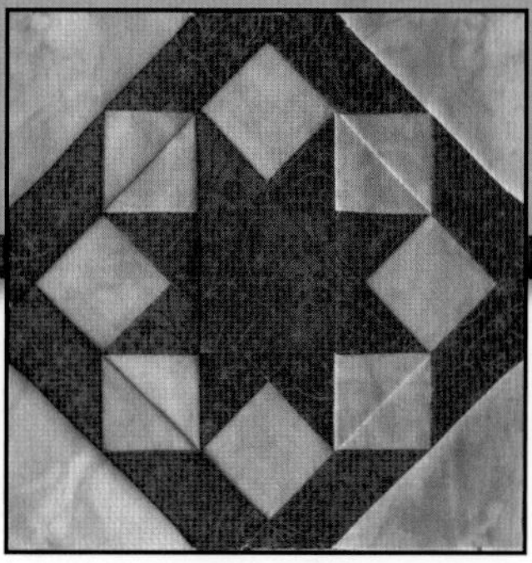

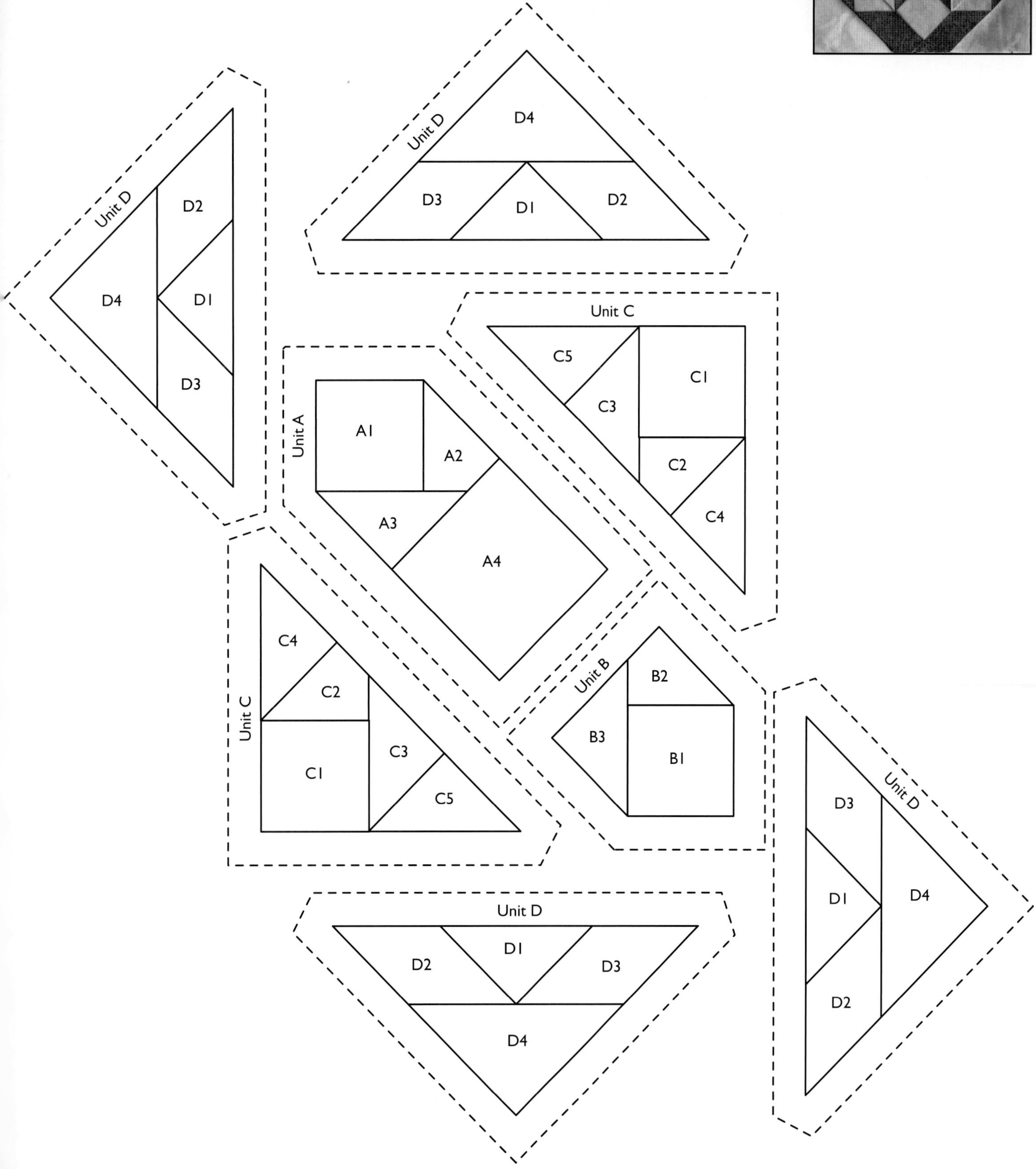

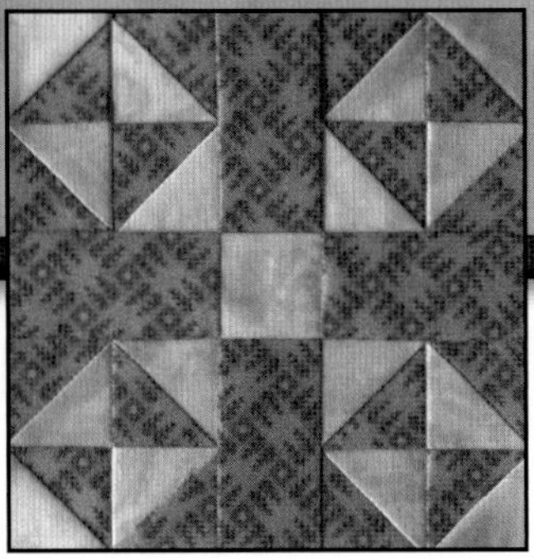

The Bright Jewel

PATTERN FOR 4" BLOCK ON PAGE 70.

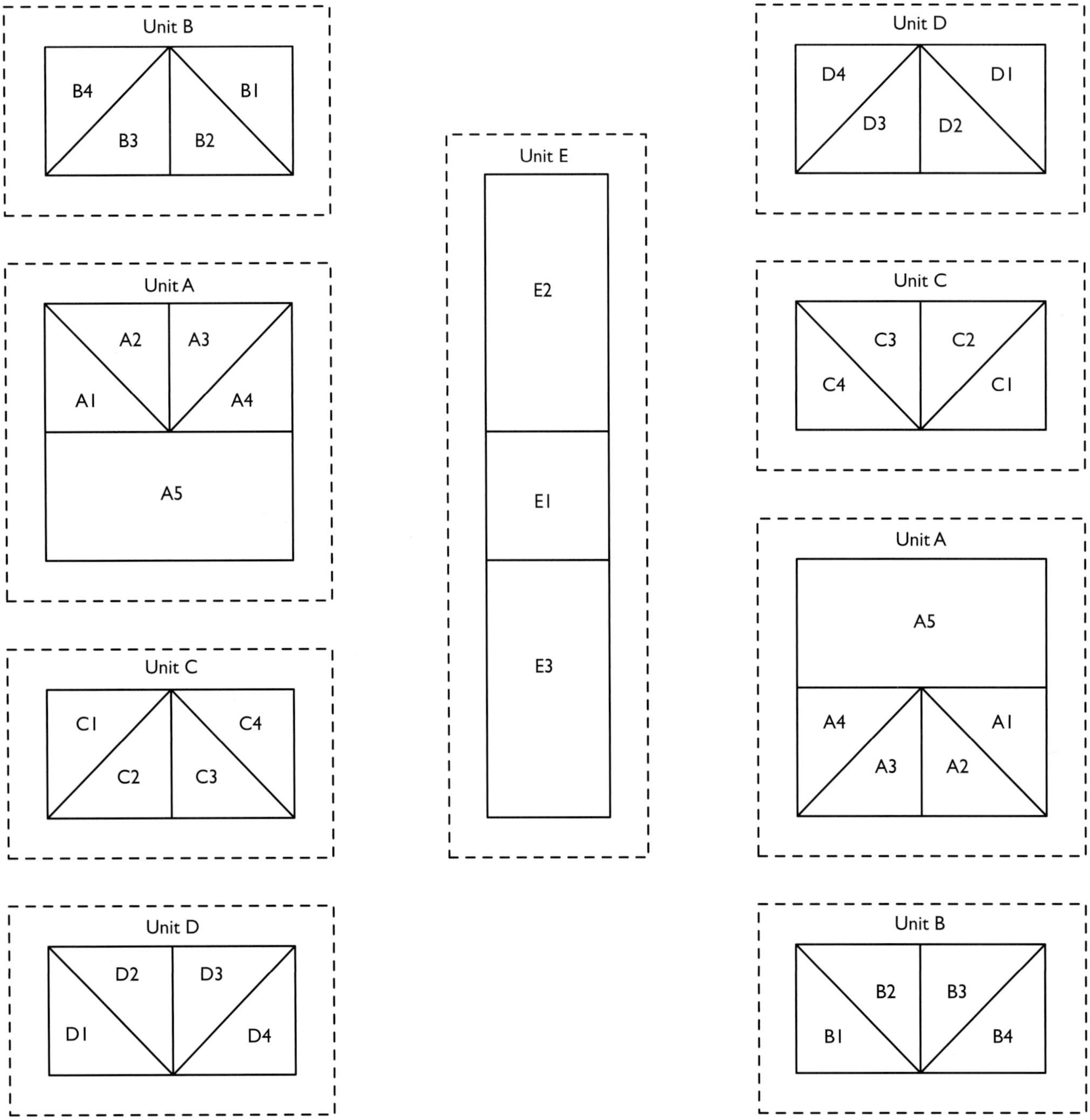

Mona's Choice

Pattern for 4" Block on Page 47.

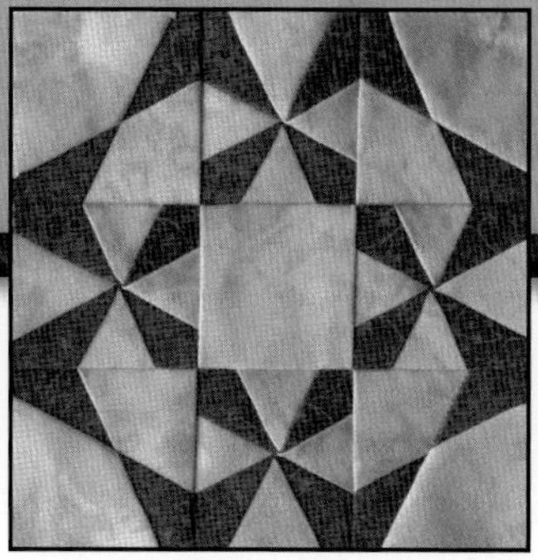

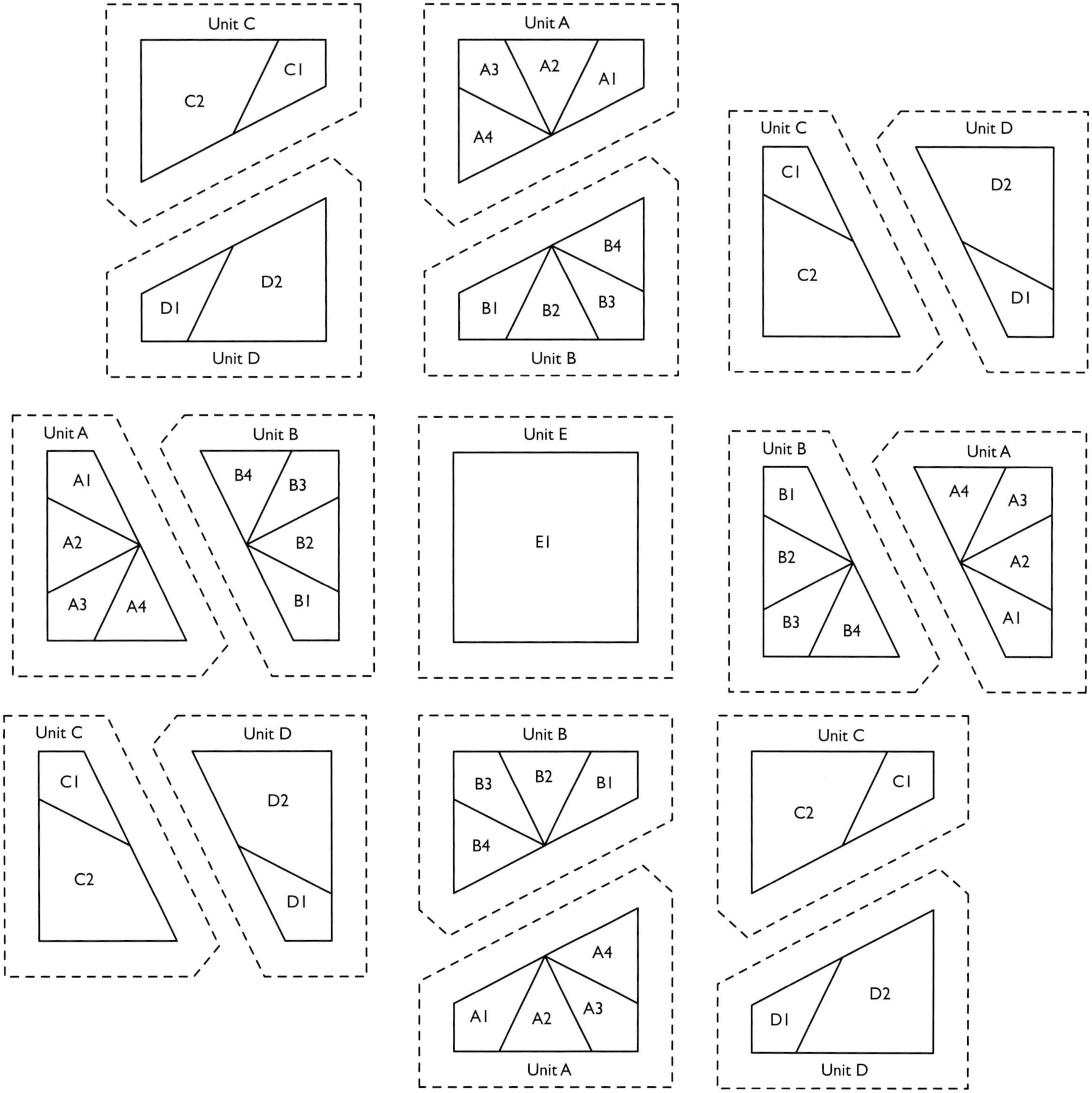

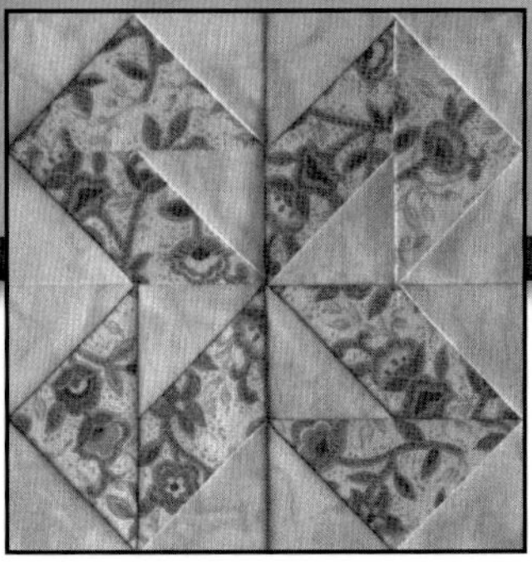

The Colorado Quilt

Pattern for 4" Block on Page 48.

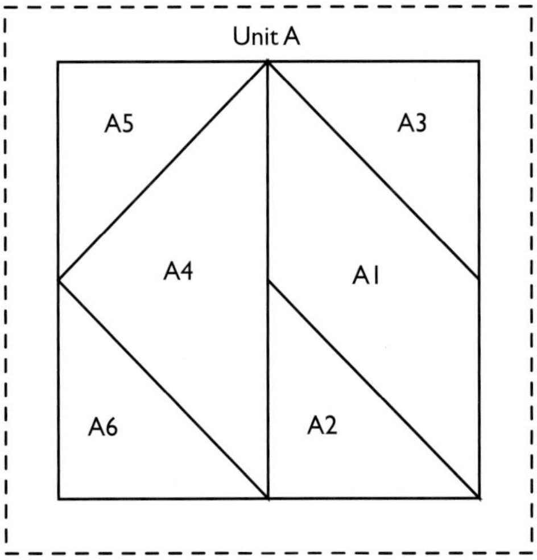

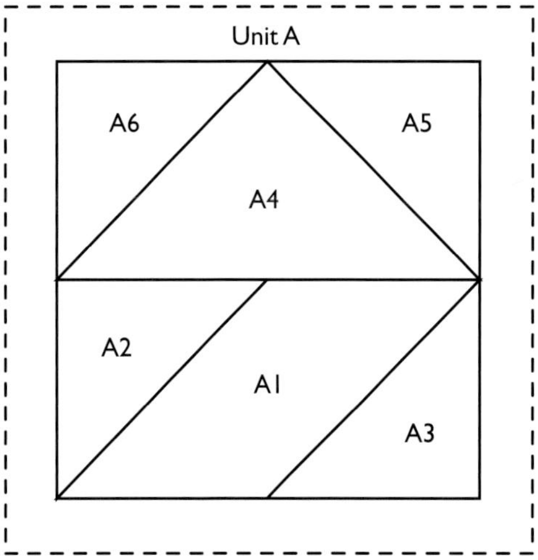

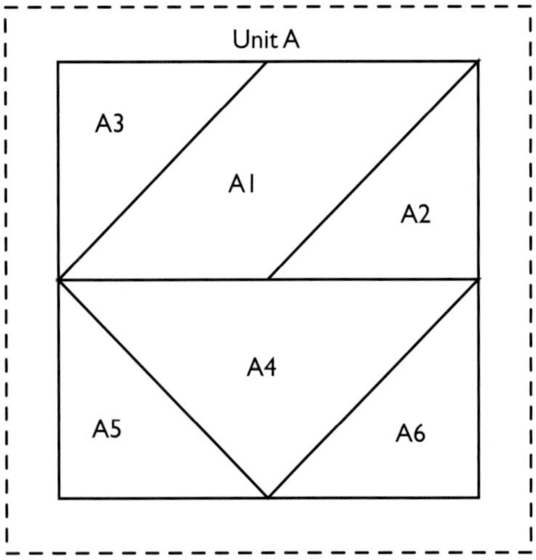

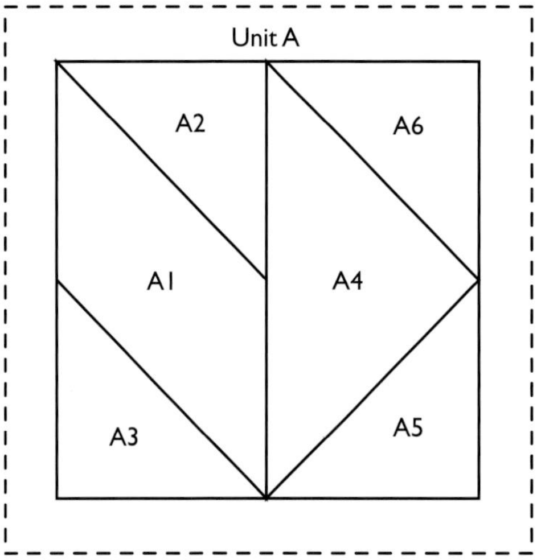

Anna's Choice

Pattern for 4" Block on Page 49.

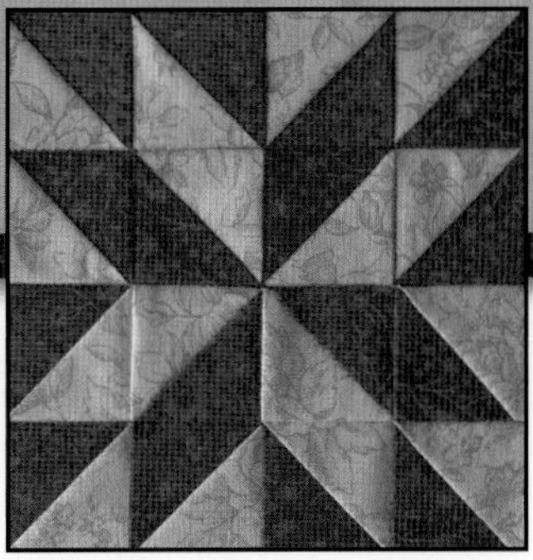

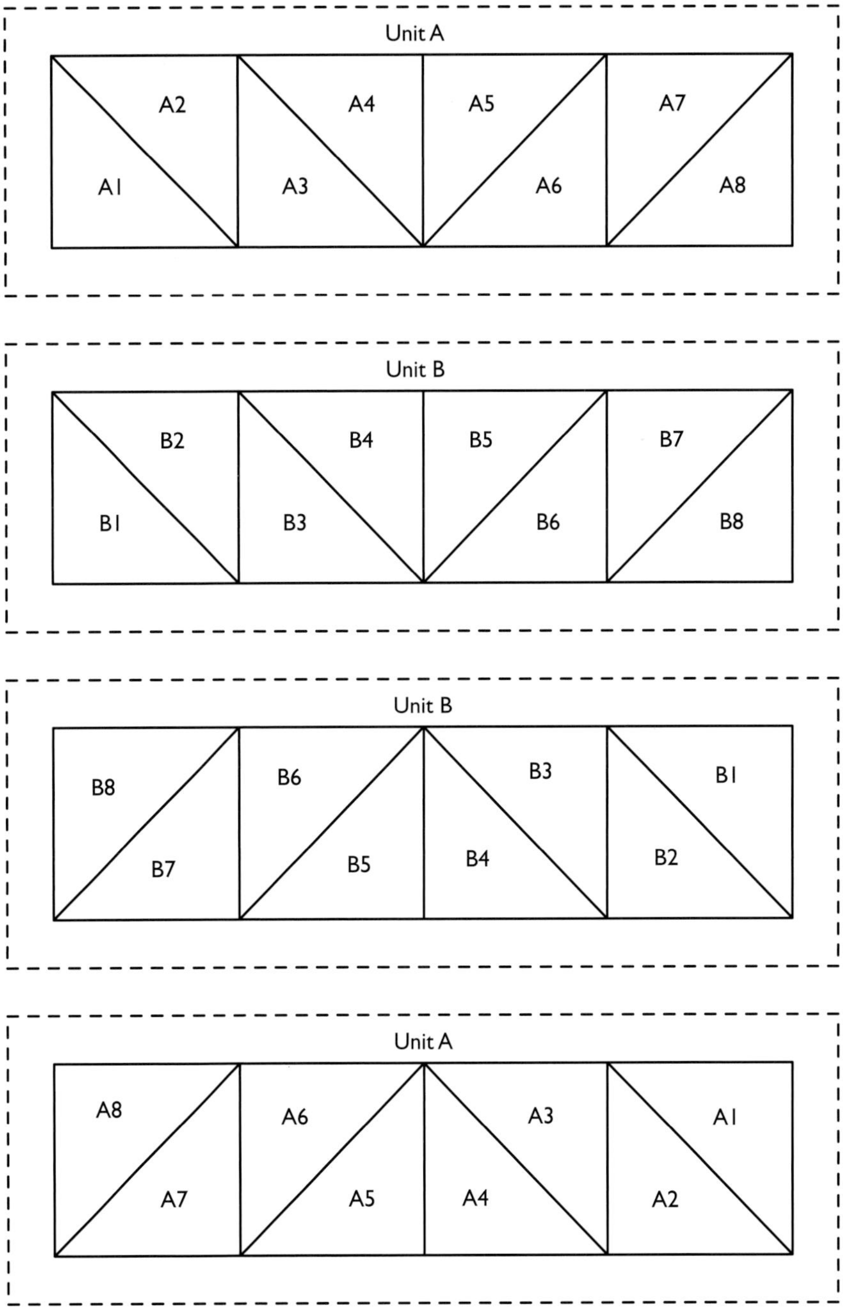

The 1941 Nine Patch

Pattern for 4" Block on Page 50.

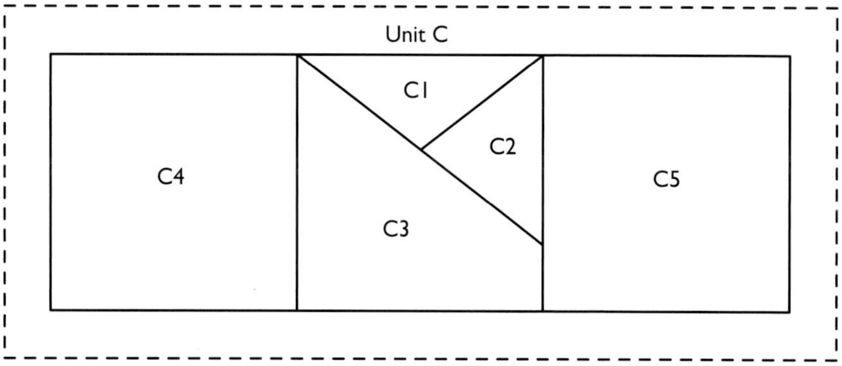

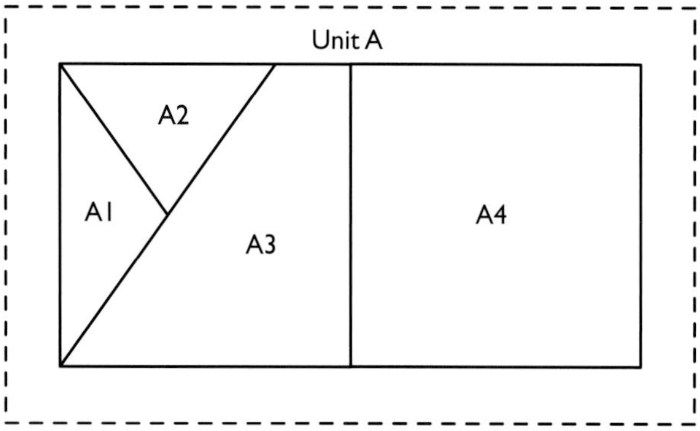

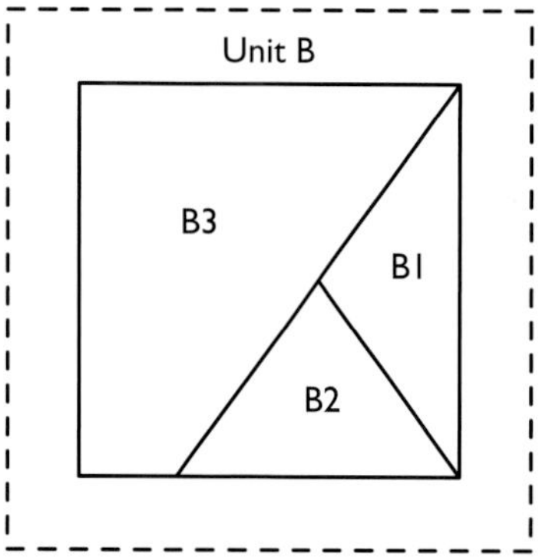

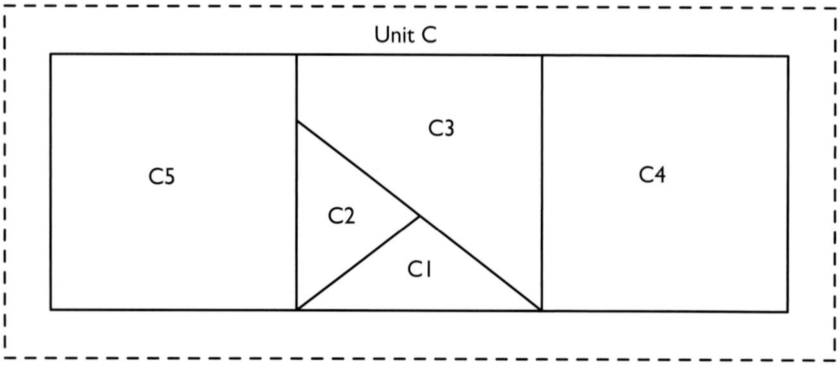

Sunlight and Shadows

Pattern for 4" Block on Page 52.

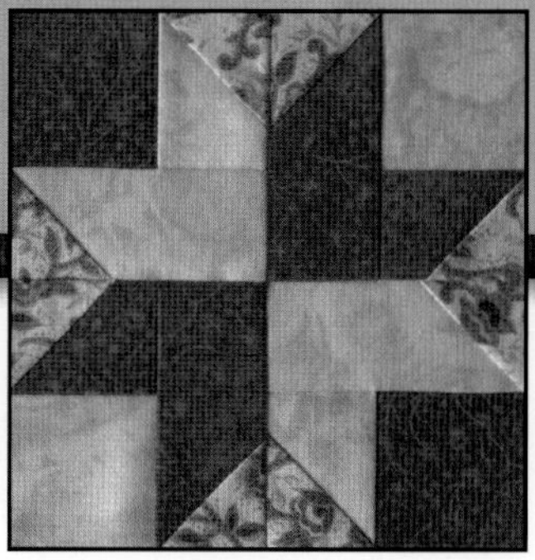

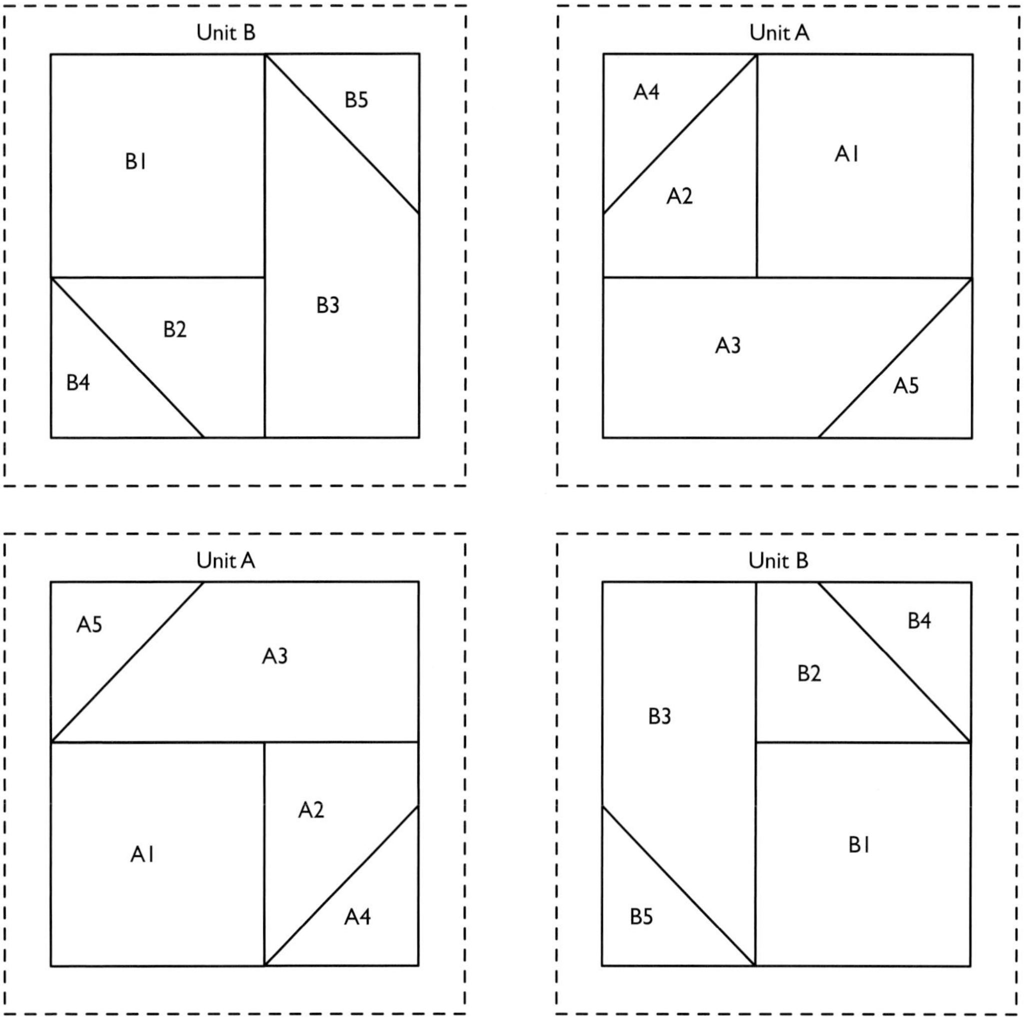

A Salute to the Colors

Pattern for 4" Block on Page 54.

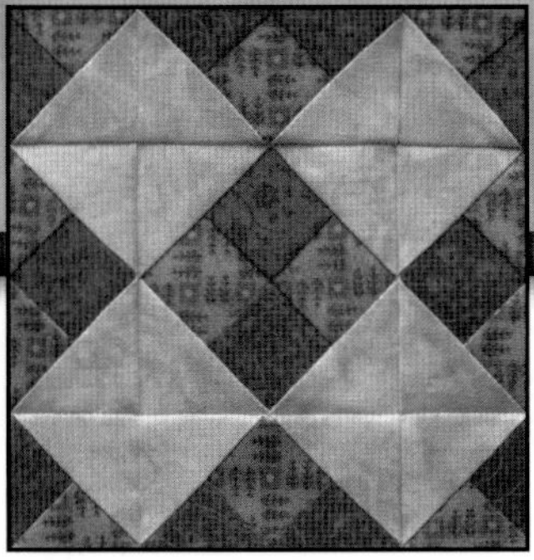

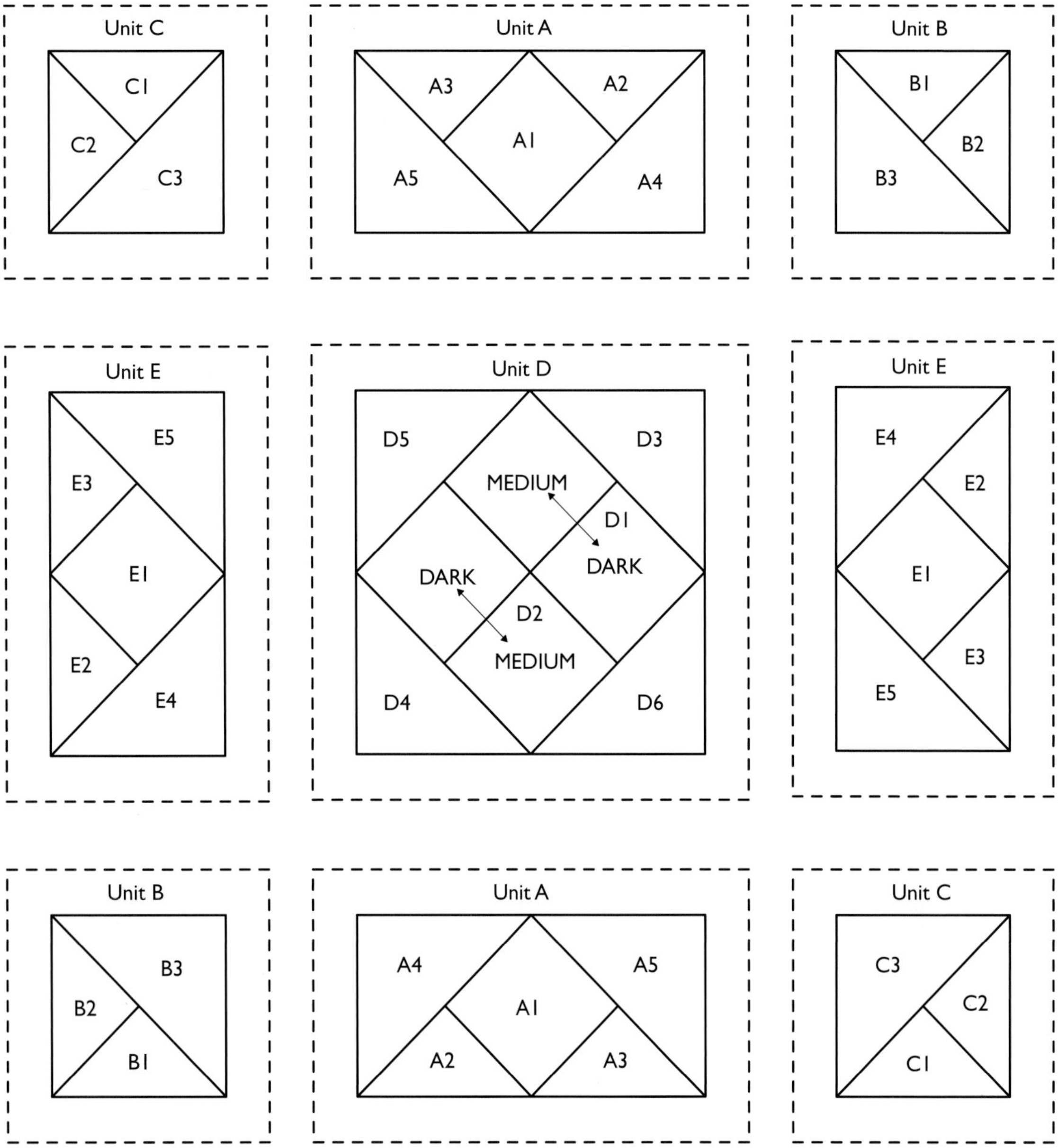

Shepherd's Crossing

Pattern for 4" Block on Page 51.

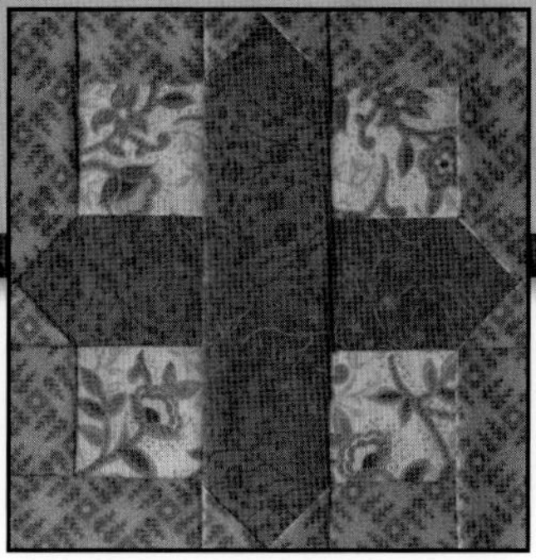

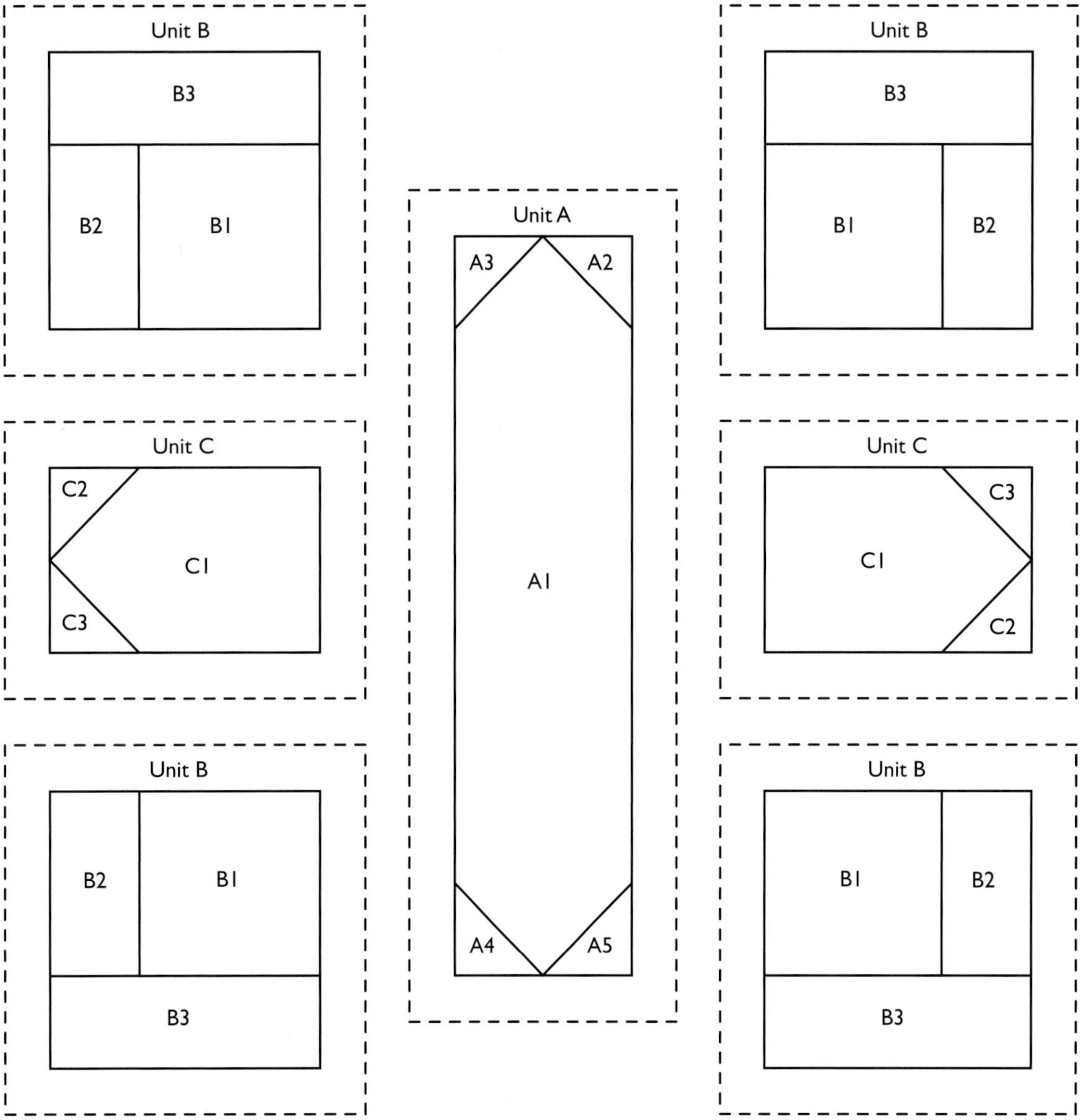

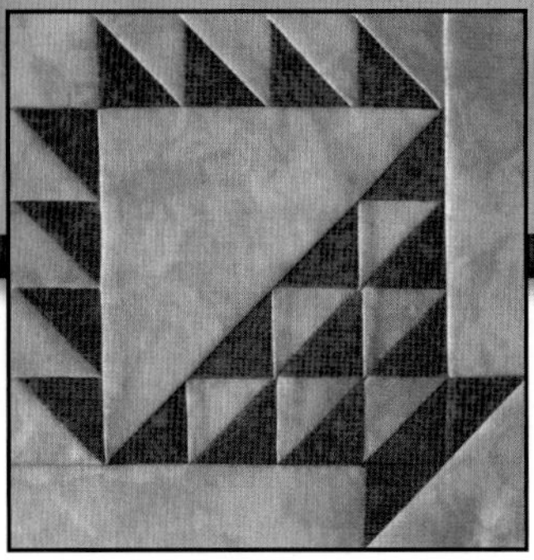

A Basket Quilt in Triangles

Pattern for 4" Block on Page 56.

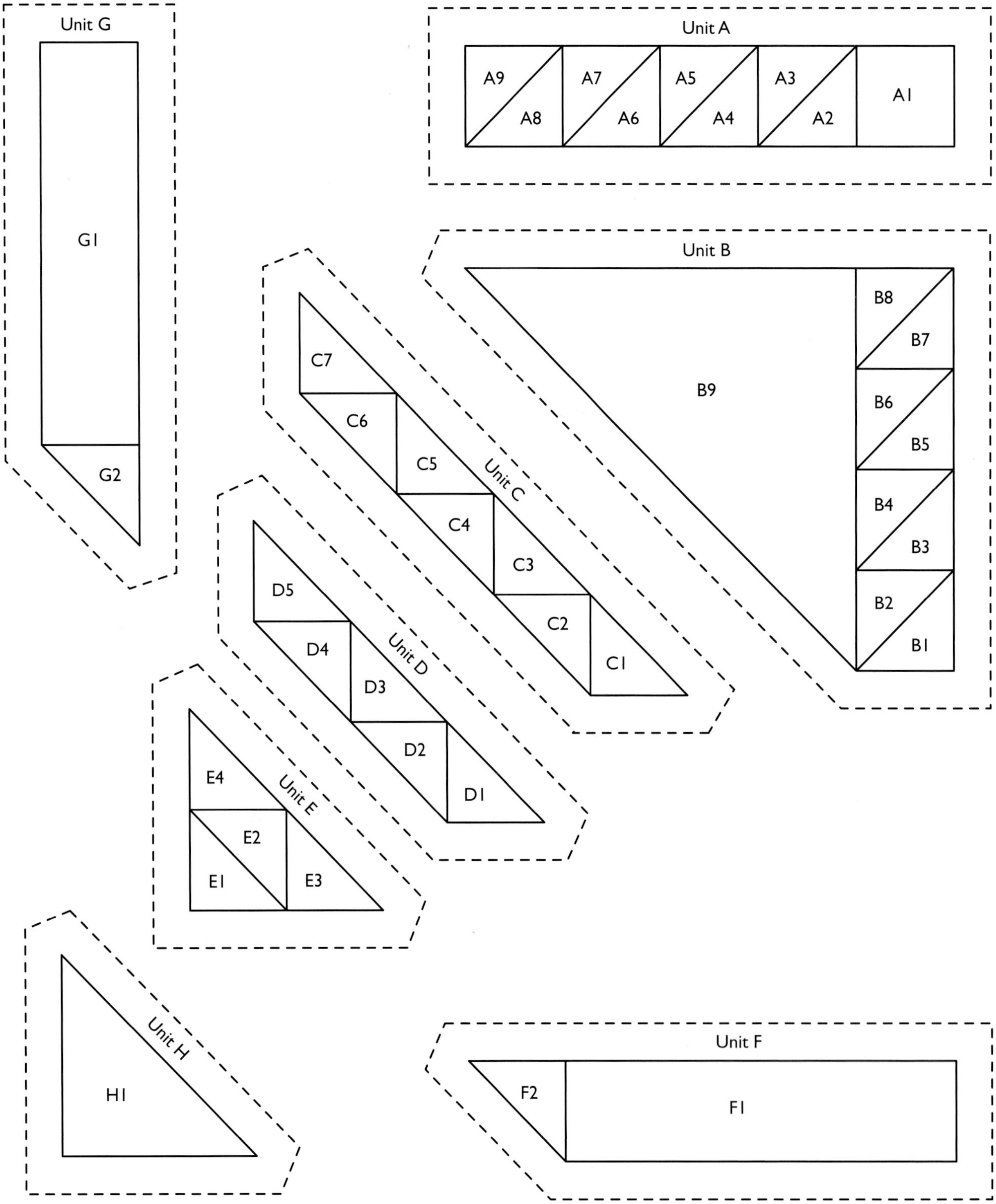

The Army Star

Pattern for 4" Block on Page 53.

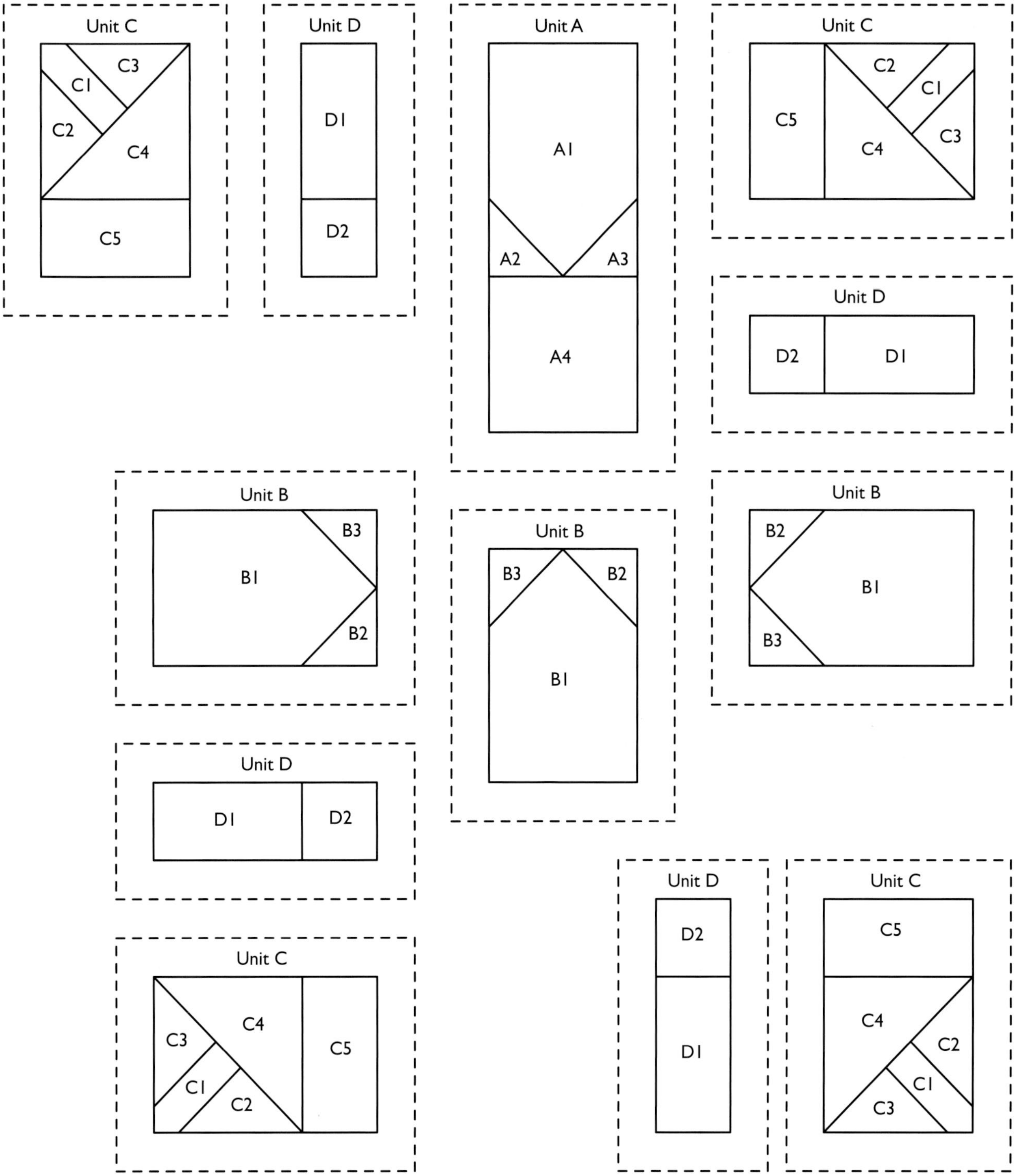

The New Four Pointer

Pattern for 4" Block on Page 58.

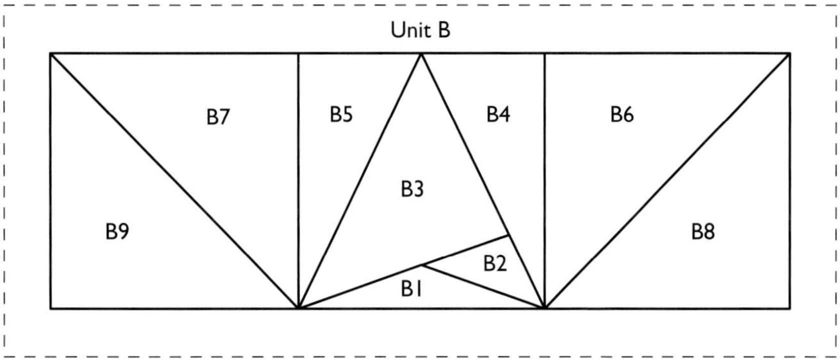

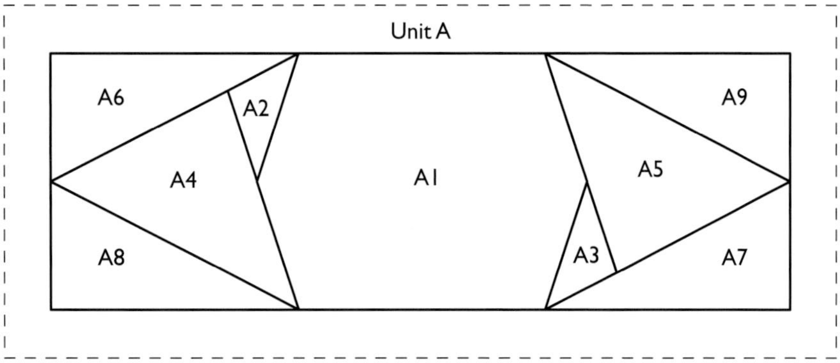

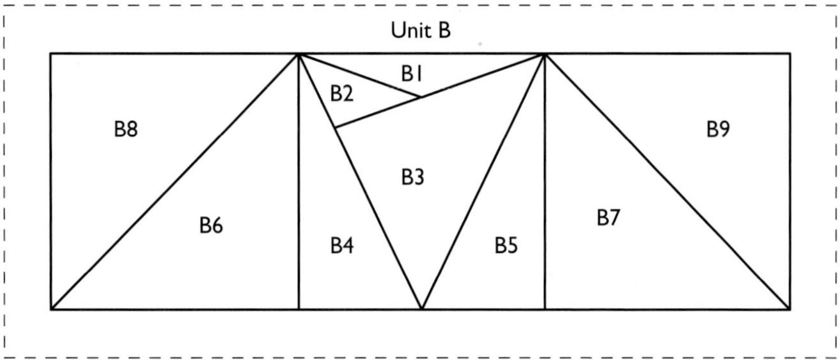

A Quilt Mosaic

Pattern for 4" Block on Page 59.

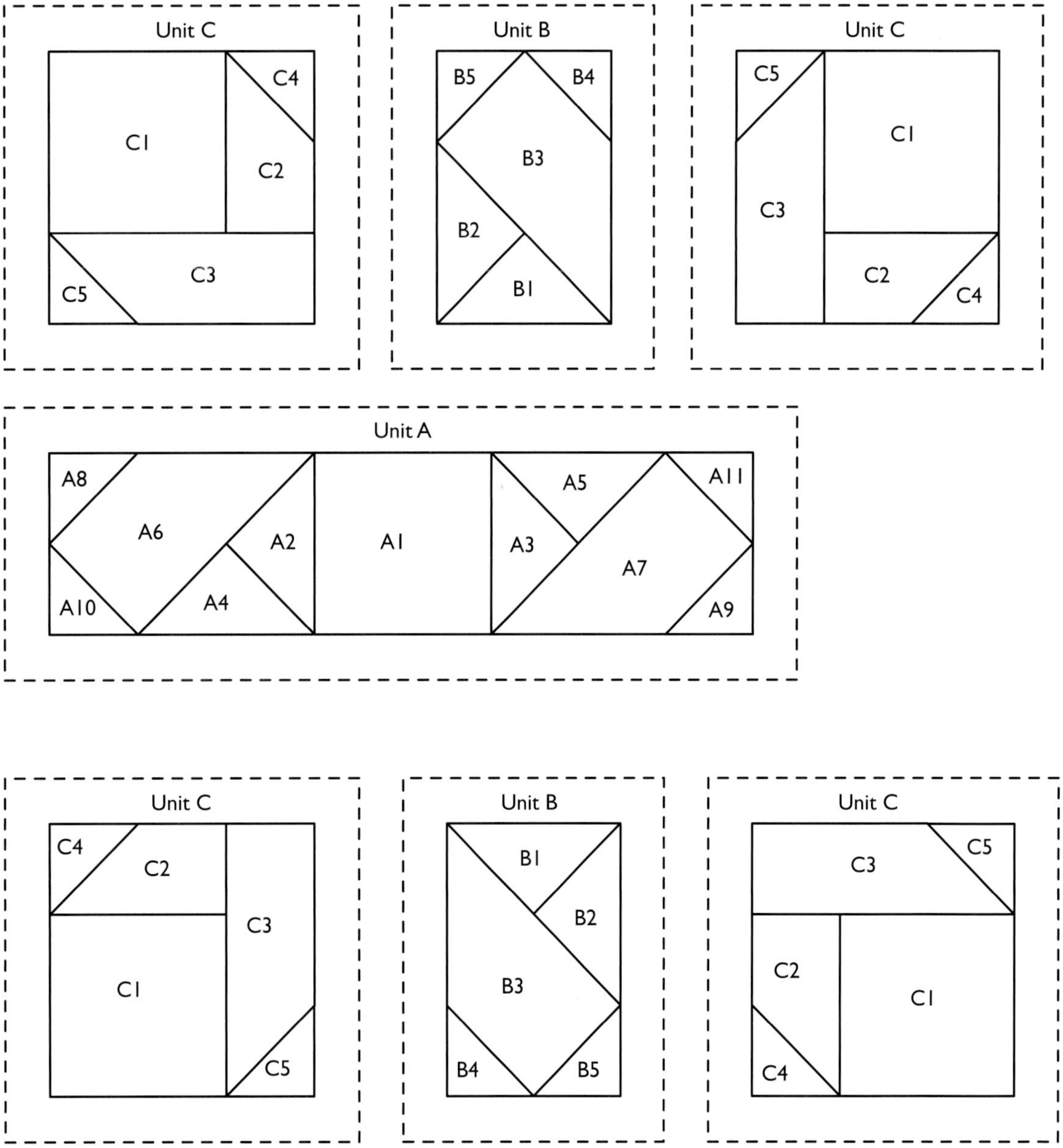

Return of the Swallows

Pattern for 4" Block on Page 60.

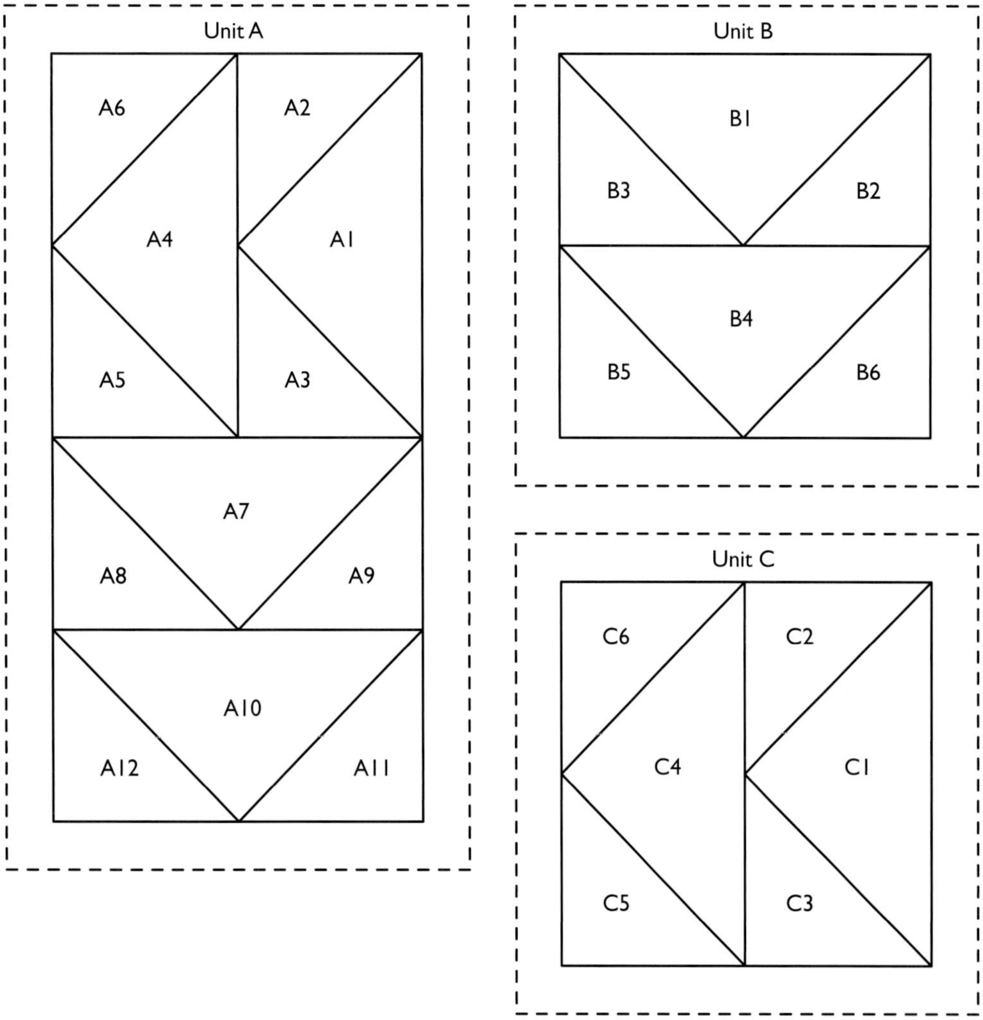

The Christmas Star

Pattern for 4" Block on Page 62.

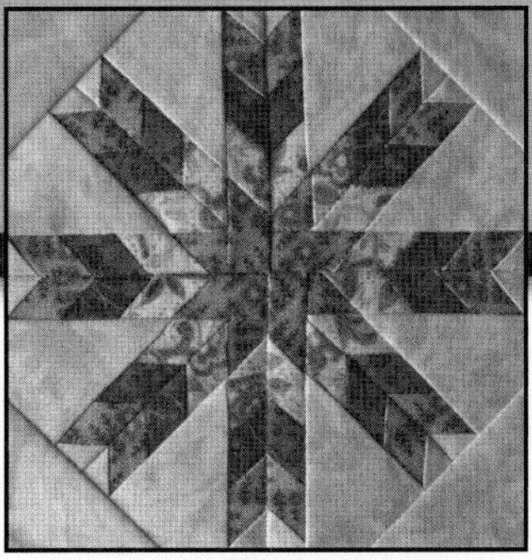

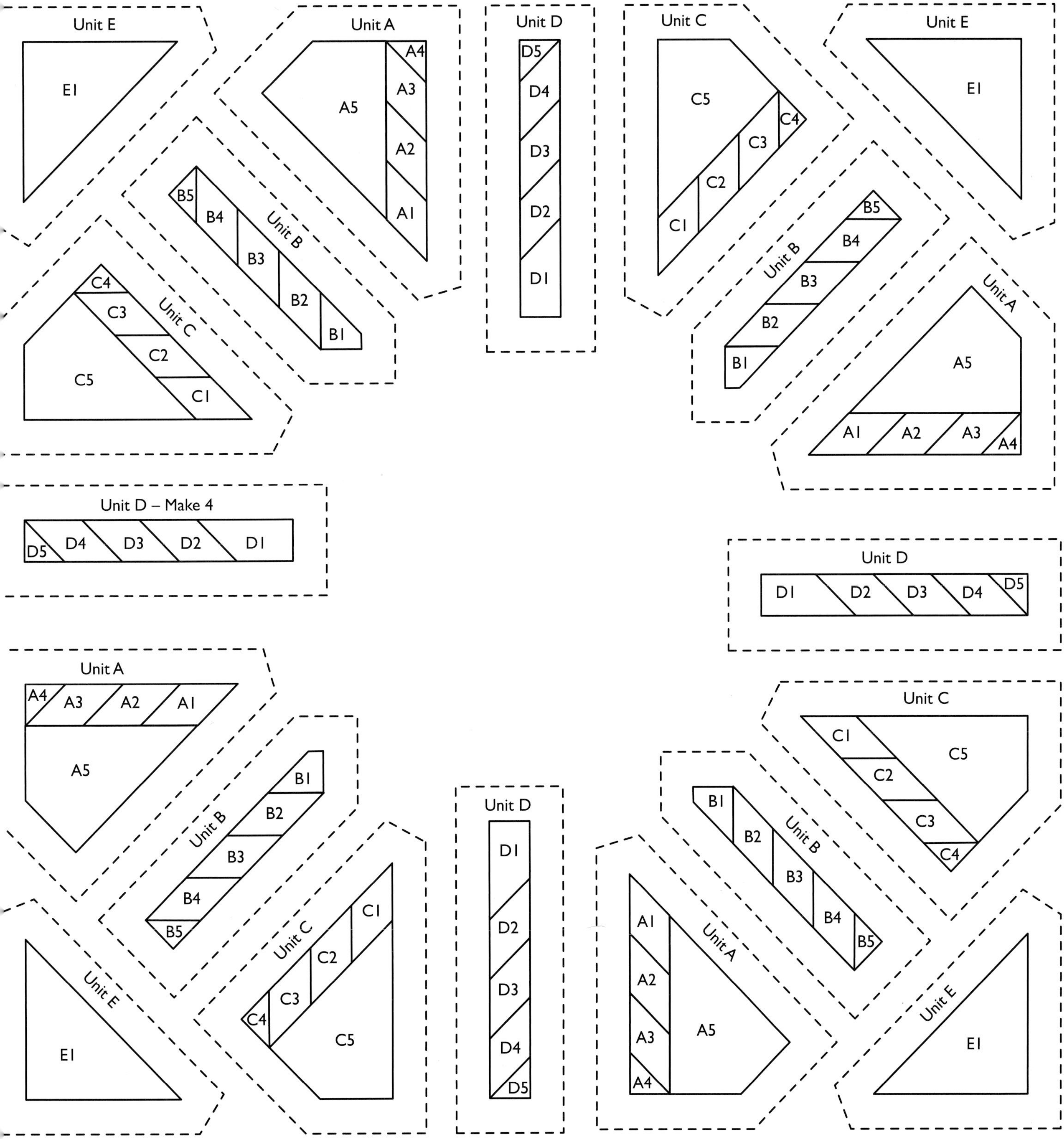

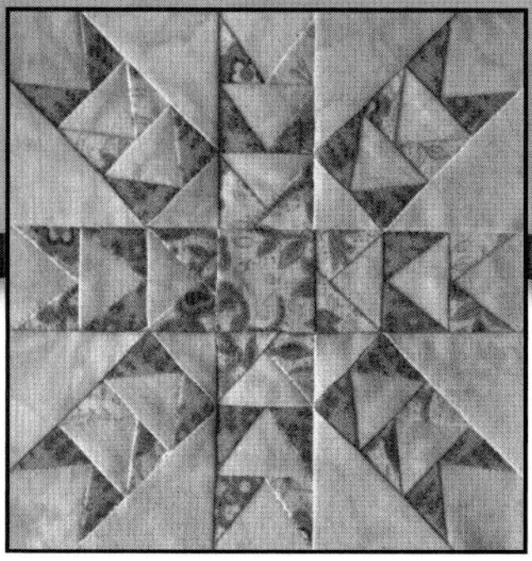

The Spider Web

Pattern for 4" Block on Page 64.

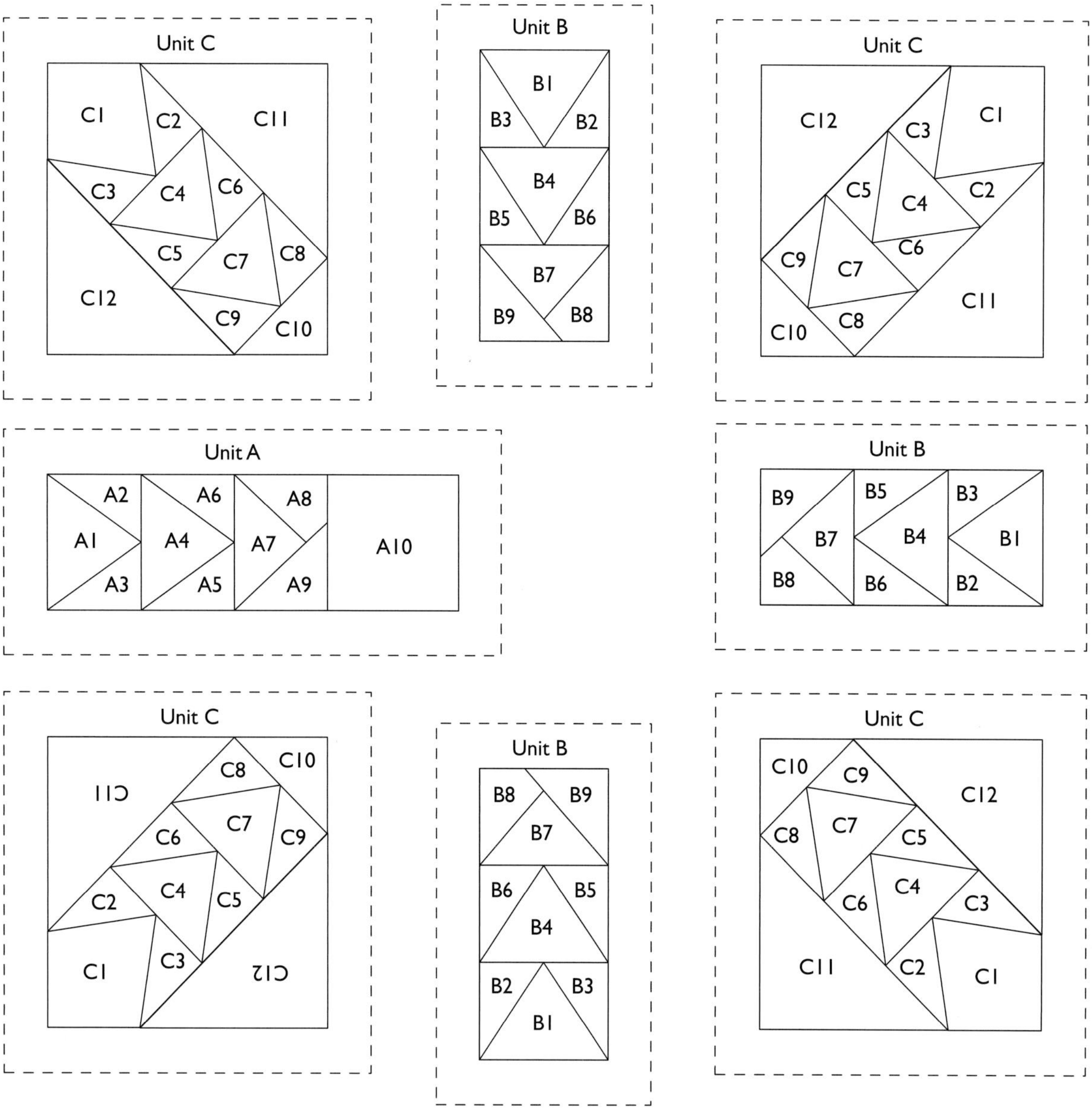

The North Star

Pattern for 4" Block on Page 61.

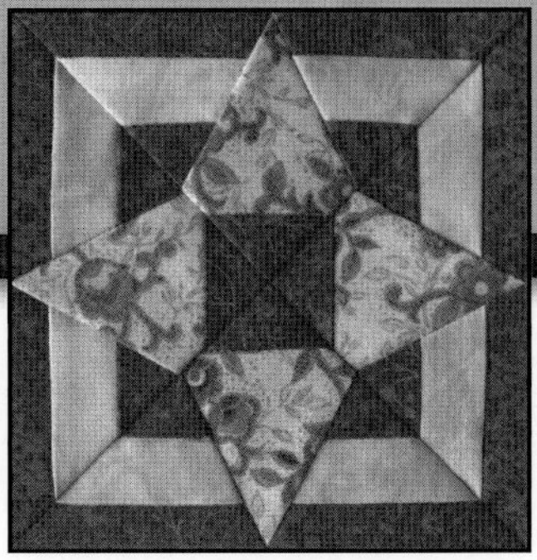

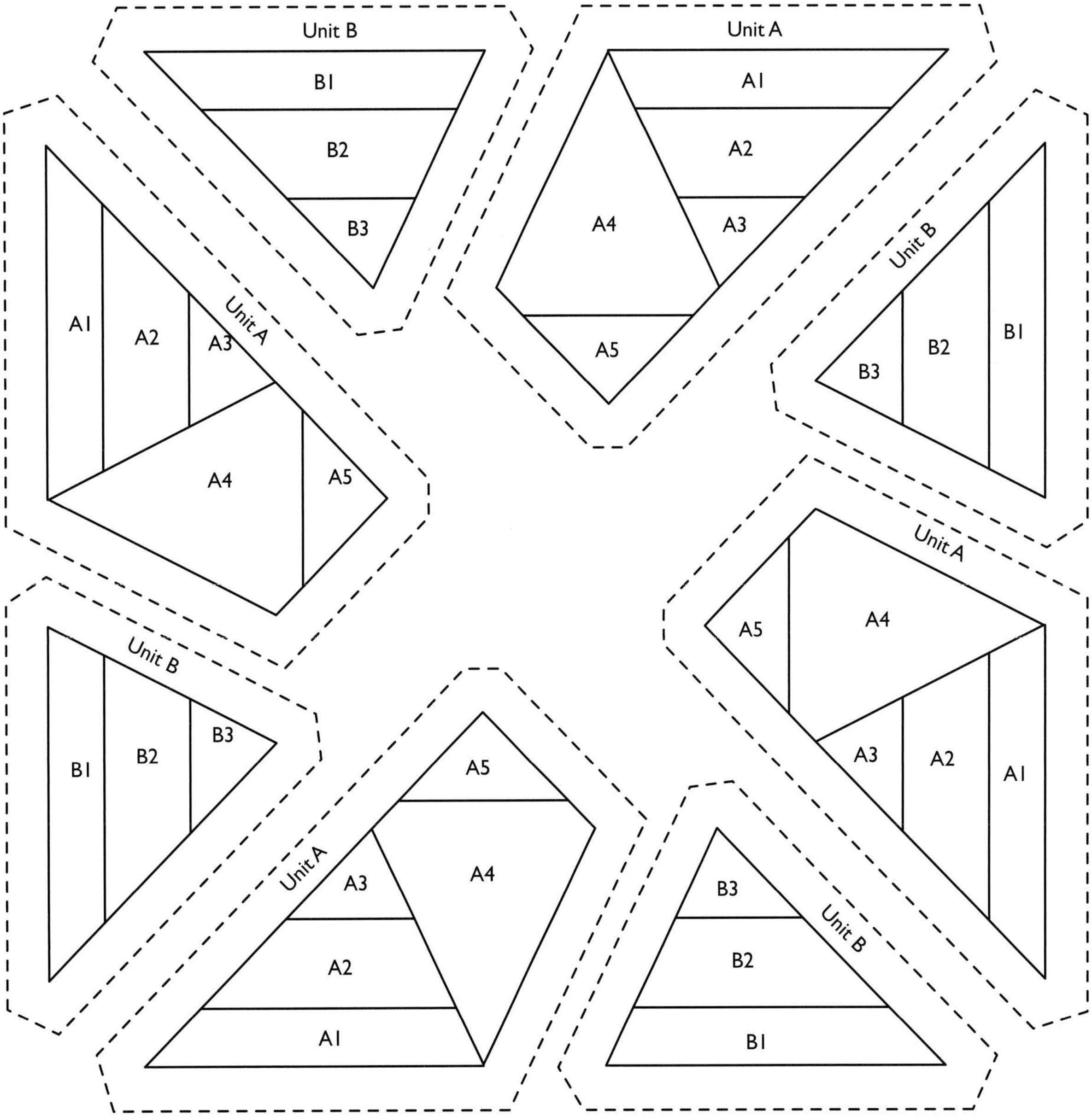

A Flash of Diamonds

Pattern for 4" Block on Page 66.

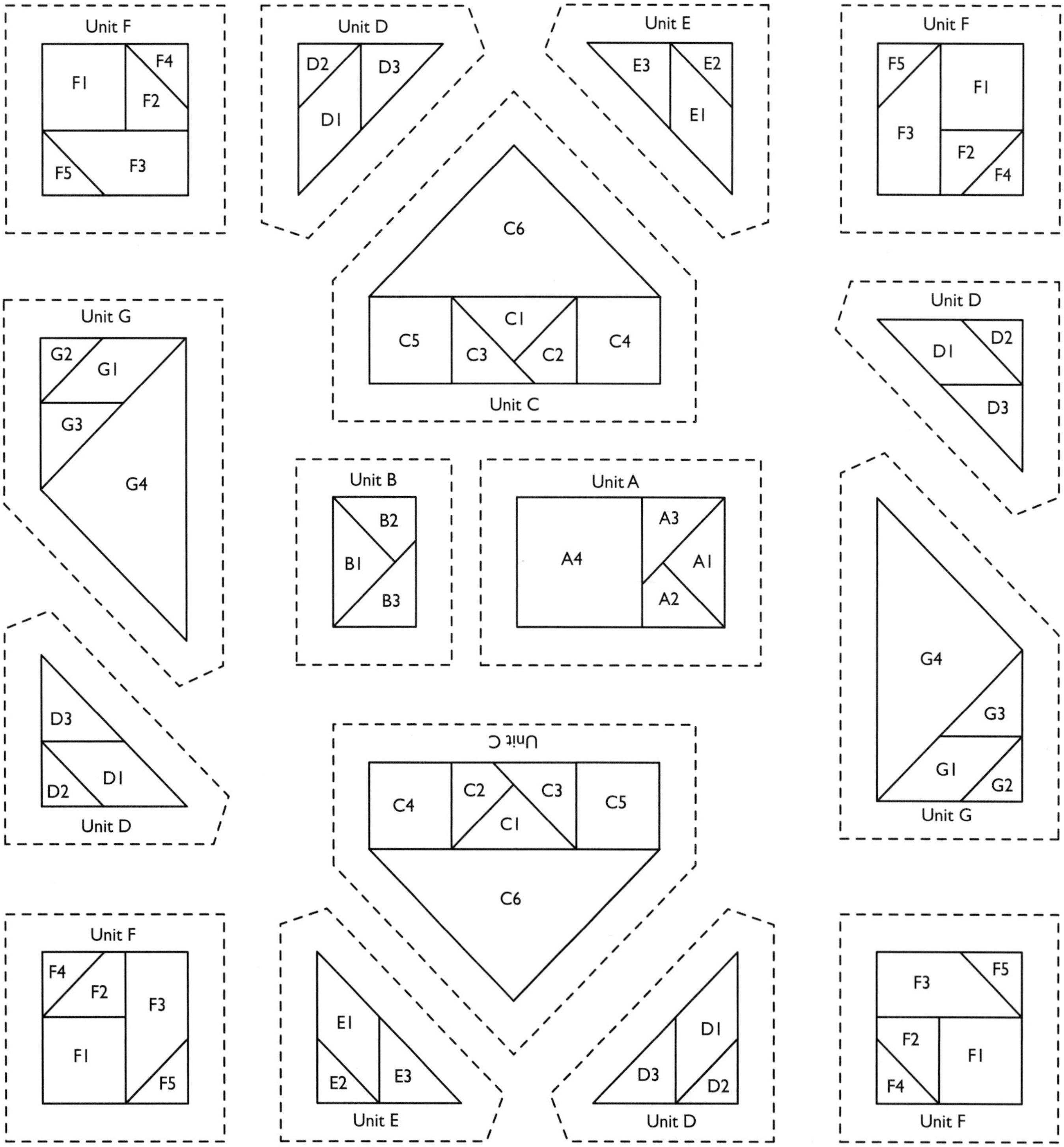

The Kansas Star

PATTERN FOR 4" BLOCK ON PAGE 68.

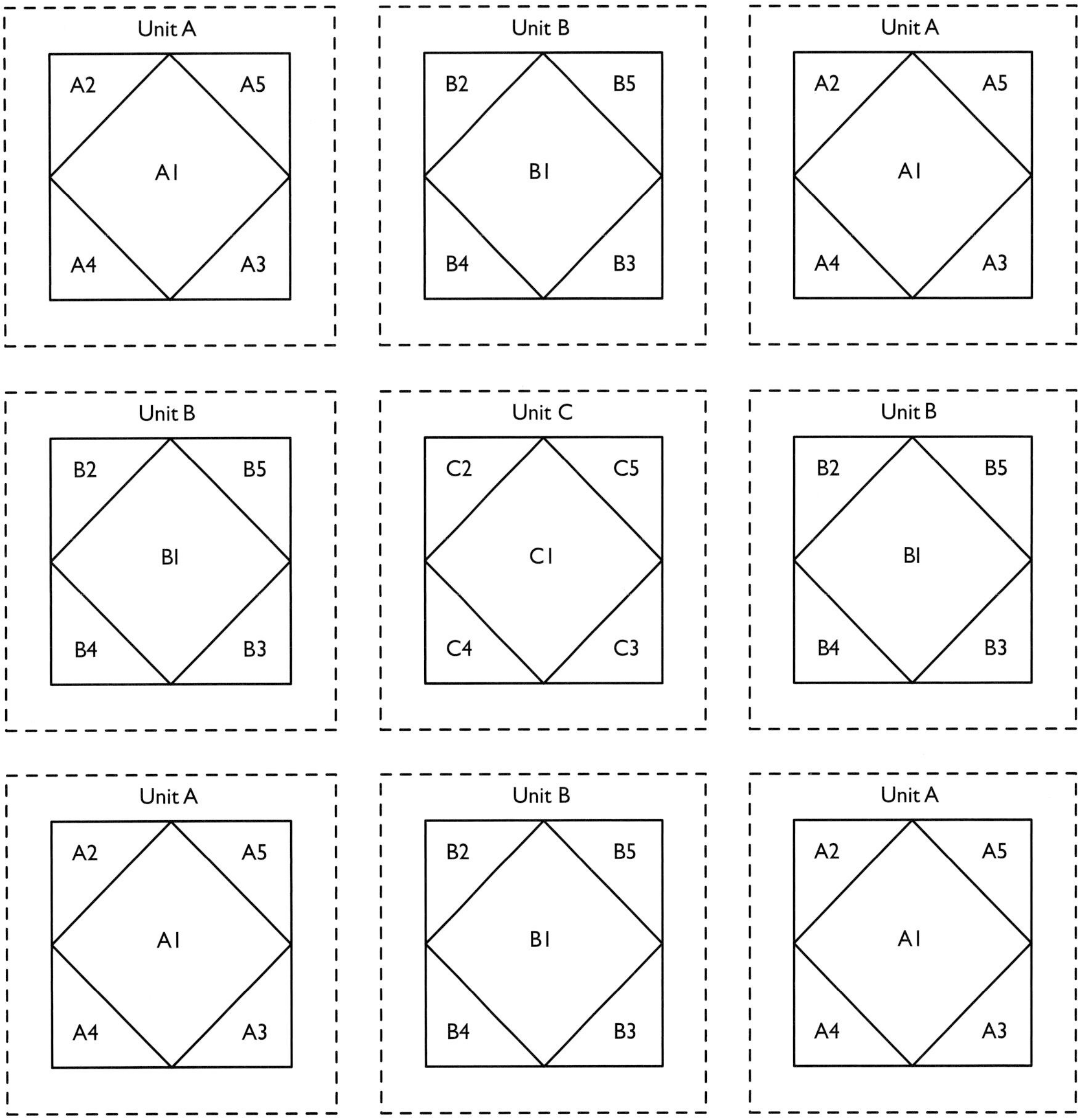

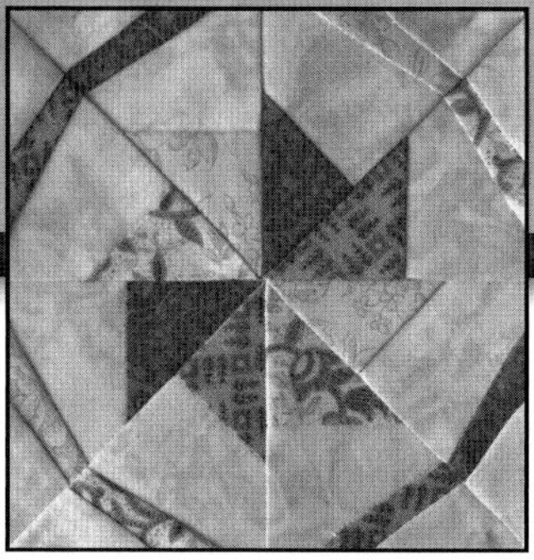

Crazy Anne

Pattern for 4" Block on Page 69.

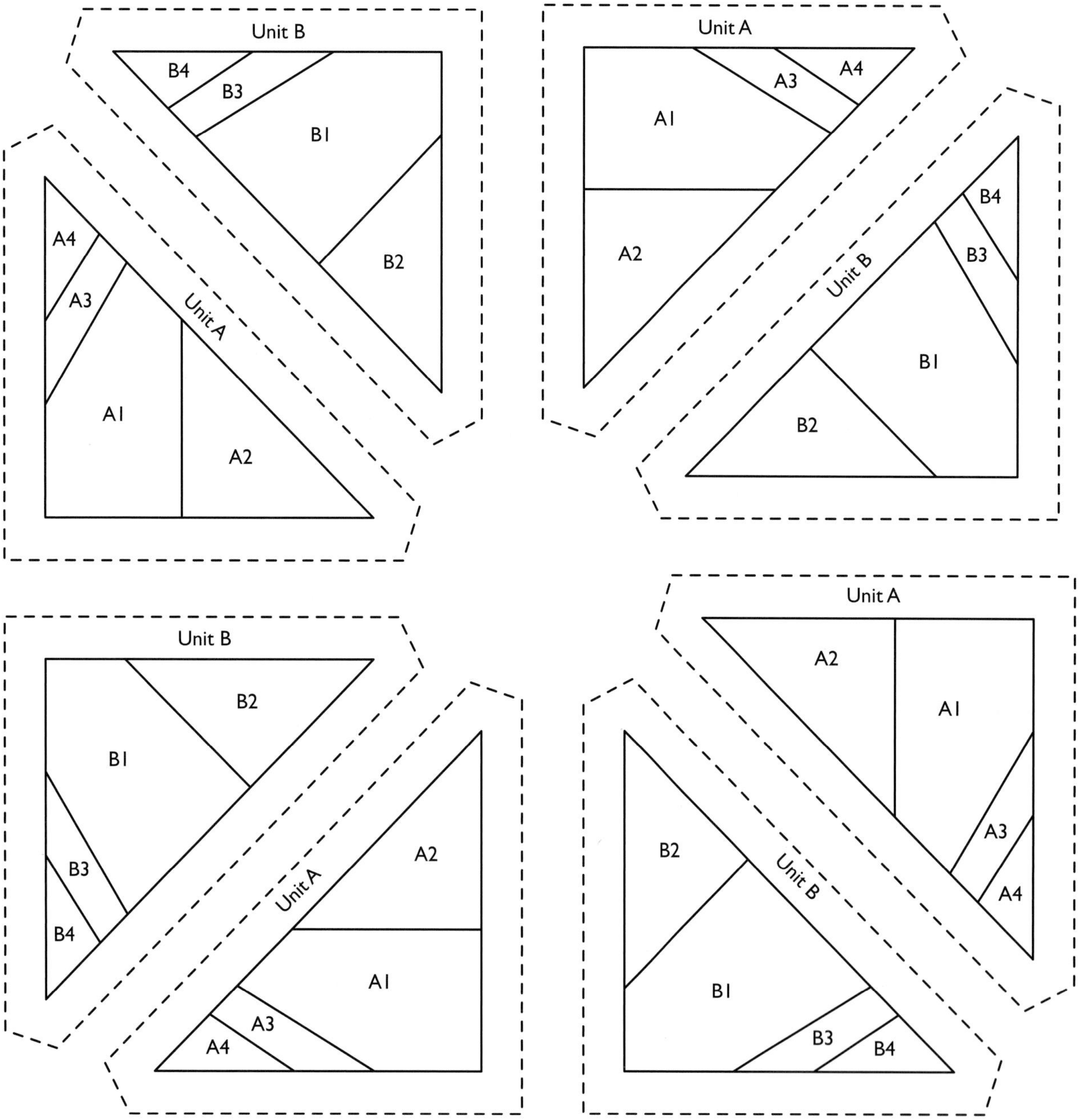

This version of Return of the Swallows was made and quilted by Jennie Maze, Parker, Colorado.

Above: This sampler using six 4-inch blocks was made and quilted by Carolyn Cullinan McCormick, Franktown, Colorado. Opposite: Sampler Quilt by Ginny Rafferty, Carol Bonetti, Jeanette Davis, Polly Somers, Brenda Phillips, Kathy Rutkosky, Jeannine Glendenning, Evie Scott, Nancy Orth, Marilyn Vap, Meriellen Joga, Carol Herriek, Claudia Harrison and Julie Lilly, quilted by Carol Willey, Castle Rock, Colorado.

Above: This little wall hanging, made and quilted by Carolyn Cullinan McCormick, Franktown, Colorado, uses only the 4-inch Mother's Favorite Star pattern. Opposite: Dargate Quilt Mosaic, made by Carolyn Cullinan McCormick, Franktown, Colorado; quilted by Tracy Peterson Yadon, Manhattan, Montana.

Above: Crazy Anne made by Marie Huber, Glendive, Montana, and quilted by Jan Holden, Glendive, Montana. Opposite: Kathy Braun of Rosholt, South Dakota, set three basket blocks on point and made and quilted this lovely table runner.

Resources

Add-A-Quarter™
Add-An-Eighth™

CM Designs, Inc
7968 Kelty Trail
Franktown, CO 80116
Phone: 303-841-5920
Web: www.addaquarter.com

Fabric:
Reproductionfabrics.com
205 Haggerty Lane Suite 190
Bozeman, MT 59715
Phone: 406-586-1775
Toll-Free: 800-380-4611
Web: www.reproductionfabrics.com

Windham Fabrics
812 Jersey Ave.
Jersey City, NJ 07310

In The Beginning Fabrics
8057 – 16th Ave. NE
Seattle, WA 98115
Toll-Free: 888-523-1001
Web: www.inthebeginningfabrics.com

Timeless Treasures
483 Broadway
New York, NY 10013
Phone: 212-226-1400
Web: www.ttfabrics.com

History:
Australian War Memorial
The photo of the Australian Changi quilt can be viewed block by block on the following Web site: www.awm.gov.au/encyclopedia/quilt/detail.htm

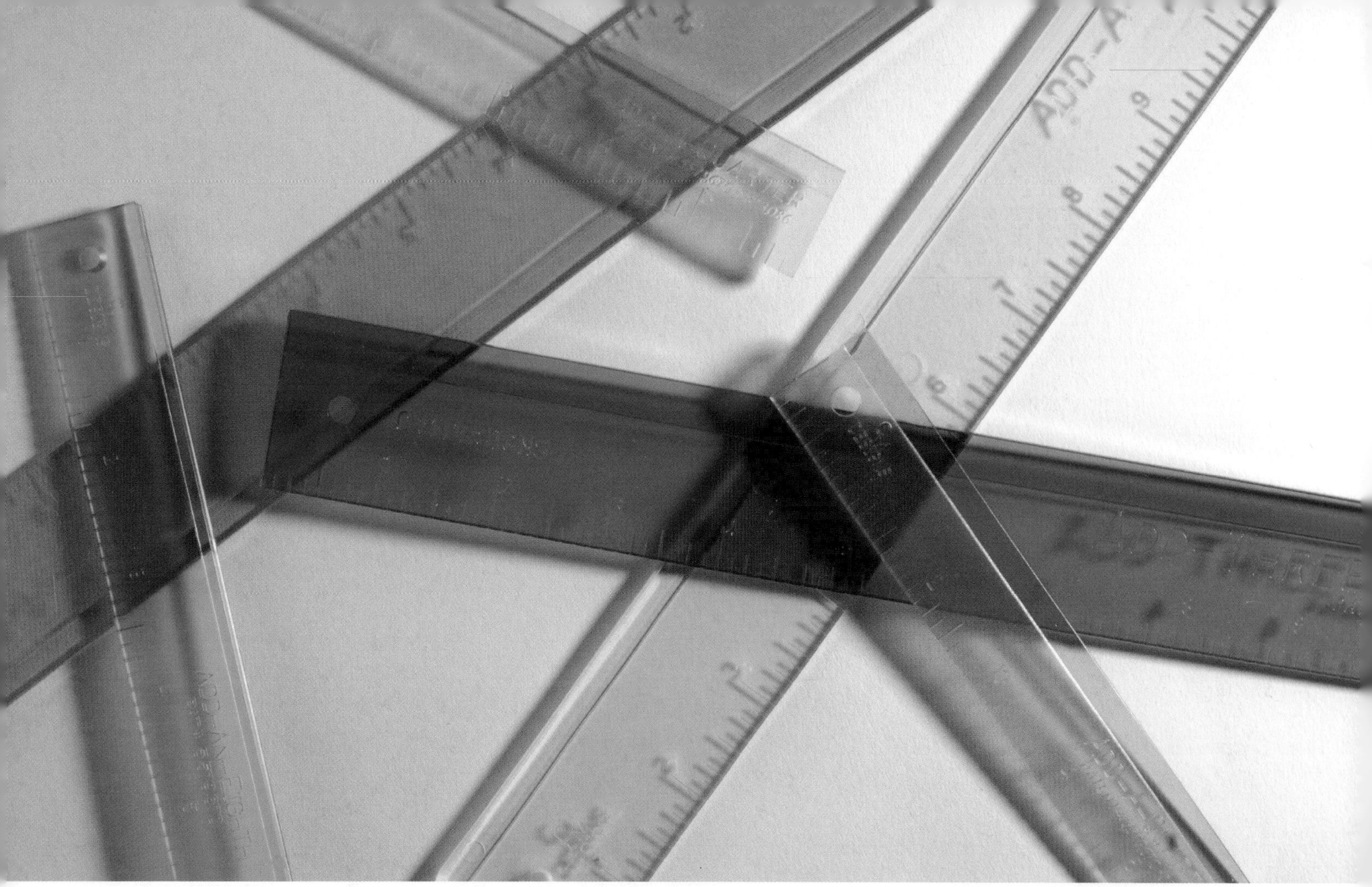

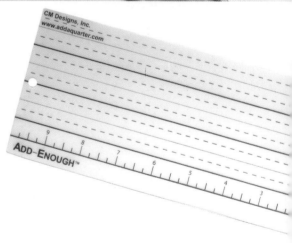